The Re-United States of America

The Re-United States of America

An Action Agenda for Improving Business, Government, and Labor Relations

DAVID A. HEENAN

ADDISON-WESLEY PUBLISHING COMPANY
Reading, Massachusetts • Menlo Park, California
London • Amsterdam • Don Mills, Ontario • Sydney

Library of Congress Cataloging in Publication Data

Heenan, David A.
   The Re-United States of America.

   Bibliography: p.
   Includes index.
   1. Industry and state — United States. 2. Interna-
tional business enterprises — United States. 3. United
States — Economic policy — 1981-   I. Title.
HD3616.U47H42   338.973   82-3936
ISBN 0-201-10527-6   AACR2

ISBN 0-201-10527-6
ABCDEFGHIJ-AL-898765432

To NERY

*Sa kanyang tiyaga, tiwala
at tulong*

Preface

AMERICANS sense that their nation is in trouble. Prospects of limited growth, rising unemployment, and swelling federal budget deficits indicate greater trouble ahead. Not only is the United States suffering from the "sick man" syndrome, but the universality of its economic ideology and of its management methods is also under attack. What had formerly been viewed as a superior model of industrialization and post-industrialization is now perceived as second best. At an alarming rate, nations of the world are turning away from the United States and to Japan, West Germany, and a handful of other countries for their lessons in modern economics. Moreover, it has become voguish to question "the American way."

What corrective actions might be taken to improve the nation's economy depends on one's analysis of the reasons for U.S. reversals at home and abroad. These have covered a wide spectrum—from loss of the Yankee work ethic to a preoccupation with the short term. But critics of the American dilemma consistently cite the failure of U.S. business, government, and labor to build a national consensus. This failure, in turn, has left America without a coherent vision of its economic future.

The Carterites embodied their remedy for our recent setbacks in the seductive slogan "reindustrialization." The Reagan administration has chosen "revitalization" to express its attempts to renew America's sagging economy. Politics aside, both concepts point to the need for a Re-United States of America, for greater collaboration between industry, labor, and government, if the U.S. economy is to move ahead.

But are the American people, particularly those who hold a key stake in the nation's economy, truly eager to reunite in shaping public policy? Do Americans sense the need to redefine government's role in the market system? Are the perceptions of our legislators and regulators different from those of the leaders of industry and organized labor? To what extent are the established interests in business, government, and labor able to accommodate a shift in economic ideology? And what is the impact of these attitudes on America's ability to compete at home and abroad?

To answer these questions, this book was written. It is based on a three-year study of almost fifteen hundred Americans, including chief executive officers and mid-level managers of *Fortune* 500 corporations, U.S. senators and congressmen, federal bureaucrats, state legislators, and labor leaders. This project began in 1979 at the request of U.S. Senator Spark M. Matsunaga, who was also keenly interested in assessing this country's commitment to forging a "new social contract." Heeding Charles E. Lindblom's advice that "the greatest distinction between one government and another is the degree to which the market replaces government or government replaces the market,"[1] I focused on alternative economic ideologies that might produce a better future for the United States. Initially, I asked participants to consider seven possibilities, ranging from laissez-faire economics to economic totalitarianism. As my research progressed, I narrowed the field to three popular—and, for all intents and purposes, the only practical—choices. They were the following: the present mixed economy (or regulated free enterprise); an "America, Incorporated" (or guided free enterprise); and a more centrally planned economy (alternatively called authoritarian capitalism, modified socialism, or a command economy). Americans from all walks of life were asked to identify which of these socio-economic futures they (1) prefer, (2) expect to dominate U.S. policy-making, and (3) feel would be most effective in solving America's problems in the 1980s. In selected interviews that followed, a number of respondents amplified their sentiments as well as their hopes and dreams for a better U.S.A.

The verdict of America's economic leaders, I discovered, is not to cast aside its seemingly slapdash, adversarial system. Nor do they seek to replace it with either the more unified approach of Japan and West Germany or the more integrated planning systems of Northern and Eastern Europe. Most prefer our present ideology, for all its limitations. While they are impressed by the recent performance of other nations, most notably Japan's, they remain unconvinced that the United States can or would be willing to adopt the cultural virtues and institutional reforms needed to shape a more organic society. Instead, they argue that a Re-United States of America must be consistent with our traditions: an open society blending Yankee ingenuity, individualism, egalitarianism, idealism, and a competitive spirit.

At the same time, however, America's leaders reject the status quo. They see only too clearly the shortcomings of the quasi-free enterprise system. This system that had performed so well in times of economic growth, rich natural resources, and narrow, domestic markets suffered badly when stagflation set in, resources shrank, and markets became internationalized. Mindful of these blemishes, Americans today are more open to ideological experimentation, albeit on a selective basis, than at any other time in modern history.

Where this experimentation may lead is the subject of this book. We begin by charting America's ups and downs in the world economy over the last thirty-five years. Special attention is given to the changing global realities of the times and the critical role of the multinational corporation. The argument is made throughout these pages that the worldwide enterprise (in Father Theodore Hesburgh's words, "the colossus of capitalism"[2]) must be the leading force in our industrial renaissance. It represents the most important instance of how ideological infighting has contributed to the U.S. malaise and why the quasi-public character of our global companies must be restored. Next, we consider some valuable lessons to be learned from others; our teachers are not only Japan and West Germany, but also a host of newly industrializing countries that are reaping the benefits of a more consensual approach to economic problem solving. Also, we examine the historical reasons for the ethos of adversarialism in the United States and explain why a rapprochement between our economic principals will not be accommodated easily. Finally, we conclude with a prognosis for a Re-United States of America: an idealized future that incorporates America's traditions with selected elements of a more collaborative society.

Two notes of caution. First, this book focuses on diagnosing the problems and analyzing the prospects of building a national consensus in the United States. By understanding more fully America's present dilemma, the underlying reasons for its existence, and the pluses and minuses of alternative approaches, better solutions, it is hoped, will emerge. Our interest, then, is more on the "why's" than on the "how to's." Any action agenda adopted by the United States in an interdependent world will prompt a series of responses from other nations. These, in turn, will trigger an American counter-response, and so on. To speculate how this sequence of actions and reactions may evolve over the balance of this decade is beyond the scope of this book.

As a final caveat, readers will appreciate that any serious effort to formulate a Re-United States of America by whatever means is not a cure-all for this country's current ills. Improving stakeholder relations is only half the loaf; the other half is upgrading the core competencies of busines, government, and labor. Thus, we must place equal attention on thorny problems, such as internationalizing corporate management, revitalizing the civil service, restoring the work ethic —and a good deal more.

Historically, America's leaders have shown the ability to respond successfully to challenge. A pragmatic resiliency is deeply ingrained in the American psyche. It has served us well in the past. If we so choose, it will serve us well in the future.

I am indebted to many practitioners and scholars who helped make this book possible. First and foremost is U.S. Senator Spark M. Matsunaga. Besides playing a major role in initiating this project, he was most helpful in making his staff available to disseminate and receive questionnaires, to arrange appointments in high places, and to support this effort generally. Jerome M. Comcowich and Patrick K. Takahashi, both of the Senator's office, were always available to expedite various aspects of my research.

Much of the writing was done at the Wharton School. I am especially grateful to Associate Dean John F. Lubin for his kind hospitality; to Steven Smith and Judith Piper Schmitt for their research assistance; and to my departmental colleagues—Franklin R. Root, Laurent L. Jacque, and Klaus O. Haberich—for their counsel. I owe a special debt of gratitude to my mentor and long-time friend, Howard V. Perlmutter. His insights into the next generation of problems confronting multinational corporations and nation-states were of great help to me, and his influence is sprinkled throughout these pages.

Parts of this book appeared in the *Harvard Business Review* and the *Sloan Management Review*. My thanks go to the editors of both journals for permitting me to incorporate these earlier pieces.[3]

William G. Ouchi and Charles E. Summer read an earlier version of this book. Despite great time pressures (aggravated, in part, by the successes of their own books), both offered valuable comments as well as kind words of encouragement. I am indebted to them in a way that I can never repay. In addition, Warren J. Keegan and Leslie E. Grayson offered helpful insights and suggestions.

My consulting experience, teaching in executive programs, and attendance at two important conferences on this subject (one at Harvard, the other at Wharton) brought me in contact with many executives who also influenced my thinking. While it is difficult to single out any individual, I would like to acknowledge Thomas O. Paine, James D. Hodgson, Malcolm MacNaughton, Robert C. Sutton,

J.W.A. Buyers, Harold R. Talbot, Jr., and Herbert C. Cornuelle. For securing midmanagement participation in various seminars around the world, I am indebted to Peter C. Peasely, Peter E. Peterson, and Reginald Garters.

On the Hawaii scene, I would like to thank Lloyd R. Vasey, Fujio Matsuda, Daniel B. Boylan, Charles Baron Shook, and Elizabeth Hirst Piper for their support. My former employer, the University of Hawaii, provided the professional setting where my writing began. The Pacific Forum provided me with the opportunity to undertake my research in Asia and the Pacific and to interact with ranking leaders of this vibrant region that I have called home for two decades. Many hours were spent collecting questionnaires, analyzing data, and related research tasks; for their help in these areas, I would like to mention Reginald G. Worthley, Patrick J. Gilbert, Loren J. Romano; and Mona Nakayama, Florence S. Nahuina, Lois A. Ikegami, Hisano Akiyama, and Sharon Pino.

For editorial guidance, I am indebted to William H. Hamilton of Addison-Wesley. His personal interest in these topics provided a flagging writer with renewed vigor. Harriet Yamamoto's competence, diligence, and unfailing good cheer through successive typings of this manuscript contributed greatly to this book's completion.

Finally, I am most grateful to my wife Nery and our children Marc and Eric for their extended support and personal sacrifice over the past three years. Although they were periodically deserted, albeit in some of this planet's most idyllic settings, they persevered splendidly.

Honolulu, Hawaii
June 1982

D. A. H.

Contents

CONTENTS

Part 1

The Problem

1

America's Dilemma

WHITHER America? In normal times, this question might seem presumptuous. But these are not normal times. One need only examine America's waning competitiveness in world markets to sense that a once-great nation is in trouble.

Symptoms of the problem face us daily. Reports of a weakened dollar, chronic balance-of-payments deficits, declining productivity, double-digit interest rates, and sagging economic growth have dominated the news—not just on the business page but on the front page as well. Underlying these problems is the widely recognized failure of our leaders to develop and implement effective public policies. Clearly, the American public shares these concerns. In a recent survey that asked which industrialized nation had the best-performing economy, only 15 percent of Americans chose the United States. A solid plurality picked Japan. Furthermore, almost nine of every ten Americans surveyed were of the opinion that drastic steps are needed to prevent a future erosion of the economy.[1]

That drastic steps are not only appropriate but critical in solving America's present dilemma is by itself a shocking admission. A mere decade ago nothing could have seemed further from the truth.

America's Ascendancy

Entering the 1970s, America had just concluded a twenty-five-year period of unprecedented economic prosperity. On the heels of its World War II victories, the United States seemed singularly qualified to assume the mantle of leadership in international affairs. Pent-up domestic demand coupled with the rebuilding of Western Europe and Asia/Pacific fueled the American ascent.[2]

The vocabulary of the times separated affluent America from the rest of the pack. We spoke in terms of "gaps"—for dollars or defense, trade or technology—to meter the distance between this country and its competitors around the world. Other nations desperately needed America's resources: its capital, technology, and managerial knowledge. The United States, in turn, responded by mobilizing these resources through a then emerging organizational form, the multinational corporation (MNC).

Make no mistake, the incentives were high for those American businesses prepared to go abroad. As late as 1965, the annual growth in per capita gross national product was largely 20 percent higher in Europe than it was in the United States—and a whopping 285 percent higher in Japan. What is more, annual surveys conducted during this era by Booz, Allen and Hamilton and others revealed that the returns on foreign investments significantly outpaced those back home. Therefore, the temptation was strong for U.S. companies to invest where the growth was—to go multinational on a major scale. By the same token, the Japanese and Europeans had every reason to stay at home and reap the rewards of reconstructing their war-torn domestic economies.

What is especially significant is that for the first time in American corporate history, senior executives tended to conclude that the prospects for long-term growth were superior outside the United States. All things being equal, Bogota defeated Boston in a race for senior management's attention. Being more multinational than one's major competitors was the way to go, although precise definitions of "multinational" were to remain elusive for most American businessmen.[3]

These were the days when, with great delight, a company president would hoist another national flag in front of corporate headquarters to signify the penetration of yet another alien market. To invest in an elaborate international network was to be in touch with the times. And invest they did!

From 1945 to 1970, the book value of foreign direct investment multiplied almost tenfold as American MNCs were hell-bent on reaching global markets. Full speed ahead was the rule, and contraction or withdrawal from foreign markets was tantamount to failure. The by-product of America's wanderlust was a milieu of multinationals circling the globe. The smallest exploited their unique skills in niches that ranged from musical instruments to ornamental flowers. The largest were the megafirms: the IBMs, Exxons, and Goodyears that have consistently dominated America's overseas efforts. (By 1970, for example, just fifty U.S. enterprises accounted for over one-half of U.S. foreign direct investment.)

Notwithstanding the impact of these corporate giants, America's greatest export was its management talent. A legion of U.S. experts promoted American business interests abroad. Among their ranks were the business healers—management consultants, accountants, engineers, and others—eager to peddle their prescriptions to interested foreign buyers. From Arthur D. Little, Inc., to McKinsey & Company, the knowledge brokers prospered, and their overseas offices assumed a Vatican-like aura. Even U.S. academics—Argyris, Drucker, Hertzberg, and others—became household names in the far-flung corners of the world. Matrix management, MBO, discounted cash flow, and other concepts made in the U.S.A. entered the lexicon of businessmen from Berlin to Bombay. By the end of the sixties, the overseas operations of U.S. professionals and their firms accounted for roughly one-half of their total revenues; and the U.S. current account benefited handsomely from the export of our management know-how.

With few exceptions, the American government encouraged the geographical adventurism of its industry. Multinationalism, American style, meant prosperity back home, and the relationship between business, government, and labor could be categorized as benign.

Although no "Japan, Incorporated," the United States—its politicians, bureaucrats, and the public-at-large—tended not to intervene in the world of international trade and investment. Accommodating attitudes by all major sectors of American society fueled the ascendancy of U.S. business.

America's commitment to globalism and its subsequent successes did not go unnoticed. Foreign financial editors feasted on the global reach of U.S. business. In his popular book *The American Challenge,* Jean-Jacques Servan-Schreiber prophesied that U.S. multinational corporations in Europe were well on their way to becoming the world's third ranking industrial power after the United States and the Soviet Union.[4] At the time, the overseas appetite of U.S. enterprise seemed insatiable, and "multinationalism" became synonymous with "American."

Success abroad quickly spelled success at home. Repatriated earnings and ideas added to the stock of national wealth. Even local companies disinterested in things foreign benefited from the gains of their more adventurous peers. "If the streets were not actually paved with gold," one commentator of the times noted, "Americans could at least expect that a pot of plenty lay just over the horizon."[5]

"The affluent society," John Kenneth Galbraith quite precisely called us. Our standard of living and sense of self were never higher. A cornucopia of goods and services competed for the attention of American consumers; prices were affordable; and most of our countrymen were gainfully employed and still vested with the Yankee work ethic. As we entered the seventies, our economic future seemed well assured.

The Party's Over

By the late 1960s and early 1970s, the seeds of America's decline in world markets were already visible.[6] Slowly, U.S. executives became openly dissastisfied with international business and the glitter and gleam that it once represented. Complains O. Pendleton Thomas, chairman of B. F. Goodrich Co.: "The rate of return on investment in overseas operations just isn't at the level we'd like to see it at."[7] So discouraging, in fact, are the prospects of overseas profits that Goodrich and many other American multinationals are nervous about making additional foreign investments, while others are selling off or liquidating their overseas operations.

"Where the going gets tougher, Johnny may go home or just decide not to play," says Anne Harrington, director of the American Chamber of Commerce in Brussels.[8] Belgium benefited most from the 1960s wave of American investment in Europe. Now it is a textbook case of second thoughts. Since 1976, three-quarters of all American manufacturing investment in Belgium has been in existing facilities—only one dollar in four has gone to new plants. Besides, one-half of the largest U.S. concerns there are reported to be considering leaving Belgium.

In his research on Corporate America's loss of confidence in Belgium and other foreign parts, Professor Brent Wilson of Brigham Young University found U.S. multinationals to be divesting themselves of overseas affiliates at an increased rate.[9] From 1971 to 1975, they sold off almost fourteen hundred affiliates (or nearly 10 percent of all their foreign subsidiaries), and U.S. foreign divestments actually increased 25 percent each year over this period.

Many examples of the American retreat can be found. Among them:

☐ The well-publicized sale by Chrysler Corporation of its European operations to Peugeot-Citröen, followed by smaller liquidations in Australia, Colombia, and Venezuela.

☐ In the tire industry, massive cutbacks in Europe by Firestone and Goodyear, with Uniroyal and Goodrich virtually closing up shop.

☐ Bell & Howell Co. and General Foods Corp. both exiting Japan and selling their assets to local companies.

☐ The pullout of Reynolds Metals from British Aluminum; Kaiser's from Alcan Booth Industries; and W. R. Grace's liquidation of its European consumer products division.

7

☐ SCM's sale of its European photocopier division; Gulf, its Spanish refinery; and the Liggett Group, its European cigarette operations.

The rash of American divestments, one-third of which occurred in Western Europe, were motivated more by inadequate earnings than by any other single factor. In its 1976 study on the subject, *Business International* found that 94 percent of U.S. multinationals involved in this massive pruning effort cited "poor performance and prospects" as the key factor triggering divestment.[10] Similarly, Jean J. Boddewyn of the City University of New York discovered: "Economic factors definitely predominate when it comes to explaining divestment."[11] And there is no letup in sight.

"Foreign earnings of U.S. multinationals are down and should stay there awhile," reports the *Wall Street Journal*.[12] That, at least, is the consensus of executives of American MNCs as they assess the prospects this year and beyond. "It's probably true that we're at the bottom, but it's hard to say what the diameter of the disk is," says John A. Klacsmann, vice-president of international operations at Du Pont Co.[13] David Mahoney, Norton Simon's chairman and chief executive officer, agrees with these pessimistic projections, saying that his company sees "no significant strengthening of worldwide economies, as they relate to our business."[14] Gone, it would seem, are the days when the foreign units of many American multinationals outperformed their recession-bound domestic counterparts and buoyed overall corporate profits.

To be sure, the sputtering earnings afflicting many U.S. enterprises are largely explained by the renewed vitality of their competitors from around the world. Predictably, the uniquely strong position that had created a wide disparity between the United States and other nations would give way. "Our multinational enterprises," says Harvard's Raymond Vernon, "had an abnormally high rate of growth from 1950 to 1970. . . .[A]fter an enormous expansion you're having the typical shakeout and consolidation."[15]

The shakeout, as it were, is perhaps timely. "Divestments are not bad," says Professor Boddewyn. "They constitute a part of the normal product life cycle."[16] The boom-or-bust era of multinationalism that pervaded the postwar decades matched many American companies with markets, geography, and cultures that they did not fully understand and hence were ill equipped to manage over the long term. Were it not for the competitive void that persisted for some years following World War II, U.S. multinationals would have begun to streamline their foreign operations much earlier.

The cautious withdrawal of American businesses from overseas ventures should not be interpreted as a full-scale retreat, though. American corporations deciding to liquidate their foreign operations are still in the minority, and U.S. investments abroad are projected to rise 11.4 percent in 1982, slightly below the previous year's increase. Nevertheless, many executives agree that profits from abroad probably will never reach the levels of the 1945-1970 era. Company officials add that they will have to manage their foreign operations much more tightly and identify the markets that they enter much more carefully. For the great majority of U.S. multinationals, the party's over—or, as Professor Vernon puts it: "Gone are the cash cows of yesteryear."[17]

American companies, by and large, were continually herding and milking their international operations (the "cash cows"), convinced that they were the most efficient and innovative producers on the face of the earth. The 1970s began to obliterate the false premises upon which this country's earlier superiority had been built. Today, U.S. companies are much more selective in choosing their foreign markets. With increasing precision, they are asking: What are our competitive advantages for the longer term in any given country? What are the relative political risks in particular countries? What governmental responses might be expected for a particular action? These questions are not readily answered. Rather, they are prompting considerable introspection in corporate boardrooms across this country.[18]

Selective expansion and, in many cases, rationalization will characterize America's international business strategy for the balance of this decade. A recent Louis Harris & Associates survey, conducted for Marsh & McLennan, Inc., confirms this viewpoint.[19] Only 11 percent of U.S. corporate officers of leading American multinationals and 7 percent of their investors and bankers said that they intend to increase their investments abroad over the balance of the 1980s. On the other hand, 29 percent of corporate respondents and 47 percent of investors and lenders confirmed their plans to increase domestic investment. On the whole, however, 56 percent of corporate executives revealed their intentions of leaving their overseas operations at the present level; 44 percent of the bankers surveyed echoed these sentiments.

The days of full-speed-ahead internationalism and flag-raising outside of corporate headquarters are over for the lion's share of U.S. multinationals. Many companies are openly questioning their earlier decisions to go abroad and all that it represents: alien cultures, customers, and competitors. Introspection overrides U.S. thinking today, with renewed interest being shown the domestic market. While many American MNCs (IBM, Citicorp, and Caterpillar Tractor, to name a few) are clinging to their long-standing commitments to multinationalism, a growing number of others are returning home to lick their wounds and to recoup from global combat.

One such firm is the H. J. Heinz Company, the large food processor. Its senior vice-president for finance, Frank M. Brettholle, says, "We'd rather spend $1 in Podunk than 75 cents in Sicily, and if we have $10 million to invest, we're going to look in the U.S. rather than in Uruguay, Argentina, or Brazil." "We just feel more comfortable," he adds, "in our own economy."[20] International Telephone & Telegraph Corporation, the archetypal multinational, is also pulling in its overseas horns. As the European economy is slumping, Herbert C. Knortz, ITT's comptroller, concedes that overseas "funds are being brought back to the United States for reconsideration of investment opportunities here."[21] Du Pont Co., Texaco, Inc., and Standard Oil Co. of California recently announced exactly the same strategies.

From Bell & Howell to Boise Cascade, American companies are shifting their preferences from foreign to familiar markets.[22] These prodigal sons of American industry might take heart from this "better-the-market-you-know" strategy were it not for the changing configuration of the U.S. marketplace.

The Buying of America

It was inevitable that, on the basis of America's reversals overseas, foreign corporations would test the U.S. economy. What better way to deflate the American balloon than by attacking the home market? With a vengeance, outsiders are taking their wrath out on their American competitors where it hurts the most—in the United States.

For the past decade, foreign investors have been flocking here in record numbers. Last year the Department of Commerce estimated that close to $10 billion made its way into the country in the form of direct foreign investment. The department's calculations include any purchases that yield direct or indirect ownership of 10 percent or more of a business as well as purchases and development of real estate—but not of individual private residences. On this definition, the recorded book value of all foreign direct investment is somewhere between $60 and $65 billion, or roughly a quarter of the book value of total direct investment by American companies abroad. This represents more than a fourfold increase over 1974, when foreign investments in the United States were a mere $14 billion.

Of course, the actual foreign stake in the United States runs much higher. When indirect investment (purchases of U.S. corporate stocks and bonds, Treasury securities, and other bank assets) is included, total private investment by foreigners in America approaches $200 billion. By the most conservative estimates, U.S. investments by members of the Organization of Petroleum Exporting Countries totaled nearly $70 billion as of mid-1981. But it is the rush of foreign direct investments that raises eyebrows. Perhaps more than any other phenomenon, it signals the increasing vulnerability of American economic power and the hard realities of global competition.

Few sectors of the U.S. economy have escaped the almost decade-long influx of foreign capital.[23] To illustrate:

☐ Royal Dutch-Shell's $3.6 billion takeover of Belridge Oil, the biggest in American history; the Kuwait government's $2.5 billion purchase of Santa Fe International; the $363 million acquisition of Fairchild Camera by the French Schlumberger family; the $350 million purchase by the Dutch insurance company National-Nederlander of the Life Insurance Company of Georgia; and the $311 million takeover of Flintkote, a building company, by the Canadian group Genstar.

☐ In automobiles, Renault assumed a controlling 46 percent interest in American Motors Corporation, with the option of increasing its holding to 59 percent at any time it wishes. (Ironically, France's other automaker, Peugeot-Citroën, acquired Chrysler Corporation's failing European business.)

☐ Much the same for trucking, where AB Volvo, the Swedish company, acquired the heavy-truck business of the financially troubled White Motor Corporation. The agreement makes Volvo the latest European company to establish a bridgehead in North American truck manufacturing. Others are Italy's Fiat, France's Renault, and West Germany's Daimler-Benz, which reached agreement in April 1981 to take over Consolidated Freightways' Freightliner truck-making operation.

☐ The Statue of Liberty's welcome also applies to foreign bankers, where the latest overseas takeover took place last year with the U.K.'s Midland Bank's $820 million purchase of 57 percent of Crocker National, this country's thirteenth largest bank holding company. This followed the move by Standard Chartered, the large British bank, to acquire Union Bancorp, the sixth largest bank in California, and Hong Kong and Shanghai Bank's 51 percent stake in Marine Midland Bank. All told, there are twelve foreign-owned banks among America's one hundred largest.

☐   Even agriculture is experiencing this unique version of carpet-bagging. The Department of Agriculture estimates that about 7.8 million acres of choice U.S. topsoil, or six-tenths of a percent of the nation's 1.4 billion acres of farmland, are now in foreign hands.

Not since British loans helped finance the building of the nation's canals and railroads in the nineteenth century has the United States displayed a more magnetic attraction to overseas investors.

The weakness of the U.S. dollar against major European and Japanese currencies aided the transoceanic takeover spree. With the softening of the dollar by 45 percent in the last ten years, America's corporate assets were bargain-basement buys. Even now the composite market value of the thirty stocks that make up the Dow Jones Industrial Average is only 90 percent of book value. This massive undervaluation of U.S. share prices means that we can look for more, not less, overseas interest in American business. Still, one should not overstate the role of a weakened U.S. dollar in accommodating the alien influx. Other factors are equally important: the lure of the rich American market, with greater prospects of profits and growth than overseas markets; increasingly favorable manufacturing costs in the United States; availability of American labor, management, and technology; the hedge against rising U.S. protectionism; and greater geographical diversity.

With so much to gain, chief executives of foreign MNCs openly admit their preoccupation with the U.S. market. Says Dieter Zur Loye, senior executive vice-president and chief operating officer of Hoechst, the world's largest chemical company: "Our top priority is to increase our share of the American market."[24] For Francois Michelin, chairman of the French tire giant, corporate survival may even be at stake. "Without our American operations," he admits, "Michelin would be bankrupt!"[25] Evidently, Mr. Michelin's advice is swaying his friendly bankers.

"Without any doubt," writes Ann Crittenden of the *New York Times*, "the fastest growing segment of American banking is not

American at all, but foreign institutions that have established a physical presence in the U.S."[26] In the past five years, the American assets of foreign branches, agencies, and subsidiary banks have soared nearly 300 percent, against a 64 percent gain for U.S.-owned banks. Even more startling is that foreign banks now make between one-fifth and one-sixth of all the business loans in the country, double their market share of only seven years ago. In New York, California, and Florida, where foreign banks are the strongest, that figure jumps to about 30 percent.

Their competitive sting is being felt deeply. Says Roger E. Anderson, chairman of Chicago's Continental Illinois Corp., the nation's seventh largest bank holding company: "Foreign banks are our keenest competitors for commercial and industrial loans. And this pattern shows every sign of continuing."[27] Bemoans crosstown rival Theodore H. Roberts, executive vice-president of Harris Trust & Savings Bank, "American banks became competitive overseas in the past decade. Now that is returning to haunt us."[28]

The haunting, as it were, hardly goes unnoticed. Just as the American challenge captured front-page headlines in the 1960s, so too has the recent European and Japanese revenge. Americans are reminded constantly that if they are consuming Mounds candy bars or Baskin-Robbins ice cream, dining out at Lum's or the International House of Pancakes, shopping at Ohrbacks or Saks Fifth Avenue, or staying at a TraveLodge or Howard Johnson's inn, they are fattening foreign wallets.

Foreigners are making their presence felt, whatever the form. Whether it is Perrier's splash in mineral water or Panasonic's being slightly ahead of our times, overseas companies are demonstrating the knack of converting Americans to their wares. They are discovering that the U.S. market, once thought to be impenetrable, is very much up for grabs.

Changing Global Realities

"For the first time in American history," says Henry Kissinger, "we can neither *dominate* the world nor *escape* from it."[29] Humiliation

14

at home and setbacks abroad signal the hard realities of world business and the lessons of interdependency. The United States, for better or worse, is inextricably linked to the political and economic dynamics of the new world order. And Grassroots America now concedes the critical bond between success in the international marketplace and solutions to the more popular issues back home: unemployment, inflation, and a full-fledged recession.

Small wonder. There are, after all, many reminders of the crucial importance of world business to the U.S. economy. World trade has expanded tenfold over what it was a decade ago. As a proportion of gross national product, the increase in exports and imports was 44 percent for Japan and 36 percent for West Germany—but a whopping 140 percent for the United States. Today, more than 25 percent of the U.S. economy is involved in international trade, or double the 1970 level. Millions of American jobs depend on exports: one in five for agriculture, one in eight for manufacturing. On the imports side, this nation depends on foreign oil and strategic minerals for its industrial sustenance. So, too, for U.S. direct investments overseas, which produced $40 billion in revenues last year—roughly five times the 1970 figure of $8.2 billion. Taken together, almost one of every three dollars of corporate profits derives from the international trade and investment of American firms. And, as mentioned earlier, foreigners are contributing to the domestic economy in a major way.

While it is easy to wax over the internationalization of the U.S. economy, one must also wane over America's inability to keep pace with its industrial competitors. To illustrate:

☐ The U.S. share of world exports has plummeted since 1970. In terms of its impact on dollars and jobs, this country has lost an estimated $125 billion and over two million jobs to foreigners.

☐ As other nations rebuilt their industrial machines, America's productive base went to seed. The average age of U.S. plant and equipment is sixteen to seventeen years compared to twelve years for West Germany and ten years for Japan.

☐ By almost any measure, the growth of U.S. productivity ranks last among the major industrial powers—averaging 2.3 percent over the past decade. By comparison, productivity growth in Japan and West Germany averaged 5.2 percent for the same period.

☐ American enterprise also lost ground. In 1963, U.S. corporations accounted for two-thirds of the world's largest companies and for three-fifths of the 500 largest. By 1979, their membership had dropped to less than one-half of each group.

☐ Nor was America's decline limited to the industrial giants. In banking, for instance, the U.S. accounted for forty-four of the top one hundred banks in the world in 1956; last year, only thirteen made it into the top echelon. Similar stories can be told for other service sectors—from airlines to construction.

Whatever the yardstick, it became clear that the *pax Americana* that shaped modern economic history was disintegrating. Many wondered, "What ever happened to the American challenge?"

What Went Wrong?

As a people, Americans are prone to occasional self-flagellation, particularly when Yankee ingenuity begins to take a backseat. Realistically speaking, the relative dip in the U.S. influence around the world was simply inevitable. "The 1970s began to obliterate features that distinguished the United States from other industrialized countries," explains Harvard's Vernon.[30] "For one thing, European and Japanese income levels were rising rapidly and no longer trailed far behind those of America. Gone, too, were the differences in cost structures that had distinguished the United States—from other countries. Labor was almost as expensive in Europe as in the United States. Capital, thanks partly to the burgeoning Euromoney market, was plentiful on both sides of the Atlantic. And as Americans began to rely increasingly on imported raw materials, their historic advantage in the prices of such materials was also evaporating."[31]

Professor David P. Calleo, from the Johns Hopkins School of

Advanced International Studies, tells a similar version of the story. "As Europe and Japan have revived and the Third World develops," he advises, "the international system has grown more plural. These changes," Calleo continues, "have inevitably affected America's world position. They represent not so much the decline of America as the revival of the world."[32]

The rest of the world's revival notwithstanding, America's slippage from global leadership cannot be dismissed lightly. "It seems to me," warns former Treasury Secretary John B. Connally, "that we have reached a stage where there is cause for deep concern. History offers too many examples in which maturity evolved into stagnation, decline and decadence."[33] Obviously, corrective action must now be taken.

Just what these actions might be depends on one's assessment of the problem. The fault behind declining U.S. economic power lies, of course, with many people and many events. But my reconstruction of America's postwar troubles places the blame on the inability and unwillingness of our key economic stakeholders to put America's house in order. The greatest disappointment: their failure to develop a national industrial policy and the strategies and programs that go with it. Rather than agree on an industrial game plan at the federal level, an economic counterpart of our foreign and domestic policies, our leaders in business, government, and labor clung religiously to the orthodoxy of the past. They agreed to disagree, to maintain the arm's-length, if not adversarial, posture of bygone days—even though the changing global realities had rendered such old ideological dogma obsolete. From this failure of national vision on all fronts sprung a series of economic crises, each seemingly more difficult than the last. In an increasingly interdependent world, the United States suffered all the domestic stresses that accompany a fall from the global pecking order: chronic trade deficits, rising unemployment, budgetary cutbacks, popular resistance to expansive government, loss of confidence in our leaders, and a heightening level of tension and infighting among self-interest groups for shares of a pie not growing as fast as their needs or expectations.[34]

What to Do?

John and Jane Doe are deeply troubled about the prospects of prolonging this gloomy scenario. "The state of mind of the public is worried sick and in a panic," says Daniel Yankelovich, chairman of the opinion research firm of Yankelovich, Skelly & White, Inc. "In that condition, people know that there is something wrong. That pushes them into working out accommodations that make economic sense."[35]

What these accommodations might be is, of course, a matter of interpretation and not easily resolved. Jesse W. Markham of the Harvard Business School puts it this way: "The central issue confronting the United States is whether there is a policy remedy for its declining performance in the global economy . . . and, if so, what form it should take."[36]

To the Carterites, the policy remedy took the form of the clever catchphrase "reindustrialization"; to the incumbent administration, "revitalization" is the way to go. Both camps, though, agree that the starting place for America's renewal is a redefinition of the adversarial axes upon which its economic principals converge. The Cambridge Reports, Inc., reached similar conclusions in a survey conducted for the Union Carbide Corporation.[37] Their pollsters found that Americans from all walks of life are strongly convinced that the most important first step in solving our problems is to develop a greater degree of cooperation among *all* groups and institutions in our society. The average citizen believes that business, government, and labor do not work closely enough on economic problems, and he wants them to cooperate in stimulating growth and prosperity.

Ever mindful of the public pulse, President Reagan joins in the chorus for greater collaboration. "Consensus is a word you will hear often in the months ahead," he promised shortly before assuming office.[38] "When it comes to goals shared by American institutions and constituencies that may have other goals not in common, consensus building is the only way to gain widespread support from the people, thus making the attainment of goals possible."[39]

Presidential promises aside, the jury is still out on the administration's real commitment to shape a national consensus and the industrial policies that go with it. For one thing, the White House remains intensely ideological in its belief that business is the majordomo of our modified free enterprise system. Repeatedly, the President has announced that resources must be shifted from the public sector to the private sector if national prosperity is to be restored. Therefore, any partnership that evolves will be an unequal one, with Washington and the Halls of Labor relegated to subordinate roles. Of the various ways to organize our industrial system, the Reaganites are placing their bets squarely on the forces of capitalism, on our mixed economy, where, ideally, there is a maximum use of free markets and a minimum of government controls. In confidence, they admit that some form of public-sector involvement in the economy is inevitable—in fact, even desirable. But on balance, chapter and verse of the Reagan revolution is to curtail sharply Washington's role in business affairs and to unleash the captains of industry to revitalize the economy.

In addition, the philosophical principles that swept the Republican party into office stress not only the limits of amiability among business, labor, and government but also the creative tensions of the adversarial system. In many quarters of the White House, a partnership (or consensus) is ideologically unacceptable, even heretic. Irving Kristol is one trusted adviser to Mr. Reagan who openly dismisses the calls for consensus. "At the moment," he insists, "I am for 'dissensus.' "[40] Even less conservative elements of the GOP are sensitive to the severity of potential charges of deserting their free enterprise principles for a pyrrhic partnership among what historically have been strange bedfellows. Hence, one cannot be bullish about the likelihood of closing the wide schism between our central economic institutions.

It is the prospect of this separatist scenario that bothers many Americans. While recognizing the primacy of private enterprise, this group looks longingly at alternative approaches, most notably from Japan, where government's visible hand paves the way for business.

19

What the United States needs, they contend, is a different strand of capitalism: free enterprise by consensus. Their "better way" is an America, Inc., roughly analogous to Japan, Inc. For them, only such a strong symbiosis between Big Business and Big Government can ensure the proper framework within which an economic blueprint can be sketched, then shaped.

Admittedly, this departure from Reaganomics has a distinctly partisan flavor. As the Democrats saw it in the Carter days and continue to see it now, any well-functioning capitalist system needs cooperation and compromise. Japan and West Germany prove their point: When the economic institutions of a society work together, spectacular gains are possible. New Jersey Senator Bill Bradley is one party spokesman who is especially frustrated by the White House's traditional — and in his opinion obsolete — view of a world in which the U.S. economy is delineated into two disparate sectors, public and private. Japan, West Germany, even France — where private corporations are assisted by government in their pursuit of markets — are Bradley's idealized models. "If you're operating in a world where you have government entities joined with the private sector in competition for third markets around the world," the Senator says, "then you have to look at your national perspective. . . . You either curtail the other countries' aiding their industries or you find some way to do that for your industries."[41] The way to aid American industries, the Senator and his colleagues insist, is to fix our economic compass on a more collaborative, less adversarial heading.

Others would take this argument one step further. Their vote is to force a national consensus by erasing the "false dichotomy" between the public and private sectors in one dramatic move: a shift to a centrally planned economy. Variously termed authoritarian capitalism (Brazil), modified socialism (Sweden), or a command economy (Yugoslavia), this option would place the economic reins in the hands of the bureaucrats. Business and labor, in turn, sacrifice their self-interests for the national good. When it works, a state-controlled system has several alleged advantages: more effective setting of economic priorities, better resource allocation, more consistent foreign and domestic policies, and a more professional civil service. At its worst, this alternative can lead to the litany of economic woes so often associated with Eastern Europe—no growth, low productivity and innovation, minimal entrepreneurship, consumer dissatisfaction, and labor unrest. Hence, even the most left-leaning pundits in America's halls of ivy, trade unions, and other campsites openly admit their reluctance to jettison the enterprise system in any major way. What they are seeking is a variant of capitalism—one that would promote, indeed guarantee, an economic coalition among disparate groups in our society.

A Need to Unbend

Where ideology and revitalization will meet is open to question. But most Americans believe that to prolong the present crisis is to ensure the continued decline of U.S. influence and standing in the world. We need to establish a forum where the leaders of the various groups that make up our post-industrial society can agree on a strategy to rebuild the economy. What is much less clear is what government's role should be in the recovery process—and beyond. Should Washington's presence be minimized, maximized, or fall somewhere in between these philosophical extremes? The answer depends on two forces: the emergence and crystallization of public attitudes on the one hand and institutional reaction on the other.

The direction of popular sentiment is difficult to assess. Simply stated, America is in the midst of making up its mind on these matters, of rethinking the proper economic functions of government. Yet one can bet safely that the United States is not likely to abandon its fundamental commitment to the individual; to Japanize its industrial and financial systems; to reduce its reverence for relatively free enterprise; to replace private institutions with public ones. "What people are saying," says pollster Louis Harris, "is that they want to give capitalism—the private section—a real chance to

21

work out the recovery and the future development of the economy."[42] By the same token, Americans are genuinely eager to tilt this nation toward a new spirit of cooperation, consensus, and common purpose. Just how far and in what directions are the subjects of this book. But we should not be surprised to discover a new ideology emerging—one that contains some of the old values of market-oriented economics and some of the more ameliorating aspects of a collaborative economic society.

The portrait, then, is of America in transition, at the beginning of an attitudinal revolution. Inevitably, this means reprogramming our economic institutions as well as their historical habit of divergence. America's success at home and abroad will be measured largely by the effectiveness of its multinational corporation.[43] These ultimate purveyors of capitalism are, after all, the lubricant of world trade and investment. As such, they represent an especially important prism through which this country's ideological evolution and reunification may be viewed.

To date, Washington's practice has been to let its MNCs fend for themselves. In instances where the bureaucracy does not actually hinder U.S. multinationals, it does precious little to help them. By contrast, foreign governments (and organized labor, too) stand foursquare behind their global companies, often treating them as policy arms of the public sector. Therefore, if America's multinational corporations are to effect their necessarily dominant role in the revitalization processes, these national distinctions in public policy must be obliterated.

To sum up, the forces underlying the end of America's economic euphoria appeared at first quietly, but persistently nevertheless. These forces signaled a major transformation in the global industrial system and, with it, a new role for this nation. More important, they galvanized the United States to reappraise its economic principles and ideological hardline and to search for better approaches. As in any philosophical search, the risks are great and the outcome is uncertain. But is there any alternative? Most Americans think not.

The outlook for the United States is dim, unless we make a dramatic change of direction—which we are fully capable of doing. "If in 1990, we can look back on the 1980s as a time of genuine economic renewal, we will have something to be proud of," says Xerox president David T. Kearns.[44] "A society once great will have achieved the most difficult of all tasks in history: finding the will to be great again, and then doing it."[45] How others are doing it—and what we can and must learn from them—are the subjects of the chapters that follow.

Part 2

Lessons from Abroad

2

Avis Strategies Win Out

T HIRTY-SEVEN years ago, allied military power crushed Japan and Germany. Both nations started from scratch after World War II, and the odds were weighted heavily against their recovery to prewar levels, let alone to superpower status. But survive and prosper they did—creating an unprecedented social and economic miracle. And today, Japan and West Germany are outperforming the rest of the world in a different theater of battle: the world of international trade and investment.

What bodes critically for the United States is not simply the penetrating inroads made by both nations in markets that were once the exclusive province of American enterprise but the manner in which Tokyo and Bonn have carefully orchestrated this process. Throughout their recovery and beyond, a coalition between business, government, and labor emerged in each country to plan and implement a coherent, well-thought-out industrial policy. While West Germany and Japan are dissimilar in many ways, both nations possess the common elements of the kind of socioeconomic consensus needed, it seems, to compete in today's global marketplace. Let us examine the Japanese and German return to prosperity as well as the underlying reasons for their recent success.

Empire of the Rising Sun

As he enters his eighties, Emperor Hirohito must view his nation's postwar transformation with wonderment. Today, the Japanese economy produces:

- ☐ More steel than the United States or any other nation in the free world.

- ☐ More automobiles and color televisions than any other country in the world.

- ☐ More watches than the Swiss.

- ☐ More cameras and optical equipment than the Germans.

- ☐ More ships than America and Western Europe together.

And the list goes on.[1]

Japan's former image as the junkman of Asia—a country whose cheap labor produced vast amounts of cheap goods—has given way to far more flattering illusions. "Made in Japan" nowadays is a distinct plus. Japan's abilities, Ezra F. Vogel reminds us, are not limited to a narrow range of products: "In pianos, hardly a traditional Japanese instrument, in bicycles, tennis and ski equipment, snowmobiles, pottery, glass, machine tools, Japan is a strong competitor. In calculators and office copying machines, Japanese advances are impressive. In industrial robots, [it's] the world's leader."[2] From tape recorders to zippers, products bearing Japanese labels enjoy international supremacy.

Whatever the dimension studied, Japan is on the rise. Its gross national product exceeds one trillion dollars and is second only to that of the United States. Crime rates are falling, and Tokyo is the world's safest major industrialized city. Life expectancy is the highest in the world; infant mortality, the lowest. Population growth hovers around 1 percent annually, and unemployment (if measured directly as in the United States) would be about 4 percent. Perhaps more impressive, Japan is the only advanced economic power that has managed to industrialize without disrupting the sociocultural fabric of what is one of the world's most homogeneous societies.

LATE STARTERS GONE WILD

"Japanese corporations have emerged as multinationals, both suddenly and recently," writes Professor Terutomo Ozawa in his comprehensive book on the subject, *Multinationalism, Japanese Style*.[3] A late starter to the world of overseas production, Japan launched its postwar expansion in 1951 with a modest iron ore development project in Goa. For the next decade and a half, its investments overseas continued at a moderate level and were usually earmarked for the developing countries of Asia and Latin America. These markets, contemptuously neglected by major MNCs from other advanced nations, proved to be safe havens for the first round of Rising Sun multinationals. Besides, the emerging countries' most abundant factor, cheap labor, matched up well with Japan's rapidly maturing industries: textiles, machinery, shipbuilding, and iron and steel.

By the late 1960s, Tokyo's trade balances began to reflect surpluses in the billion dollar range. The rapid accumulation of the foreign reserves that followed left Japanese policymakers with two fundamental choices: to restrict exports or to export their surpluses as foreign investments. As we know, Japan's economic ministries opted to step up overseas investments. Shortly thereafter, the revaluation and floating of the yen acted as a further inducement to invest abroad, as Japanese companies were able to acquire foreign productive assets at relatively cheap prices. Tokyo's economic offensive had begun.

Later, following a 1974 report on Japan's industrial structure, Tokyo adopted a series of new economic directions that were to have an equally profound effect on Japanese multinationalism. The days of accelerated, unrestricted economic growth would give way to the

29

changing climate of the 1970s and 1980s: slower, more programmed economic growth. In so doing, policymakers decided to restructure Japan's industry from "pollution-prone" and "resource-consuming" heavy and chemical industries toward "clean" and "knowledge-intensive" industries. Targeted by the Ministry of International Trade and Industry (MITI) as high flyers are nuclear power, pollution abatement systems, medical equipment, and any electrical goods based on integrated circuits. For these "sunrise" or "target" technologies — that is, those sectors expected to be tomorrow's rapid growth industries — government's helping hand reaches out in many directions.

In computers, for instance, Japan is intensifying its challenge to the United States for world supremacy.[4] That was the clear message given on April 1, 1981, when the Japanese kicked off their fiscal year with a federal budget that included three new major research and development programs — the latest in the country's ambitious efforts to focus business and government resources in the drive for leadership of the fast-growing computer business. The research money comes from MITI, which has pledged more than $400 million over the next decade to develop the "supercomputer," the world's fastest computer, plus the so-called fifth-generation computer.

This is by no means the first time the Japanese government and industry have joined forces in computer-related research. It made $239 million available from 1971 to 1976 to its large-scale mainframe manufacturers for basic research; approximately $250 million for development of the Very Large-Scale Integrated Circuit (or VLSTI) during the 1976 to 1979 period; and an estimated $100 million is projected for related software development between 1979 and 1984.[5] Receiving the government's help to establish the VLSTI Technology Research Association are Nippon Electric Co., Toshiba, Hitachi, Fujitsu, and Mitsubishi Electric. In addition, the best and brightest government scientists are being assigned to various corporate projects designed to enhance Japan's position in the computer industry.

Such support by MITI and other government agencies is vital if Japan is to challenge the United States seriously in computers and other target technologies.[6] Without the ministry, most of these priority projects would never get off the ground. "The top decision-making people at private companies cannot decide to do such fundamental research because they cannot tell whether it will lead to profits," explains Makoto Nagao, a professor at Kyoto University's electrical engineering department. "But," he adds, "when MITI says that research is vital and hands them the money to begin, they cannot turn it down."[7] Rarely, if ever, does Corporate Japan turn down Tokyo's generosity. In computers, as in business generally, industry's interests are usually synonymous with the public interest.

Much the same process takes place for the noncompetitive segments of the economy. In Japan, even the losers win.[8] The so-called sunset industries, identified as structurally troubled (*kozo fukyo gyoshu*), fit one or more of the following categories:

1 Those having excessive production capacity with little prospect of demand rising substantially in the future (among them: steelmaking, shipbuilding, plywood, and nonferrous metals).

2 Those suffering from the high cost of raw materials and energy (aluminum smelting, sugar refining, polyvinyl choride resin, and chemical fertilizer).

3 Those threatened by foreign competition from the developing countries (textiles and machine tools).

Under the aegis of MITI, public-sponsored aid to depressed companies takes many forms: low-interest loans to enter other businesses, grants for job retraining, help in forming cartels to reduce excess capacity, and so forth. Rather than being cast adrift to weather the storms of the international marketplace, endangered enterprises in Japan benefit from the largess of Big Brother.

The carefully planned and articulated strategy of restructuring Japanese industry has had the effect of assigning overseas investment a new role—that of housecleaning the economy. By exporting the obsolescence of its structurally depressed businesses to the "second Japans" (South Korea, Taiwan, Singapore, and others), Japan is able to extend the longevity of its stagnant labor- and pollution-intensive industries.[9] This tactic not only preserves an especially powerful segment of Japanese society, the small business community, but it also sidesteps the thorny task of euthanasia by public fiat.

National planning in Japan consistently encourages industries that hold the promise of future competitiveness and discourages aid and comfort for those on the decline. Targeting winners as well as losers is the first step in industrial policymaking. On closer examination, however, history reveals that Japanese leaders have been reluctant to bite the bullet for "sunset" industries. Phaseouts, even at a modest level, are rare; and a far more preferable antidote is the "guided" relocation of companies in structurally depressed industries to the developing countries of Asia. "Government is hesitant," Professor Ozawa admits, "to let the senile industries take their natural course and quickly die out."[10] Backing the winners and soothing the losers would be a far more accurate description of the Japanese planning ethic, which sacrifices rationality for humanitarian gains. This asymmetry, as it were, is in keeping with the "dual industrial structure" in Japan.

On the one hand are the large-scale, supergiant firms engaged in capital-intensive and, more recently, knowledge-intensive industries; on the other are the small-scale firms engaged principally in labor-intensive operations.[11] Those in the former group, which includes the Teijins, the Toyotas, the Hitachis, and others, have the resources and expertise to compete effectively on any level, foreign or domestic. On the whole, they are self-reliant and unsolicitous of government help. The latter, however, are particularly vulnerable to the swelling strength of the newly industrialized countries. Composed mainly of small and medium-sized companies, this second tier of Japanese industry carries substantial political clout, which it is not reluctant to call upon. Receiving various kinds of assistance, Japan's mini-multinationals are rapidly migrating overseas.

Today, some two thousand Japanese small businesses manufacture worldwide. They are canning sweet potatoes in the Philippines, distilling vinegar in South Korea, and building safes in Thailand.

Defined as firms with fewer than three hundred employees or capitalized at $4.8 million or less, small business represents $381 million of the $4.6 billion of Japan's current stock of foreign direct investment. Japanese companies in this category are expected to venture further overseas—employing two million workers in seventeen thousand projects by the end of the decade.

To be sure, Japanese small businesses have a distinct preference for nearby markets. South Korea remains the largest single target (with 27 percent of the pie), followed by Taiwan and Hong Kong. "There is a clear trend toward investment in other Asian countries," says Takeo Matsunaga, managing director of Japan Overseas Development Corporation, a semi-official organization that subsidizes foreign ventures by smaller Japanese companies.[12]

Less threatened but even more interested in the art of global reach are Japan's major corporations. For them, too, there is no turning back. "We must become multinational," says Akio Kohno, senior economist at Daiwa Securities Co. "Otherwise we cannot survive. With increasing trade barriers, we have to enter the [international] market to produce."[1]

FULL SPEED AHEAD

Retreat, it would seem, is not in the minds of Japanese businessmen and government officials. Aided by its stockpile of foreign exchange reserves, the yen float, and industrial restructuring, Japan has embarked on a program of direct investment abroad unmatched by any other industrial company.

By 1970, Japan's foreign direct investment was just $3.6 billion. In 1978 alone, by contrast, its overseas projects hit a record $4.6 billion. And much the same for 1979 despite the yen's fall from 180 to the dollar (late in 1978) to 250 to the dollar (in 1979). Fully one-half of the nearly $33 billion that Japanese firms have ventured overseas has come in the past five years alone—and that stake could quadruple by the decade's end.[14] In fact, projections by the prestigious Japan Economic Research Center show total Japanese overseas stakes soaring to $155 billion by 1990 (see Exhibit 2.1). In December

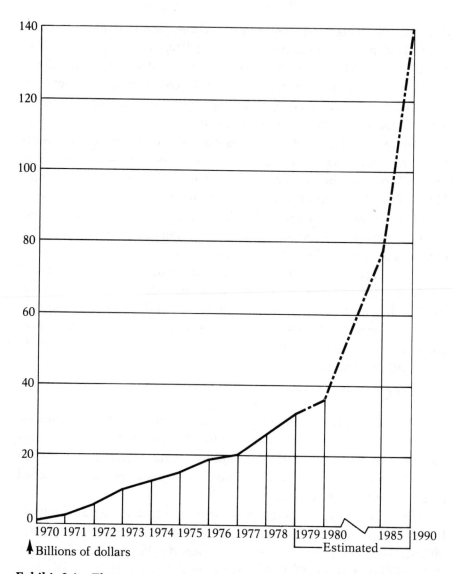

Exhibit 2.1   The soaring overseas stake of Japan's multinationals, 1970-1990 (in billions of dollars). *Source:* Reprinted from the June 16, 1980 issue of *Business Week* by special permission, © 1980 by McGraw-Hill, Inc., New York, NY 10020. All rights reserved.

1980, the Japanese government liberalized its foreign-exchange law to encourage further ventures and to make the figure achievable.

In publicizing the rise of Japanese enterprise, *Business Week* commented: "This investment drive, like the similar thrust of United States multinationals in the 1950s and 1960s, will radically reshape both Japan's domestic economy and the competitive atmosphere of world business in the 1980s."[15] As one indication of their swelling ranks, Japan dominates the *"Fortune* non-American 500" listing: 121 Japanese companies are included, far outpacing the United Kingdom (88), Germany (62), France (42), Canada (32), and Sweden (26).[16] Names like Panasonic, Sony, and Honda strike fear in the hearts of any of their head-to-head competitors.

None more so than their United States rivals, for it is the North American market that holds special appeal for Japanese businessmen. Approximately $8.5 billion, or 37 percent, of Japan's overseas investment is in North America, mainly the United States, and that figure is expected to increase 145 percent by 1985. In fact, Japanese industry controls, wholly or in part, 225 American manufacturing companies with operations in 42 states and a combined work force approaching 60,000, while Japanese investment in United States enterprise was practically nil in 1970.[17] Japan's leadership is mindful of Peter Drucker's warning that no manufacturing industry has ever been able to maintain a substantial market in a developed country by exports alone. To maintain its market, it has to become a producer in that country.[18] Whether it is Nissan Motor Co.'s decision to manufacture Datsun trucks in Smyrna, Tennessee, or Fuji Bank's broadening its corporate banking services in New York City, indications abound of the global appetite of Japanese enterprise and of the special importance of the United States market in their plans for future growth.

Tokyo's contemporary corporations, unlike their predecessors, need the sophisticated skills and resources of advanced nations such as the United States. The industrialized world is ideally suited not only to consume but also to produce the future wares of Japanese industry. Besides, these affluent settings pose few political risks. As a result, Japan is reshuffling its worldwide investment priorities to reflect the special appeal of the industrial West.

Forming the advance guard for Japanese business in its spread across the globe are the ubiquitous trading companies.[19] With roots that go back to the 1870s (when Japan resumed international trade after more than two hundred years of self-imposed isolation), these once-unique Japanese enterprises developed because of the growing dependence of the Rising Sun on foreign raw materials and markets as well as the difficulty for each individual company to develop for itself the necessary language skills and an adequate worldwide purchasing and selling network. Although six thousand firms qualify to be classified in this group, it is the "big ten" or general trading companies (*sogo shosha*) that dominate the scene. Among their ranks are Mitsui, Mitsubishi, and Marubeni, and it is not unusual for the annual turnover of the general traders to account for 30 percent of Japanese GNP.

Trade intermediation is their primary business, and the general trading companies are actively involved in transportation, freight forwarding, and warehousing, as well as in the marketing of Japan's exports and imports. More recently, however, they have assumed a new role: trade and investment creation. From developing iron ore sources in Australia to the site selection of textile plants in Taiwan, Japanese traders represent a well-developed system for seeking out and expanding international business opportunities. To illustrate: Mitsubishi International's U.S. affiliate is America's *largest* trading company![20]

In the years to come, we can expect even more changes. Harvard's Thomas Lifson suggests three new directions for the *sogo shosha:* "One is to move into new commodity areas, specifically oil. Second is to move into what is called third country trade, for example, selling American grain to Europe. [Third] . . . is to move into what you might call project management, or sales of large scale industrial projects overseas, such as building large petrochemical facilities in the Middle East."[21]

But even in their present mode the trading companies are commercial heavyweights. Virtually unmatched is their tenacity in understanding and penetrating foreign beachheads. Their quest for the China trade is just one indication. "Look at any major Japanese trading company and you'll find a special section devoted specifically to China peopled with bright young men who speak Chinese and are well acquainted with Chinese culture and politics," says one Tokyo trade expert.[22] This kind of expertise—and commitment to internationalism—does not exist on a similar scale in the United States or in any other Western nation. It is not surprising, then, that the Japanese government smiles upon the *sogo shosha*.

Equally unique is the support of organized labor in Japan for the corporate gallop overseas. Unlike their counterparts in the United States, Japanese workers consider the pluses of multinationalism to far outweigh the minuses. They recognize that a firm foothold in the major industrialized markets of the world hedges against possible vulnerability back home. Ichiro Shioji, president of the Confederation of Japan Automobile Workers' Unions, none of whose 570,000 members is out of work, has been most adamant in demanding that Japan's automakers set up plants in the United States. His recommendations are surely in Japan's self-interest.[23] If Japan does otherwise, Shioji contends, U.S. auto-trade barriers are inevitable.

Mr. Shioji's opinions, shared by others in Japan's union hierarchy, run counter to those of Douglas Fraser, president of the United Auto Workers, and of most American laborites. The latter have been consistently in the forefront of fights against the U.S. multinational corporation and the "runaway plants and jobs" that it allegedly breeds. Japanese unions, organized along strict company lines, have a far different view of the world. For them, company as well as governmental arguments are persuasive, especially on the merits of Japan's building a global network of far-flung production units. Wages, hours, and working conditions are negotiated on a company-by-company basis with the union's clout waning as the company becomes smaller. "If the company goes bankrupt," explains

Professor Robert J. Ballon of Tokyo's Sophia University, "that's the end of the union."[24]

The harmony between management and labor, in part, is a matter of shared experience. Unlike the American case, many company executives in Japan once headed unions at their companies. Such executives include company presidents Shuzo Muramoto of Dai-Ichi Kangyo Bank Ltd., Junji Itoh of Kanebo Ltd., Takeshi Hijikata of Sumitomo Chemical Co., and Yuzuru Abe of Nisshin Steel Co. Of 313 major Japanese companies that responded to a recent survey by the Japan Federation of Employers Association (or *Nikkeiren*), 74.1 percent had at least one executive director who once served as a labor union leader.[25] That figure is up from the 66.8 percent statistic reported in *Nikkeiren*'s last survey in 1978. Experts attribute what to most Americans seems to be a bizarre finding to the so-called lifetime employment practice of Japanese industry. Under the system, executives climb the corporate ladder step by step from the bottom. Because of their leadership ability and competence, future CEOs often are elected to lead their company's labor union in their youth. For the same reasons, their companies later promote them into management, *Nikkeiren* says.[26]

It follows that "the Japanese work ethic derives from company loyalty," writes Yoshimatsu Aonuma, economics professor at Keio University;[27] and Westerners marvel constantly at the corporate allegiance displayed by Japanese workers. From the Japanese viewpoint, though, the difference is management, not labor. "There's little difference between Japanese and U.S. workers," says Yuzo Kumamota, director of administration at Toyota's mammoth Takaoka assembly plant.[28] But what is different is the collective self-reliance of white- and blue-collar employees on promoting the welfare and productivity of their employees. "In the U.S., labor-management relations are a matter of combat," writes *Forbes*'s James Cook. "In Japan, they're a pursuit of consensus. Far from trying to win something at the other's expense, Japanese management and labor try to resolve their divergent interests in the best interests of the company."[29] Typically, these resolutions go well.

Japan is the picture of a stable, dedicated work force. Absenteeism rates and labor turnover are extremely low by U.S. standards. Labor unrest, too, is infrequent. In 1978, for example, the United States lost 39 million workdays because of strikes, while Japan lost just 1.4 million. Much to the chagrin of their American counterparts, Japanese workers are also unmatched in their progressive substitution of automation for labor. Union leaders and their constituents realize that by cutting back the number of manual workers, automation minimizes the basic weakness of Japan—the incurably high labor costs of manual work in a developed country.

If mechanization displaces a worker in Japan, he is simply transferred to another company unit. Hitachi, for instance, is designing robots to assume 60 percent of its assembly functions in five years. A step toward total plant automation, the initial stage would reduce the assembly work force by 70 percent—freeing it to fill an expected shortage of software workers. These reallocations are in keeping with human relations, Japanese style. Valued workers receive lifetime employment, a guarantee that makes them far more willing to accept new technology that others might view as threatening to their jobs.[30] An added payoff, these same values carry over to managerial employees.

In his highly popular book, *Theory Z: How American Business Can Meet the Japanese Challenge*, Professor William Ouchi calls attention to the distinctive features of Japanese management systems and their impact on organizational effectiveness.[31] Lifetime employment, collective decision making, and nonspecialized career paths underlie the penchant for long-range planning that pervades Japan's business institutions. American companies, on the other hand, are trapped by a short-term perspective and the drive for quick and highly publicized profits, forcing them into a bonus system which has made management itself too expensive. Akio Morita, founder of Sony Corporation, agrees with Professor Ouchi's conclusions. "In Japan, we can't pay a bonus to management," says Morita. "At Sony, I say management should not worry about year-by-year profits. Maybe every three years, I review my managers' wages."[32] By looking ahead, by avoiding the trap of pursuing compulsively day-to-day, short-run profits, Japanese managers and their companies are ideally tempered to cope with the vagaries of contemporary business.

In their *Art of Japanese Management,* Professors Richard Tanner Pascale and Anthony G. Athos reach similar conclusions.[33] They use the "Seven Ss" to describe Japanese managerial success versus American management practices. The "Seven Ss" are Strategy, Structure, Systems, Staff, Style, Skills, and Superordinate Goals. While American firms are considered to be particularly strong in the "hardball" Ss—strategy, structure, and systems—the Japanese are described as superior in the "soft" Ss—staff, style, skills, and superordinate goals. More important, the Japanese excel at integrating all Seven Ss, that is, at interdependence. The Japanese focus on tending the environment in which the team works and on making sure that they have a good team.

Building esprit de corps at the enterprise or national level is something the Japanese do best. Clearly, an investment plan of the proportion envisioned by Japanese industry requires governmental sanction and support. This Japan has in spades. Throughout modern time, the Rising Sun's stepped-up expansionism has had the steady prodding of government.

"Japan, Inc.," the somewhat overblown description of the nexus between business, government, and labor, is still an important catalyst behind growth in foreign direct investment. Multinationalism, says Terutomo Ozawa, is "a national desideratum for Japan, a policy officially encouraged and wholeheartedly supported by the Japanese public—including labor unions."[34]

One unique dimension of the simpatico between Japanese enterprise and government is what Ozawa calls "resource diplomacy."[35] In its worldwide search for new supply sources, Japan is trying a variety of approaches. Bargaining ploys center on political support, easy financing, commercial links, and offers to overhaul the local infrastructure. Many believe that the Japanese have launched a global resource offensive that makes the efforts of its economic rivals pale in comparison. Consider, for instance, the mammoth Asahan River project in Indonesia.

In the quest for refined aluminum, Prime Minister Tanaka visited Djakarta in 1974 to lend official commitment to Japanese businesses eager to become prime contractors. In July 1975, both governments agreed on the principles of this $1.3 billion project. Just three years from completion, this project, the largest single venture abroad by Japan, involves the construction of a huge dam and hydroelectric power station on the Asahan River, an aluminum refinery that uses the power generated, and related infrastructure facilities in Sumatra. No wonder the project is publicized as "the TVA of the Suharto government."

For its part, the private sector is represented by a twelve-company consortium: the initial participants (Sumitomo Chemical, Nippon Light Metal, Showa Denko, Mitsubishi Chemical Industries, and Mitsui Aluminum) along with seven leading trading companies as co-investors. The Japanese government, in turn, will provide credits covering approximately 70 percent of the project's total cost, along with its ever-present assistance in economic diplomacy.

On the heels of this much-publicized and highly successful "Asahan formula" are a variety of other showcase projects: in Brazil, a $1 billion effort in electrical power generation and aluminum refining; a 23-company petrochemical consortia valued at $800 million for the Singaporean government; and in Saudi Arabia, a 54-company venture (also in petrochemicals), at a tab of $1.25 billion.

Tokyo's aid to industry comes in many packages. It may take such forms as low-interest financing and guarantees from a variety of quasi-governmental agencies, help in forming corporate consortia, assured domestic markets, or insurance against political and foreign-exchange risks. But perhaps most significant are the ongoing efforts of Japanese diplomats in aiding overseas ventures. From the prime minister to the most junior commercial attaché, all members of the Japanese civil service stand by ready, willing, and able to encourage the global resource offensive of the private sector. As long as the project carries long-term significance for Japan, the officialdom of the Rising Sun sooner or later comes to the aid of industry.

In Japan, getting help from government carries no stigma. It is considered perfectly natural for government to encourage and support its most important industries. Yet, write Douglas R. Sease and Urban C. Lehner, "U.S. executives often view the close links between government and industry in Japan as something short of free enterprise. Some even think that Japanese industrialists blindly take their marching orders from MITI and build their remarkable plants with government loans."[36] Nothing could be further from the truth.

"Americans have some prejudiced views that the Japanese government is helping all Japanese industry. But that's not true," argues Sony's Akio Morita. "The reason the Japanese computer electronics industry became strong was the competition, among Japanese companies. . . . We like to create competition. But we don't rely on the Japanese government for assistance."[37] By almost every standard, the Japanese economy is equally or more competitive than that of the United States. And "in almost every industry where Japanese companies have done well in export markets, they have honed their teeth in fierce domestic competition," says Ken Ohmae, managing partner of McKinsey & Co.'s Tokyo office.[38] To illustrate:

☐ In cameras, at least half a dozen major Japanese companies— Nikon, Canon, Olympus, Minolta, Pentax, and Konica—compete vigorously for shares of the domestic market.

☐ In color televisions, industry leaders such as Matsushita, Sony, Toshiba, and Hitachi must contend with close runners-up such as Mitsubishi, Sanyo, Sharp, and Nippon Electric.

☐ In hi-fi audio equipment, Technics (Matsushita) and Pioneer slug it out in Japan with Aurex (Toshiba), Lo-D (Hitachi), Sansui, Sony, and many others.

☐ In autos, Toyota and Nissan (Datsun) strive for first place, with Mitsubishi, Toyo Kogyo (Mazda), Honda, and Fuji (Subaru) nipping at their heels.

And the list continues. Therefore, to understand why Japanese companies do so well in world markets, it is important to recognize that they have built up their competitive strengths in perhaps the world's most competitive domestic marketplace.[39] "Our secret is our ability to combine cooperation and competition," says a highly placed MITI official. "[Japanese] companies compete fiercely with each other. But they realize that on big research and development projects, for example, they have no choice but to cooperate."[40]

American misconceptions notwithstanding, MITI cannot and usually does not protect the Japanese from each other. True, the ministry has aided Japan's growth and success. But MITI is just one of many institutions that form the framework within which the economy has thrived. Besides the trading companies mentioned earlier, the banks and trade groups have played important roles, too.

Industrial capital in Japan normally comes from the banks rather than from external capital markets, and banks not only lend money, "but also take equity interests in their creditor companies — less as a token of ownership than as an indication of the mutual support corporations extend each other."[41] Financial institutions, for instance, hold 61 percent of Nissan's equity; corporations another 30 percent. Though individual banks are permitted to own only up to 5 percent of a company's stock, they can still exert considerable clout.

"Stock purchases," Peter Drucker advises, "have nothing to do with financing the business. The financing is [a] bank loan. . . . But the Japanese distinguish, without ever saying so, very sharply between the part of the bank loan that is loan and the part that is equity. The bank doesn't buy shares but gives a loan that is 80% or 90% of the company's capital. And the bank and the company both know that half of the loan is equity, which means that it may not be called normally."[42] Through this method, banks, especially long-term credit banks like the Industrial Bank of Japan, allow Japanese firms flexibly and rapidly to undertake massive investments such as those made to sustain an 8 percent increase in integrated-circuit production capacity between 1977 and 1979.

In its thirty years of existence, the Japan Development Bank's lending capacity has grown 34-fold, from 30 billion yen in 1951 to 1,077 billion yen in 1981. During that period the JDB has financed such projects as the successful commercialization of Sony's Trinitron tube for color television and the Wankel engine for cars.[43] Currently, its focus is on energy resources and high technology, and the bank lends only to projects that fit into articulated government policy and are located in Japan. While there is much evidence of government-orchestrated financing of priority industries, public officials claim that this perception is all nonsense. Kiyoaki Kikuchi, former deputy minister of foreign affairs and now ambassador to Mexico, "object[s] very much to . . . the idea of Japan Inc.—government, MITI and businessmen—using the taxpayers' money [to fund priority sectors]."[44] Yet he admits that government money accounts for *only* 30 percent of total research spending"[45] (italics added). There is no question that over the years Japanese banks and public institutions have helped to reduce the financial risks involved in industry's plunging ahead with much-needed capital expansion programs.

The trade groups also make their presence felt. "Major business federations like *Keidanren* with substantial staffs make policy proposals and help to orchestrate Japan's increasingly complex resource-oriented [democracy]," explains Harvard's Kent E. Calder.[46] In each major sector, an industry association (*gyokai*), representing major firms in the sector, stands ready to provide MITI with current data on the industry's condition, to help administer depressed-industry cartels, capacity reduction, and voluntary-restraint agreements.

Taken together, these institutions underscore the commercial collectivism behind the Japanese challenge. In charting the future course of the steel industry, for instance, the companies, banks, and other interested parties participate actively in the making of steel policy. The forum: an advisory council to MITI called the Industrial Structure Deliberation Council and its several subcommittees, each including industry, financial, academic, government, and other representatives.[47] In the consensus-building process, the aim is to settle a position that nearly everyone can support.

"It is axiomatic to practically every Japanese," Peter Drucker observes, "that Japan's dependence on imported fuel, food and raw materials demands close collaboration between government and industry and a basically merchantist philosophy. . . . Hardly anybody in Japan would argue for a traditional laissez-faire economy."[48] Indeed, it would be inaccurate as well as naive to describe the Japanese model in Friedmanian terms. Nevertheless, it would be equally imprecise to overstate the hand of Big Government in Japan's rise from the ashes. "Contrary to . . . conventional wisdom," Professor Calder notes, "Japanese success is in fact a powerful argument for less government, rather than more. The times demand efficient, minimalist, market-oriented government—which can nonetheless coordinate the changes required to restore our national competitiveness. It is precisely this sort of minimalist government, with the low taxes and scope for private initiative, which has been a crucial element in Japan's dynamic industrialization."[49] By coupling private-sector initiatives with a "minimalist" government, Japan stands ready to extend the force of its trillion dollar economic machine into the 1980s and beyond.

The Rebirth of the Reich

From a commercial wasteland three decades ago to the dominant economy in Europe today, West Germany has also won the respect of nations on the rise. As with Japan, the odds makers had all but counted it out. It would take a miracle, the pundits said, for war-wrecked Germany to reemerge among the industrial powers—even by the end of the century. But miracles, on occasion, do happen, and Prussian determinism created one: the *Wirtschaftswunder* (economic "miracle").

West Germany's transformation from a destroyed nation to an economic superpower was carefully designed. Its primary architect: Dr. Ludwig Erhard. In July 1948, Professor Erhard, chairman of the Economic Council of "Bizonia," the combined American and British zones of occupation, met with Lucius D. Clay, the military governor of the American zone.[50] Heeding the advice of Freiburg University economist Alfred Muller-Armack, Erhard envisaged a Germany in which free market forces laced with welfare statism would govern.

45

At Erhard's urging, General Clay abolished wage-and-price controls and postwar rationing; and to Clay's surprise and to the dismay of his closest advisers, it worked. West Germany—and Ludwig Erhard—never looked back.

Next came the creation of the Federal Republic of Germany (FRG) in September 1949 and, with it, the concept of a social market economy. As economic minister to Chancellor Conrad Adenauer, Dr. Erhard handcrafted new policies directed at achieving *Soziale Markwirtschaft*, a socially responsible free market economy.

"Capitalism with a conscience," as it is now called, is the foundation of Germany's present economic philosophy. It represents a form of capitalism designed to foster a dynamic partnership between labor, business, and government by combining cradle-to-grave social benefits and vigorous public-sector investments with a firm commitment to marketplace competition.

Undoubtedly, the memory of just how badly democracy fared in the Weimar Republic created a greater willingness by the German people to favor such an economic philosophy of compromise over combat. "Consensus rather than confrontation," says Harvard's Guido Goldman, "has typified the internal political and economic life of the FRG. . . . The state, labor and business leadership coalesce in ways that have fed effective economic collaboration."[51] The result: the German version of a "Japan, Inc."

Unions, for their part, have usually refrained from making wage demands that are unjustified by productivity increases. "Concerted action" brings together labor leaders, managers, and government officials on a regular basis to discuss issues of mutual interest. Through codetermination (*Mitbestimmung*) workers appear as co-equals with managers on boards of directors.[52]

This unique form of "industrial democracy" evolved from a 1951 law covering the steel and coal industry. At that time, labor received equal voting power with shareholders on the supervisory boards of German concerns—giving workers broad rights of consultation on working conditions, layoffs, and personnel policies. Later, in 1976, the West German parliament raised from one-third to one-half the portion of worker representatives on the supervisory boards of firms with more than 2000 employees.

To its advocates, industrial relations, German style, represents the wave of the future. Some of its proponents argue that the German board system sets for workers and blue-collar participation in shop-floor decision making and gives employees more control over their lives. For others, codetermination has encouraged worker motivation and contributed rightly to Germany's high industrial productivity and low incidence of industrial strife. James C. Furlong, author of *Labor in the Boardroom: The Peaceful Revolution*, goes so far as to suggest that codetermination has been the secret of West Germany's monetary stability and high growth rate.[53]

Despite some evidence of labor's turning to greater militancy in the last few years, Reinhold Stoessel, chief economist of the Dresdner Bank, points out that "unions are more concerned with the size of the economic cake than fighting about how it's shared."[54] Hence, German workers have deferred pay increases and allowed their employers to plow profits back into modernizing plants, increasing productivity, and guaranteeing employment. Organized labor, on the receiving end of one of the world's most far-reaching and expensive social benefit systems, usually prefers to collaborate, not confront, German business interests.

Consider, for instance, how Germany profits by its unique apprenticeship program, which weaves financial and organizational support from labor, management, and government.[55] With its roots in the craft guilds of the Middle Ages, this system benefits from Germany's educational system, which sets occupational paths at ages as early as ten. Apprenticeships start with the end of compulsory schooling at age fifteen. Then, with advice from local industry, unions, and government, youths who want to take a two- to three-year apprenticeship course select from over four hundred possible occupations. What is more, about 80 percent of the apprentices who finish their programs stay with the companies that trained them.[56]

Employee staying power is characteristically German. From company-sponsored sports to low-cost vacations, employers excel at keeping their workers happy. What's in it for business? Loyalty, at least. The average BASF employer, for example, is forty and has been with the company for almost fifteen years.[57] One expects that he is probably a far more dedicated worker than his peer in the United States. In addition, Germany has been a leader—along with Japan—at building worker involvement in the production process. Volkswagen, Germany's largest automaker, is the latest company to initiate a switch from traditional mass production techniques—the assembly line—to building complete automobiles by small groups of workers.[58] With the backing of its major union, IG Metall, and at an annual cost of over $15 million, VW anticipates that up to 60 percent of its work force could be organized along these lines within the next few years. Even if work groups boost productivity by only 2 percent, the scheme will pay for itself. Anything above 4 percent will be full profit. "Our workers are now fully behind this 'work-enrichment' program, as we like to call it," a Volkswagen spokesman claims, "and labor is consulted at every stage. We fully expect this plan to be the model of the future, to increase VW's income in the long run, and perhaps to be a model for the West as Japan has been for the East."[59]

Government, too, stands ready to accommodate the private sector. Resource diplomacy, German style, also parallels the Japanese approach described earlier. With some envy, Reginald Jones, former board chairman of General Electric Co., notes that "whenever the chancellor of West Germany goes abroad, he has a number of major commercial proposals in his briefcase."[60]

Also supportive are government's enlightened attitudes in the administration of antitrust policy. The public sector has consistently encouraged conglomeration to ensure that West German industry remains competitive in world markets. When, for instance, the Germany Cartel Bureau ruled in the early 1970s that Volkswagen could not acquire Audi, the government overruled it. That decision, as Jean Ross-Skinner recalls, "proved to be VW's solution. Sales of its famed, but obsolescent Beetle slumped badly shortly thereafter. But a whole new series of cars already on Audi's drawing boards helped Volkswagen to recoup quickly."[61] In another case, the Bonn government acted to bring about a merger between Vereinigte Flug-techninsche Werke and Messerschmidt-Bolkow-Blohm, making the joint entity the third largest aircraft manufacturer in Europe.[62] By so doing, public officials hope that the combined company will compete more effectively with its American and European rivals.

Bigness, in the eyes of both West Germany and Japan, promotes competition, especially where world markets are concerned; and economic concentration is a central feature of the German system. The chemical, electro-technical, and automotive industries are dominated by monolithic giants, who have emerged as important multinational players.[63] Here, the interplay between size and commanding export performance has been of immense strategic value to the nation; and all three industries export more than 40 percent of their total production.

Economic concentration in West Germany is increasing, slowly but steadily.[64] The three largest companies in each major sector of the economy accounted for 26.9 percent of sector turnover in 1977 as against 25.3 percent in 1975. Alternatively, West Germany's one hundred largest companies raised their contributions of total economic turnover from 21.7 percent in 1972 to 24.2 percent in 1978. The accommodation of the Bonn government is largely responsible for these trends, but permissive banking legislation also plays an important role.

Unlike in the United States, there is no separation of the deposit-gathering and investment banking functions in West Germany. As a result, German banks are in a position to acquire a significant stake in the companies to which they lend as well as to build the supergiant firms that rule the economy.[65] Directly, and through shares of its customers deposited with it, the Deutsche Bank, for instance, probably controls 50 percent of Siemens's share capital. This phenomenon gives Prussian banks a distinct edge over their international competitors. The provision of massive funds by private banks permits more long-term, stable planning for industry; and German firms are not nearly as adversely affected by the collapse of stock prices as are their American counterparts. In fact, share prices are irrelevant to the German lenders, who are much more concerned with the long-term viability of their clients.

"Banks and companies," says Harvard's Goldman, "work together to rationalize when desirable and to salvage when necessary. A bankruptcy such as Rolls Royce would not occur in the FRG."[66] By the same token, *World Business Weekly* reports: "If Chrysler Corp. had been a West German company, its frantic and highly visible quest for bank loans to fend off imminent bankruptcy might never have occurred. Nor would it have had to wolf down humble pie while beseeching the government's support."[67] A hypothetical West German Chrysler, it adds, "could have quietly and confidently relied on its banks—which would also be among its major shareholders— to provide bail-out funds."[68]

Besides this advantageous partnership between banks and their key corporate customers, the prevailing winds permit allegiances and relationships that would not be possible in the United States. On any score, the hands of Big Government and friendly labor are highly visible in West German affairs.

LOOKING AHEAD

Taken together, government's support, labor's cooperation, and industry's resourcefulness fueled West Germany's economic miracle. Today, West Germany accounts for one-fourth of Western Europe's GNP, and it is often referred to as "the engine of Europe." In contrast to other industrialized countries, its economic indicators remain impressive: inflation is on the rise, yet still is only 5.3 percent; unemployment is below 6 percent; exports shot up an estimated 13.7 percent last year; and work force productivity (as measured by the value of production per hour) is exceeded only by that of the Netherlands. On the surface, Germany seems to be doing very well.[69]

But to the critics, these figures tell only part of the story. There is, they argue, good reason to be nervous about the impending condition of the West German economy.[70] The deutsche mark, once in a state of continuous appreciation, has faltered badly. It has lost 7 percent against the dollar since 1978 and 26 percent last year, and it has also slipped against such one-time weaklings as the British pound, the French franc, and even the Italian lira. Real devaluation rates are even higher when one takes into consideration the fact that inflation in West Germany has been lower than in the United States, let alone other European countries.

Looking ahead, one sees that economic growth went negative for the first time in 1981, but it should bottom out by midyear. The balance-of-payments deficit, which was $1 billion in 1979 after fourteen years of continuous surpluses, was $28 billion in 1980—far higher than any other industrialized nation. A big reason is that West Germany paid OPEC member nations $30 billion more for oil that year than in 1979, despite a 20 percent reduction in consumption. The results were even worse in 1981.

Burgeoning public debt adds to Bonn's problems. Soaring welfare costs dampen the entire economy. Doomsayers claim that the "Swedish disease" has struck West Germany; and, no doubt, years of social democracy (and all of its obligations) are now taking their toll.[71]

With Chancellor Helmut Schmidt's Social Democratic Party safely restored to another term of office, Bonn has been taking steps to tighten its belt. Schmidt decided on an $8 billion cut in last year's public spending and withdrew his NATO pledge to raise military spending by 3 percent annually for fifteen years—a move that was greeted with great dismay in Washington.

The Bundesbank has also left no doubt that combating West Germany's recent reversals is the No. 1 challenge. With its characteristic independence, the bank has resisted all pressure to cut the discount rate. Tight money along with reduced government spending are projected for some time.

At Bonn's insistence, industry's pricing policy must be moderate, and unions have been advised to keep their wage demands low. Both sides, in typical Germanic fashion, seem to be living with this message. For instance, organized labor has not repeated last year's widespread demands for wage hikes above and beyond those agreed to in routine wage negotiations. If the recent agreement by IG Metall, West Germany's largest union, for a 4.2 percent pay hike is an indicator, labor should settle for something in the order of 5 percent pay increases this year.[72]

SEARCHING FOR SOLUTIONS

For its apparent failings, the alleged "German decline" is the kind of misery most other industrialized economies would be happy to suffer. True, growth has slowed. In the 1960s, West Germany scored "only" the average economic growth rate of the industrial world; in the 1970s, its GNP rate of growth was below average. Yet, as the *Economist* points out, "after a series of energy crises that took the price of oil from $2 a barrel to over $34, this energy-dependent economy was in 1979 booming beyond expectation and it still had inflation under control. Neither the U.S., nor Britain, nor Italy, nor the West Germans' closest neighbor, France, could boast the same combination."[73]

Put in proper perspective, the softening of Germany's economic muscle may not be so serious. And we should be careful not to wrap more black crepe around this remarkable nation. What does merit careful scrutiny, however, is the role that the coalition partners of "Germany, Inc.," will play in moving the economy ahead. The fundamental question facing Bonn, writes *Business Week*, is "whether the laissez-faire government philosophy and the business institutions that nourished the German 'miracle' in the fast-growing world economy of the 1950s and 1960s are still valid—or whether Germany must seek new ways in the 1980s to sustain its industrial momentum."[74]

Those new ways, in large part, will require new industrial strategies for the West German economy. The soft underbelly of German industry remains its reliance on several mature industries: chemicals, automobiles, mechanical and electrical machinery. The problem, according to Robert J. Avila of New York's SAGE Associates, is that Germany does not have firm footholds in today's high-growth, high-technology industries, from electronics to biochemicals. "Demand for German's prime exports is declining, and there is increasing competition from Japan at the high technology end and from the developing countries at the low end," Avila says.[75] West Germany, he warns, could become "the Ohio Valley of Europe."[76]

Realistic? Perhaps not. Still, the timing may be right for Bonn to reassess its current industrial policies, as Japan did in the mid-1970s. Even the Federal Republic's economic minister, Otto Graf Lambsdorff, concedes that the German economy must be "substantially restructured."[77]

Midcourse corrections rather than profound redirections will characterize this restructuring process. Unlike its wartime partner Japan, West Germany understates the role of government in, for instance, targeting sunrise and sunset industries. Which industries are so identified, Count Lambsdorff advises, "is not a question you should ask the German government. We feel it is the task of industry itself, of the entrepreneurs, to find new products, new fields of activity, and new markets."[78] Bonn, he adds, "can assist in technology research, and we do. But we do not want to prescribe and certainly not to order."[79]

The relatively unobtrusive posture of the West German bureaucracy allows free market economics to move the nation in the right direction, and it underlies government's deep-seated belief that businessmen, who are active in their own markets on a day-to-day basis, know best where their future challenges and opportunities lie. Faith in the capitalists with a conscience has worked in the past; and its advocates, who constitute the bulk of West German society, favor its continued application.

With a profile that is considerably lower than that of their Japanese counterparts, government officials in West Germany are gingerly nudging industry to scan for new fields of opportunity. So far, the private and public sectors are in agreement, and their conclusions closely mirror Tokyo's earlier findings—namely, a preference for (1) knowledge-intensive and energy-reliant industries (at the expense of mature, energy-consuming businesses), and (2) overseas markets in advanced economies, particularly the United States.

At the present time, the West German government is offering a multitude of incentives aimed at spurring industrial diversification, corporate research and development, and innovation generally.[80] Here the role of the Federal Ministry of Research and Technology (a post which does not exist in the U.S. cabinet) has become increasingly important. With a hefty budget, the ministry is actively underwriting high-technology fields that range from microelectronics to silicon chips.[81] It has also funded a variety of projects aimed at upgrading the competitiveness of mature industries (such as chemicals) and at subsidizing the modernization of steel-producing equipment (as, for example, at Hoechst).

But it is in lessening West Germany's dependence on imported crude oil that the Ministry of Research and Technology and related governmental agencies deserve especially high marks. No other industrialized nation has been as skillful in the art of oil diplomacy.[82] When it became clear to West Germany that its major supplier, Iran, could no longer be counted upon for crude oil supplies, it immediately solicited other OPEC countries (including Iraq) and restored the continuity of precious petroleum. Concurrently, the German foreign service cleverly negotiated long-term supply agreements with the Soviet Union and Algeria for natural gas imports.

Equally impressive are the German successes in nuclear energy, synthetic fuels, coal gasification, and the equipment needed to run these sectors. In each segment, West Germany ranks among world leaders, and it is No. 1 in coal-mining productivity. Germany's coal miners were among the first to automate, and they are capitalizing their expertise at home—and abroad. Three examples:

☐ The recent decision of Hemscheidt Maschinenfabrik to build its first plant in the United States at a site near Pittsburgh.

☐ The plans of Krupp Koppers, a leader in coal gasification, to enter the U.S. market with a Kentucky plant for the International Coal Refining Co. of Allentown, Pennsylvania. The U.S. Department of Energy will underwrite 92 percent of the $1.49 billion project, and Kentucky another 2 percent.

☐ The plans of Saarbergmerke AG, a government-owned coal and energy company, to acquire a 25 percent stake in Ashland Coal Inc. for $102.5 million.

These cases, however, represent just the tip of the iceberg.

Since 1968, West Germany's foreign investment has grown at a 14.2 percent clip each year (see Exhibit 2.2). In fact, last year the FRG's overseas investments amounted to three times those made in West Germany by foreigners, although this trend is unlikely to continue for the foreseeable future. Nearly three-quarters of all West German foreign investments (72.5 percent) are located in the industrialized world with the United States and Canada receiving increasing attention in recent years. North America now has more than one-quarter of the stock of West Germany's foreign holdings, and nearly one-half of new overseas investments made by Germany in the past eighteen months were U.S.-bound.

To be sure, the United States offers many advantages to German investors. The recurring themes underlying America's special appeal are the size and attractiveness of the U.S. market, the rising value of the deutsche mark versus the dollar, and lower labor costs. Whether it is Volkswagen making cars in Pennsylvania or Daimler-Benz building trucks in Virginia, West Germany's assault on the American market takes many forms. Consider, for instance, the acquisitions appetite of German multinationals:

☐ The takeover of the Budd Company by the steelmaker Thyssen.

☐ Bayer's purchase of Miles Laboratories.

☐ BASF's triple pickup: New York's Fritsche, Dodge & Olcott, America's third largest maker of flavors and fragrances; Detroit-based Cook Industrial Coatings Corp., a major supplier to the auto industry; and Allegheny Ludlum's pigments division.

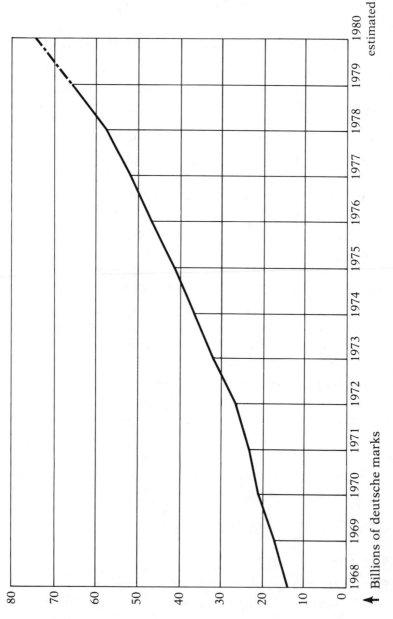

Exhibit 2.2 West Germany's global reach—foreign investments, 1968-1979 (in billions of deutsche marks). *Source:* Andrew Hargrave, "West Germany, a Top Investment Partner," *New York Times,* October 28, 1980, p. 12. © 1980 by The New York Times Company. Reprinted by permission.

Then, there are the joint ventures. For example, the linkage of West Germany's largest contractor, Philipp Holzmann, with the J.A. Jones Construction Company of Charlotte, North Carolina, created a $3 billion conglomerate. (In April 1981 this duo added Lockwork Engineers Inc. of Spartansburg, South Carolina, to its family.)

Whether it is through acquisitions, joint ventures, or other vehicles, the cream of West German industry is committed to the American market. Says Hoechst's Deputy Chairman C. Kurt Lanz, "No market in the world is more important to Hoechst today than the U.S. Our hope and aim is to have American Hoechst rank as a major chemicals and pharmaceuticals company in its own right."[83] Hermann-Josef Strenger of Bayer agrees, "We expect our U.S. operations to produce 20 percent of Bayer's world sales in the course of the next five years, versus 14 percent now."[84]

It is not coincidental that leaders from the chemical industry are among Germany's staunchest supporters of an all-out attack on the American market. By allowing their experience curve advantages to take hold, the so-called "Big Three" — BASF, Hoechst, and Bayer — became least-cost suppliers. Over time, they have been able to secure a dominant market share in the United States at the expense of American multinationals like Du Pont, Union Carbide, Dow Chemical, and others. (Du Pont, for example, was the world's largest chemical producer in 1969. A decade later it had been leap-frogged by each of the German Big Three.)

True to form, chemicals are leading Germany's forays overseas. Its level of foreign investment (DM 10.5 billion) easily surpasses the runner-up, the electrical industry (DM 6.8 billion). Still, other mature industries in West Germany are following the lead of chemicals by exploiting their scale economies and market share victories — first at home and, later, abroad. Iron and steel, motor vehicles, and transportation are just a few cases in point. If Bonn can complement these historical winners with a cadre of new, high-technology industries, West Germany's place in the global economy should be assured.

Summary

The economic performance of Japan and West Germany, as measured by all the conventional indicators, has been superior to that of the United States from 1970 on. By trying harder, both nations are demonstrating the effectiveness of "Avis strategies" where world markets are at stake. But sweat alone did not breed the economic comebacks of West Germany and Japan. In both cases, several other elements accompanied their success.

First and foremost, both countries pursue a collaborative approach of business, government, and labor to economic nation-building. Each of these major forces is able to put aside any misguided ambitions it might have for the benefit of the country-at-large. Whims of personal aggrandizement are muffled, and the ranking leaders of the major economic stakeholders are committed to rapprochement.

The primary integrator in making these coalitions go is government. Tokyo and Bonn provide more incentives to private saving, investment, and international business than Washington does. The West German government, especially, exercises its clout through tax revenues and expenditures, which represent a much larger share of GNP than in Japan or the United States. The Japanese government, with a relatively small public budget, opts to flex its muscle in other areas: industrial planning, resource diplomacy, and explicit administrative guidance to business.

In addition, German and Japanese companies are more dependent on banks than on equity markets for financing. Consequently, their governments are most influential through their decisions regarding monetary policy. Tokyo and Bonn can prime the investment pump in any desired direction.

Second, neither nation is inclined to leave its economic fate in the hands of market forces. Industrial policymaking receives serious attention in West Germany and Japan. How to leverage maturing industries, what new technologies to tap, and which foreign markets to plunder are questions that are asked and reasked in both countries.

The answers, of course, do not come easily. They touch upon such thorny areas as industrial restructuring, plan relocations, and planned layoffs. Nevertheless, the officialdom of West Germany and Japan does not shy away from making these difficult and far-reaching decisions.

Naturally, there are style differences. Japan, as we have seen, yields to its government the chore of setting industrial policy. Germany, on the other hand, permits the private sector to uncover the new market niches upon which future generations will depend. In both cases, the vital tasks of redefining the axes upon which economic prosperity can be perpetuated are not left to chance.

Third, a highly effective system of intra- and inter-sectoral institutions encourages close communications and understanding between the German and Japanese coalitions. Whether it is Japan's *Keidanren* or West Germany's consultative arrangements, both nations have pioneered elaborate networks of conciliatory organizations, to say nothing of their many ad hoc special-interest groups. From position papers on environmental protection to recommendations on national tariff policy, these agencies are able to speak with a common tongue on any current topic of national interest. They easily outdistance their counterparts in the United States or, for that matter, those in any industrialized nation.

Fourth, one of the main reasons that Germany and Japan have had a relatively strong track record is that they have less antagonistic labor-management relations than those of rival nations. The German and Japanese systems of corporate governance weigh carefully shareholder and employee interests. Managers are more fully committed to the firm, to productivity and product quality, and, in the final analysis, to economic performance. The concept of workers as coequals with business and government represents an important advantage to Japan and West Germany.

Fifth, both nations possess a civil service of the highest caliber. These elite bureaucracies are able to snatch the best and the brightest from their nation's bosom. Unlike the United States, the public sector is often viewed as the fast track, and dual careers are quite visible in Japan and West Germany. A pyramid of human contact and shared experience characterizes dealings between the private and public sectors. This reciprocity of respect between the members of business and government goes a long way toward making coalition politics work.

Finally, Japan and West Germany recognize that economic success at home depends on success abroad, and not the other way around. The leaders of both nations are able to look beyond their national noses and to seek out opportunities overseas. Recognizing the rising costs of domestic manufacturing, Japan and Germany are pacesetters when it comes to selecting low-cost foreign sites for their mature industries. At the same time, they are developing new technologies back home in an effort to extend their comparative advantage. Simply stated, Japan and West Germany are masters at understanding the role and potential contribution of international business.

The combined force of these factors is sustaining the Japanese and German assault on world markets. How exportable these methods are to the United States, of course, remains to be seen. Nevertheless, the lessons of Japan and West Germany are inspiring a growing nucleus of other countries eager to participate more actively in the global economy.

3

The Second Japans . . . and Beyond

"**F**OLLOW Japan!" This recent headline in France's leading news weekly, *L'Express*, sums up the growing conviction in government and industry that the key to French prosperity in the 1980s and beyond is to emulate Japan's postwar industrial strategy. From Paris to Taipei, leaders are shifting their allegiance from American to Japanese—and German—notions of industrialization and post-industrialization. Increasingly, the Tokyo and Bonn versions of stakeholder relations stand as the preferred model.

The envy of many nations, developed and developing, Japan especially is viewed as the economic pacesetter for good reasons—its rapid industrialization, rising currency, growing export surplus, productive work force, and overall leadership in international business. What is more, this process of economic achievement has occurred without disrupting Japan's social and cultural values. Quite the contrary, traditional Japanese norms (such as the work ethic) have tended to legitimatize its commercial accomplishments.

"Once Japan demonstrated that a resource poor Asian country could, by proper mobilization of its economy, move very rapidly to high levels of output and income," says James C. Abegglen of the

Boston Consulting Group, "other nations were able to draw on that model."[1] Simply the fact that it had been done was significant. Japan's renewal clearly demonstrated that modernization and Westernization were not synonymous.[2] With that realization, the pervasive influence of America's economic culture began to give way to concepts made in Japan.

It is no wonder, then, that a growing number of countries seeking modernization without Westernization are eager to follow Japan's course. But in what directions? Above all, these countries are opting for some version of "Japan, Inc."—that strong coalition of business, government, and labor. By the same token, they seek to avoid the hostilities that often accompany dealings between government and business in North America, Oceania, and some parts of Western Europe. As black African leader Gordon C. Chavenduka put it, "We need mixed capitalism, modified socialism."[3]

Like Japan, nations both rich and poor prefer the collaborative approach to industrialization. Among other things, this means considerable government intervention or "administrative guidance" in the economic affairs of nations on the rise.

"In a developing country, government initiative plays the leading role," argues Nam Duck Woo, South Korea's former prime minister. "It's decisive. The government must give guidance, direction, stability."[4] When you ask why the Economic Planning Board of South Korea is taking a certain policy with respect to, say, foreign investment, the answer is very often, "Well, we examined what MITI had done earlier and have adopted it." This, Dr. Nam candidly admits: "Government initiatives are indispensable in allocating financial resources, providing government guarantees, and negotiating with foreign governments and banks. No question, there's close business-government collaboration in this country—analogous to Japan."[5]

Special Asian Appeal

Following Japan's lead, South Korea and other newly industrializing countries of Asia are on the march. Variously referred to as the "second Japans," the "Gang of Four," or the "chopstick countries," South Korea, Taiwan, Hong Kong, and Singapore are parlaying a strong work ethic, efficient public administrators, political stability, and a common Sino-Japanese heritage to their advantage.[6] All are tremendously successful, with sustained economic growth rates of about 9 percent annually. Willard D. Sharpe, area economist for Chase Manhattan Bank, goes so far as to predict that by 1990 "the four stars [will be] still outshining just about every country. Their aggregate gross national product will have doubled, and their relative importance in Asia will be even greater than it is today."[7]

Jean-Jacques Servan-Schreiber, who once extolled American management methods as examples for Europe and the Far East, now feels that these aggressive Asian nations, with the help of microchip technology, could vault from underdevelopment directly into major computer societies. This is a main theme of his recent book, *The World Challenge.*[8] "It's a very shocking idea at first, but I'm not the only one who's saying it," Mr. Servan-Schreiber commented. "People in the Third World are saying it, too."[9]

Indeed, in each national instance, Japan serves as the engine of development. "It serves as engine in a very real sense: it is the source of the capital and the technology required for growth, and it is the region's market," explains James Abegglen.[10] Ongoing visits to Southeast Asian capitals by Japanese heads of state (by Zenko Suzuki in January 1981) demonstrate the importance of these markets to Japan, and vice versa.[11] On the one hand, Japan's ambassadors in business suits may seem to form a pernicious posse of industrial imperialists; but on the other, the Rising Sun is, after all, the largest trading partner, foreign investor, and source of foreign aid in the ASEAN region. (ASEAN stands for the Association of Southeast Asian Nations, which includes Malaysia, Indonesia, Singapore, Thailand, and the Philippines.) Hence, loud and frequent appeals by Japanese prime ministers to their "fellow Asians" are not likely to fall on deaf ears. Quite the opposite, the area's leaders openly acknowledge their growing economic, political, and diplomatic reliance on Japan.

"The model of Japan and its success in rising from the ashes of the Pacific war has proved increasingly attractive," writes Derek Davies, editor of the *Far Eastern Economic Review*.[12] "Japan's developmental strategy—industrialization based on the careful acquisition of Western technology and an unremitting search for export markets—has been carefully adopted by the most successful economies of Asia—Singapore, Hong Kong, South Korea, Taiwan, and Malaysia and, perhaps to a lesser degree of success, Thailand, the Philippines, and Indonesia—some of which, at one time, adopted radically nationalistic socialist policies."[13] But unlike Japan, the move away from socialist economic strategies toward more open economies by the "second Japans" has not been accompanied by a move toward Western-style democratic systems.

With the exception of Japan, Australia, and New Zealand, one finds a noticeable decline in Western parliamentarianism in the Pacific Basin since World War II. Of the world's nations, only about 18 percent (roughly thirty in number) meet any normal standard of what constitutes a free and open political society. On the issue of political ideology, most Asian nations are breaking ranks with Japan (and the United States). They favor a so-called directed democracy with its balanced authoritarianism and accompanying features: political and economic centralism, formalized national economic planning, and efficiency-suppressed egalitarianism.

"Expediency's gains spell the loss of basic human rights," the critics argue. Yet, authoritarianism need not be viewed in the same light as totalitarianism. Professor Robert Scalapino of the University of California at Berkeley warns the natural opponents of South Korea, the Philippines, and other directive Asian nations that "it will become very important . . . to try to make the distinction between quasi-authoritarian societies—ones that have certain evolutionary potential—and those that seem dedicated to dictatorship of one party to a purely statist system that has not yet offered very much evolutionary potential."[14]

The dynamism of the region indicates that this evolutionary potential exists, at least in economic affairs. Take the case of South

Korea, a target of much external criticism. For all its alleged faults, it has eliminated the discrepancy between urban and rural household incomes—a feat matched by very few other nations, including the United States. Although most of Korea's Five-Year Plans were primarily industrial in their focus, they did include provisions for improving the productivity of agriculture and the quality of life on the farm. One of the most important moves in this direction came in the Second Plan period with the introduction of the *Saemaul* (or "New Community") movement. This rural self-help program had a quite simple premise: If you were willing to work, the government would pay for the materials. The results can be seen throughout the countryside, where clusters of thatch-roofed cottages have been turned into model villages with gleaming tile roofs, fresh paint, and paved streets. But most important, the *Saemaul* movement has so enhanced farm income that it surpassed urban income three years ago. Widespread social progress in South Korea takes place on several fronts: medical care, education, and housing—all this despite what strikes most Westerners as a tight-fisted dictatorship.

Whatever their political leanings, the "second Japans" are calling on the public sector to plot their economic offensives. Indicative, rather than regulatory, planning is a basic aim of government. South Korea's Nam, for instance, believes that the proper role for Seoul is to "direct the interest and energy of our people to national economic development . . . hoping that individual firms will respond."[15] A professional cadre of civil servants works diligently to assume the necessary corporate response. "Our bureaucrats are quick, flexible and pragmatic—as well as being goal- and achievement-oriented," beams Dr. Nam. "In fact, in 'Korea, Inc.,' the bureaucrats play a more important role than in Japan!"[16]

Choong Hoon Park, president of the Korean Traders Association, also speaks highly of Seoul's bureaucracy. "The Korean Government, in establishing and implementing economic policy guidelines, has consistently remained pragmatical, flexible and innovative," he boasts.[17] Mr. Choong should know. His voluntary, nonprofit organization, modeled strictly along Japanese lines, safeguards the interests of its 2300 companies—a membership that has multipled 58-fold since its inception in 1962.

Hong Kong or Singapore?

What we are seeing in South Korea and its Asian allies are economic ties that bind predominantly open economies with activist governments and a relatively docile labor force. One wonders, what would Milton Friedman think?

In their bestseller *Free to Choose* Milton and Rose Friedman present Hong Kong as "perhaps the best example . . . of limited government and free market societies in practice."[18] Their choice may leave something to be desired. Aside from Thieves Alley, a bazaar of black-market merchandising, Hong Kong often operates much like a closely held corporation. The privately owned Hong Kong & Shanghai Banking Corporation assumes the mantle of a public institution. Among its many "official" duties is the printing of local currency. In addition, a well-entrenched cluster of a few companies dominates the central business district. The "hongs," as they are called, include such familiar names as the Swire Group and Hutchison-Whompoa, with roots in the soil of James Clavell's epic novels Tai-pan and *Noble House.* Besides the steadying influence of these mandarins, the government's size and scope are growing. Last year, for instance, public spending rose by more than the rate of economic growth and that sector's share of the colony's gross domestic product reached over 22 percent, compared with 15 percent seven years ago.[19]

The rise of direct spending is only one form of government's gaining presence.[20] There is a mounting debate about whether the bureaucracy should intervene directly with the market mechanisms to push the economy along. The trickiest area is land. Hong Kong, with its 5.07 million people crammed into 404 square miles of land, is already overcrowded, and rents have risen four to ten times in the past eighteen months. So far, government is holding back on the mounting calls for rent controls.

Hong Kong's capital markets are a different story. The city-state's reputation as the last bastion of capitalism was tarnished during the recent "Battle of the Kowloon Wharf." Profiteering entrepreneurs bought and sold 20 million shares of Kowloon Wharf even though the stock was suspended from trading on the local market. This affair (and the colony's unwanted image as the gambling den of Asia) could inhibit Hong Kong's development as an international financial center. The *Asian Wall Street Journal* editorialized: "We see no reason why Hong Kong should live by the rules of Bank of America. . . . But we do see a reason why Hong Kong tycoons should live within the rules—however voluntary—that have been established by Hong Kong's own business community."[21]

There is visible evidence that the era of voluntary restraints, self-imposed by the private sector, may give way to something far more stringent. In banking, the Hong Kong government is especially frustrated by the stubborn refusal of credit institutions to cool their lending in response to repeated admonitions. One may expect sterner measures, including changes in key banking laws. *World Business Weekly* predicts that "the clear trend is toward greater intervention. . . . Amendments to raise capital requirements and require consolidation of accounts [for supervisory purposes] for both banks and quasi-bank deposit-taking companies have [already] been introduced."[22] Also, the government recently granted statutory recognition to the Exchange Banks Association (EBA), the group that functions as an informal interest rate cartel. By fixing the rates nonbank depositors, the EBA largely determines the prime lending rate. Furthermore, deposit-taking companies were separated into two categories with different capitalization requirements and greater restrictions on their ability to take deposits.[23]

Hong Kong, then, is having some second thoughts about its not-quite-laissez-faire economy. And the status quo may be a hindrance to future progress. Enter Big Government. All along, Chief

Secretary Sir Philip Haddon-Cave has argued that pragmatic government policy has been the secret of the colony's success—and not, as the Friedmans and others would believe, the innate abilities of Chinese traders and the "no-systems system" in which they operate.[24] Hong Kong's dream is to become "the global city of the Pacific." But to do so, one observer notes, "[will mean] more regulations to control the freewheeling spirits . . . [and perhaps even] a whole new industry of civil servants."[25]

Beyond the matter of Hong Kong's commitment to what is now "semi-free" capitalism, some experts are placing their bets on the Singaporean model of economic development. Futurist Herman Kahn is just one of those who contend that "the free enterprise system [of Hong Kong] doesn't work quite as well as the welfare of the state of Singapore."[26] The latter's 2.3 million people, living in intense density in 243 square miles, have, after all, Asia's highest standard of living after Japan, with a per capita gross national product of $3,800.

Singapore's small but remarkable city-state has chosen Japan as the country that it desires to work most closely with in the future. "Japanese society," Prime Minister Lee Kuan Yew declares with admiration, "is an illustration in Darwinism evolution, the survival of the most resilient social organization."[27] The two nations, of course, have much in common: the minuses of limited land, few natural resources, and far-removed industrial markets; and the pluses of hard-working workers, amenable to regimentation, and capable bureaucrats. Similarly, the bulk of their populations subscribe to the Confucian ethic and benefit from the stability of the Asian family. In both instances, their cultures and governments tend to favor the collective good over the rights of the individual. "Like the Japanese," writes Derek Davies, "Lee Kuan Yew has managed to maintain the quintescence of a Confucian state—in which individual human rights are sacrificed for the greater good of the community—while retaining a democratic system."[28] One cabinet minister attributes Singapore's success to the fact that about three-quarters of the population are of Chinese origin. He claims, "The whole of Chinese history knows no opposition, only good government and bad government. They accept if the Government is good for them. They are not attuned to Western democracy."[29] Being out of touch with Westernism has not impeded this city's progress.

With more than twenty years of uninterrupted leadership under his belt, Mr. Lee is now plotting Singapore's "second industrial revolution."[30] Its industry, which is entirely based on imported raw materials and has specialized in being labor intensive, faces competition from South Korea, Taiwan,[31] and Hong Kong; so the objective is to increase the value Singapore adds to its products. The ultimate goal: to become a fully industrialized country by the end of this decade. Working together, industry and government have identified twelve industries for special attention. They include computer software, specialized chemicals and pharmaceuticals, electronic instruments, aircraft components, and precision engineering. In particular, Mr. Lee is emphasizing more of what he calls "brain services" in higher technology and believes Singapore's future is in computer software and a wider range of professional services in engineering, communications, and finance. By tilting the economy from labor-intensive to higher technology businesses, Singaporeans are looking for 8 to 10 percent GNP growth per annum for the balance of the 1980s. This, of course, means upgrading the efficiency of the work force, and yearly productivity increases of 6 percent are targeted. Again, Japan is the standard—in part, perhaps because the largest Japanese business community in Southeast Asia (17,000 members) is based in this island mini-state.

In his 1981 New Year's message, Mr. Lee suggested that Singapore's future seemed safe, "if, like Japanese workers, we increase productivity by ceaselessly thinking up ingenious ways of cooperating to get more out of machines and improve machines themselves."[32] The extent to which Singaporeans can become Japanese remains to be seen, but their interest in doing so extends far beyond prime-ministerial pep talk. Last year, for instance, the Japan-Singapore

Technical Center opened with the aim of transmitting Japanese work methods and values on to the locals. Essentially a vocational school, the center is supported financially by the Japanese government, and its staff includes a director from Japan's Labor Ministry and fourteen Japanese teachers. The school's two hundred Singaporean students, wearing the traditional blue uniforms and caps so identifiable with Japan, begin their day with Japanese-style calisthenics in the parking lot.

Pushups aside, Mr. Lee's focus on educating for maximum economic utility has led to widespread criticism of what is called "social engineering," the shaping of a society to make it fulfill a mission devised for it by its leaders. Writing in the *New York Times*, Henry Kamm senses that "the Government shows increased signs of showing the concern of many of Singapore's intellectuals that this emphasis [on economic output] has produced a society whose majority cherishes only material aims."[33]

Second Singapores or Third Japans?

Even for a society that supposedly "puts culture at the bottom of the list,"[34] Singapore's prowess as a "second Japan" is the open envy of the rest of South and Southeast Asia. President J. K. Jayerwardene of Sri Lanka is one national leader who has paid more than lip service to the Singapore story. He, as well as other senior officials in the developing world, are giving considerable attention to how Mr. Lee made Singapore what it is. From Indonesia to Bangladesh, Singaporean bureaucrats are lending their talents to interested nations on consultancies ranging from improving orchid yields to marketing blue jeans abroad.

Sri Lanka, especially, is using Singapore as the basis for rebuilding its once-shattered economy. The leadership of this island nation of 14 million people (known as Ceylon until 1972) openly talks about the "Singapore model" of development, emphasizing market forces,

free trade, tax concessions, foreign investment, and efficient government.[35] That Colombo's 160-square-mile free trade zone is so similar
to Singapore's Jurong district "didn't happen by accident," recounts
Sri Lanka's Minister of Trade and Shipping, Lalith Athulathmedakli.
"I remember Jurong [Singapore's major industrial area] when it was
a swamp," the minister said, reflecting on Singapore's development
since the 1960s.[36] Within the Greater Colombo Free Trade Zones, full
tax holidays are granted on income, profits, dividends, and capital
gains for up to ten years, with extensions for an additional fifteen
years. Investors are also assured of freedom from exchange controls
and red tape generally.

How have these new economic policies fared? "Economic statistics, though only for 1977 to 1980, are very encouraging," argues
Alvin Rabushka, a senior fellow at Stanford University's Hoover
Institute. "In these three years, unemployment has fallen from 20%
to 15%. Since 1977, real rates have more than doubled. Between 1970
and 1977, economic growth averaged 3.1% per year (about 1.5% per
capita). Since 1977 growth has risen at annual rates of 8.2%, 6.2%,
and 5.6%, averaging slightly less than 5% per capita, despite a severe
cyclone, drought and oil price hikes."[37] In 1981, the country posted
an income-adjustment gain of 5 percent. While Sri Lanka has a long
way to go before it can approach the success of its Southeast Asian
neighbors, it has taken the right steps toward becoming a "second
Singapore" or, perhaps more accurately, a "third Japan."

Unquestionably, Singapore's success is well deserved, and to
receive targeted treatment from one's neighbors is good for the ego.
Nevertheless, Japan is responsible for its kudos in a very major way.
By showing the efficacy of collaborative, not adversarial, relations
between economic stakeholders, Tokyo has created an ideological
ripple throughout the Pacific Basin.

Consider, for instance, the recent remarks of Boonchu Rojanasathian, deputy premier for economic affairs of Thailand. With some
rhetorical flourish, he proclaimed: "We used to talk of 'Japan, Inc.'
and of 'Singapore Inc.' . . . I would like to announce the arrival of
'Thailand Inc.'"[38] Little false bravado usually comes from this former

president of Southeast Asia's largest financial institution, the Bangkok Bank. Then, too, Mr. Rojanasathian was quick to clarify his intentions: "What I'm doing is bringing the private sector into public sector policy. We work together and move in the same direction."[39] How? "First, you have to declare your policy—that we will stick with the free enterprise system. I don't want the public sector to take too much of a role in business without thinking about private sector activities. The public sector should not compete with the private sector if it already has its activities moving in the right direction. Instead of competing with them, you should put them into your plan. You have to sit down with the private sector before you draw up any plan."[40]

Thailand's economic game plan might have come right out of Japan's playbook. What we are seeing is the transmission of "Japan, Inc.," tempered to meet local conditions, throughout the Pacific Basin—and beyond. For sure, the cloning process is not confined to Confucian societies.

Beyond Asia

From Brazil to Sweden, one finds a growing acceptance of elements of the Japanese and German models and, concurrently, a rejection of America's economic ideology. France, for example, is shifting its allegiance to indicative planning, which emphasizes export competitiveness based on advanced technologies.[41] The Interministerial Committee for Strategic Industrial Development (CODIS) is seeking to establish a position for France in the growth industries of the future. Like Tokyo and Bonn, Paris has targeted twenty-three priority sectors from robotics to biotechnology for national pursuit. Enduring results, as Paul Krauss, managing director of McKinsey & Co. in Paris, warns, "may depend on whether *le défi japonais* ('the Japanese challenge') can galvanize French industry as effectively as *le défi américain* did a decade ago."[42] Still, to most Europeans the tone is being set by Japan and its former ally West Germany—not the United States.

In his new book, *The American Disease,* French sociologist Michael Crozier presents an especially candid view of the recent decline in American power as seen through European eyes.[43] America's confidence works wonders, he feels, when there is space to be filled, when people are in short supply and resources abundant. But when conditions change, when there are more people than places and a limit on resources, then confidence turns sour. "There will be no more Big Brother," Crozier contends. "America will never be what it was."[44]

Alfred Grosser offers another European view of the United States as an economic system in disrepair: "[U.S.] prosperity seemed to justify the conception of liberalism as a harmonious confrontation of forces at the heart of a self-regulating market. This model is now decidedly tottery."[45] Why? "The explanation for the weakening of the American model in Europe is similar to that given for the general push to the left in Europe in 1945; that is, laissez-faire policies no longer seem acceptable since it is a question of getting out of a difficult situation."[46] Grosser goes so far as to predict that "the demand for a firm government policy of intervention will gain in intensity throughout Europe."[47] And if Francois Mitterand's socialist stand in France is any indication, capitalism, American style, may be on the rocks in Europe.

More and more, national leaders are being called upon to bring industry, government, and labor back together on some systematic course. This, of course, is what Japan and West Germany do best. So it comes as no surprise that a full range of countries are eager to pursue the success stories being written in Tokyo and Bonn. Nowhere is the demonstration effect more noticeable than in the emergence of a new cadre of formidable foreign competitors.

73

4

The New Multinationals

AMERICA'S losses during the decade of the seventies were not the exclusive gains of its two major competitors, Japan and West Germany. These once-defeated powers, of course, benefited the most from the decline in U.S. competitiveness. But other nations, formerly excluded from the global industrial system, also evolved as serious threats to American business by heeding directly or indirectly some of the lessons of Tokyo and Bonn. This chapter examines the emerging phenomenon of the so-called new multinationals:[1] where they have come from, where they are going, and why these institutions should be taken seriously by every American.

The Rise of Third-World Multinationals

"The multinational game will go on vigorously, but it will evolve and change," warns N. T. Wang of the United Nations Center on Transnational Corporations. "The leadership might pass from the United States to European to Japanese multinational enterprises, and might change again to some of the developing countries that are fielding multinationals—Korea, Singapore, and so on."[2]

No doubt, few observers of the international business scene were surprised when a Saudi Arabian businessman, Ghaith R. Pharaon, sought to acquire a controlling interest in Hyatt International. Pharaon, after all, already had shown his muscle in U.S. banking circles by winning control of the Mainbank of Houston and the National Bank of Georgia, First Commercial Bank, and Clayton County Bank, all of Georgia. Then, too, the multinational spread of wealthy Middle Easterners has been well publicized. Whether it is the alleged Arab takeover of London or Saudi Arabia's proposal to buy the Gaza Strip from Israel, another Middle Eastern investment overseas is no longer front-page news.

Far less publicized, however, is the fact that OPEC bloc nations are not the only developing countries that are practicing the art of global reach.[3] From Brazil to South Korea, as Dr. Wang's introductory remarks would indicate, a major move is underway to industrialize, and the engine of growth is that familiar institution once confined to the developed world, the multinational corporation. Consider the evidence:

☐ The explosion in international construction spearheaded by multinational corporations headquartered in South Korea, Taiwan, and the Philippines. Korean companies are paving roads in Ecuador, while the Taiwanese build steel mills in Nigeria. Filipino companies span the globe—from Indonesia, where they are restoring the fabled Borobudur shrine, to the Persian Gulf, where they are developing deep-water port facilities.

☐ Peking is even pursuing a multinational course. China Construction Engineering Co., the nation's largest building firm, is shipping three thousand of its one million workers abroad— most of them to build houses in Kuwait, a highway in Iran, and an office building, theater, and state guest house in North Yemen. "Wherever there is a project, we are willing to send laborers," says Yang Xinghua, assistant manager of China Construction.

☐ On a regional level, the commitment of the twenty-five-nation SELA (the Latin American Economic System) to establish multinationals in Central and South America. Special priority is being given to agribusiness, selected capital goods, and low-cost housing, as well as an inter-American data center.

☐ Even the poorest nations are getting into multinational economic development. India is a prime example. The nation's Hindustan Machine and Tools Company is helping Algeria develop a machine tools industry, while other Indian multinationals are upgrading Iran's capacity to manufacture detergents, building Libyan steel mills, and constructing electronics plants in Yugoslavia.

Many more examples could be cited. In fact, forty-one of *Fortune*'s "overseas 500" companies for 1980 were headquartered in what the United Nations refers to as "developing countries."[4]

What is more, the scope and impact of the developing countries extend far beyond the enterprise level. In fact, a growing number of them are being placed among the strongest nations in the world. According to a ranking devised by Ray S. Cline of Georgetown University's Center for Strategic and International Studies, eleven of the twenty most powerful countries are from the emerging world.[5] Make no mistake, the "newly industrializing countries" (or NICs) are on the move. With relatively little fanfare, Brazil has grown into the tenth largest economy in the world, and it is already the seventh largest auto producer. Even less noticed is the Mexican economy, which has pulled about even with that of Sweden or Belgium. More widely acclaimed are the "second Japans" (South Korea, Taiwan, Hong Kong, and Singapore) mentioned in the last chapter; they, too, are amazing the world with their resourcefulness.

Consequently, the prevailing image of the developing countries as impoverished, unstable, and in a general state of disrepair deserves reconsideration. This is not to say that the Third World has solved its centuries-old socioeconomic problems. Nor is the multinational enterprise by itself the rags-to-riches answer to these problems. The

77

contemporary corporation, however, is an essential element in the gathering strength of the developing countries. And, what is most significant of all, the Third-World multinational could play a key role in lessening the structural dualism that now exists between the haves and the have nots.

The rise of the Third-World enterprise offers both developing and developed countries a unique opportunity to gain the benefits of a truly international economy. Indeed, it is the likelihood of restoring greater balance to our present global industrial system that has made even the strangest bedfellows staunch advocates of this trend. Leading international businessmen, United Nations officials, even the hierarchy of the People's Republic of China are all openly supportive of the possibilities.

Let me emphasize that major corporations from the Third World represent still a very young phenomenon. The cost of going global, as firms from the developed countries have learned, is high. Consequently, there are few developing nations that seriously influence world business at the moment (see Exhibit 4.1 for a listing of some of the major Third-World multinationals).

ROUTES TO SUCCESS

There are three kinds of economic soil in which the Third-World enterprise is taking root. They may be categorized as follows:

1 *Resource-rich developing countries.* These nations, most notably the OPEC bloc, are eager to pursue accelerated programs of international expansion and are in a position to acquire the technology and managerial skills to do so. At the end of 1980, Arab OPEC nations had $340 billion in assets deployed around the world— triple what they had five years earlier and more than the combined assets of Bank of America, Citicorp, Chase Manhattan, J. P. Morgan, and Manufacturers Hanover Trust.[6] By 1985, these assets could rise to $1 trillion if real oil prices remain stable. With tremendous export earnings, other state-owned monoliths such as National Iranian Oil, Indonesia's Pertamina, and CODELCO-CHILE are also capable of investing at home and abroad.

To date, foreign investments by companies based in these countries has been modest, but their potential for expansion is clear. Consider the example of Kuwait Petroleum Corporation, which represents a country with an accumulated surplus of $70 billion and rising daily.[7]

In April 1981, the national oil company of Kuwait and Pacific Resources, Inc., an energy company based in Honolulu, formed a joint venture that made Kuwait the first of the Mideast oil producers to gain a major stake in a U.S. refinery. Sheik Ali Khalifa al Sabah, chairman of Kuwait Petroleum, said he views this arrangement as a way to improve the company's vertical position in the Pacific Basin.[8] Then, in October 1981, Kuwait Petroleum took another step ahead by agreeing to purchase Santa Fe International Corporation for $2.5 billion.[9] Recently approved, the transaction will far outstep any other Mideast investment of petroleum revenue in a publicly traded U.S. corporation. If these moves were not enough, Kuwait Petroleum is rumored to be seeking to purchase some of Gulf Oil Corp.'s refining facilities in Europe. Other developing countries with similar assets and aspirations are expected to follow the Kuwaitis' lead in moving offshore.

2 *Labor-rich, rapidly industrializing countries.* With limited resources and narrow domestic markets, internationalism has long been synonymous with survival for areas such as Hong Kong, Singapore, Taiwan, and South Korea. Strict adherence to the watchwords "export or die" has triggered the economic miracle of these communities, which now exhibit real GNP growth rates four to five times higher than that of the United States.

Over time, these economies have moved away from their former emphasis on being intermediary centers of trade and into sophisticated manufacturing. Combining a cheap but industrious and well-educated work force with astute political leadership, developing countries in this category have evolved from basic trading nations to more complex, production-based economies.

A significant step in this evolution occurred in the 1960s with a massive influx of "satellite plants" from the multinationals of

Exhibit 4.1
Partial Listing of Major Third-World Multinationals

Company	Country	Industry	1980 sales in estimated millions of dollars
Petroleos de Venezuela	Venezuela	Petroleum	$18,818.9
Petrobras (Petroleo Brasileiro)	Brazil	Petroleum	14,836.3
Pemex (Petroleos Mexicanos)	Mexico	Petroleum	14,813.5
Hyundai Group	South Korea	Shipbuilding, transportation, equipment	5,540.5
Chinese Petroleum	Taiwan	Petroleum	5,373.4
YPF (Yeimentos Petroliferos)	Argentina	Petroleum	4,784.1
Indian Oil	India	Petroleum	4,605.4
Kuwait National Petroleum	Kuwait	Petroleum	4,564.9
Turkiye Petrolleri	Turkey	Petroleum	4,515.6
The Lucky Group	South Korea	Petroleum, electronics, appliances	4,452.5
Samsung Group	South Korea	Industrial equipment, electronics, textiles	3,798.0
Korea Oil	South Korea	Petroleum	3,321.1
Zambia Industrial & Mining	Zambia	Mining and metal refining — copper	2,744.4

Company	Country	Industry	Sales
Philippine National Oil	Philippines	Petroleum	2,470.6
CODELCO-CHILE	Chile	Mining and metal refining—copper	2,280.8
Koc Holding	Turkey	Motor vehicles	2,153.4
Grupo Industrial Alfa	Mexico	Metal refining—steel, chemicals	2,035.0
Haci Omer Sabanci Holding	Turkey	Textiles	1,982.6
Hyosung Group	South Korea	Textiles, motor vehicles	1,950.2
Empresa Nacional del Petroleo	Chile	Petroleum	1,742.1
Ssangyong Cement Industrial	South Korea	Building materials	1,707.8
Pohang Iron & Steel	South Korea	Metal refining—steel	1,568.5
Gecamines	Zaire	Mining—copper, cobalt, zinc	1,470.0
Sunkyong	South Korea	Textiles, chemicals	1,449.0
KukjE	South Korea	Rubber products, metal refining—steel	1,358.0
Korea Explosives Group	South Korea	Petroleum	1,200.6
Valores Industriales	Mexico	Beverages, food products	1,195.3
USIMINAS	Brazil	Metal refining—steel	980.7
Empresa Colombiana de Petroleos	Colombia	Petroleum	952.2

Source: "The 500 Largest Industrial Corporations outside the U.S.," Fortune, August 10, 1981, p. 208. Includes only industrial companies that elected to officially report 1980 sales figures. Hence omitted are several MNCs, such as Algeria's Sonatrack and Iran's National Iranian Oil.

developed countries. Singapore, for example, served as a major manufacturing base for many high-technology companies, including Hewlett-Packard, Fairchild, Litton Industries, Phillips, and Hitachi. But by the 1970s, the more adventurous developing countries became net exporters of the labor, products, and ideas.

Witness, for instance, the invasion of the Middle East by South Korean construction companies and their army of 100,000 skilled expatriates.[10] Competitors are particularly astounded by how swiftly the Koreans are extending their capabilities beyond civil construction and into the more technical and lucrative engineering-related areas once dominated by major Western contractors. Today, Korean contractors have a $10 billion backlog in overseas contracts.

Some Korean companies are growing by as much as 50 percent a year in sales, and four now rank among the world's twenty largest construction companies. None of this success came without Seoul support. The Koreans, like the Japanese, play down the collaboration between business and government, but, says one foreign observer, "If there is a Korea Inc., construction is the Inc.-iest part of it."[11] But Korea's wanderlust extends far beyond construction. The Gold Star Company, a South Korean electronics concern, announced plans to open a $5 million factory in Huntsville, Alabama. It would be the first Korean plant in the United States, and Gold Star hopes eventually to hire 1,000 Americans and produce 400,000 color television sets there each year, as well as refrigerators, microwave ovens, audio equipment, and other items. The factory is scheduled to begin operations in 1982 with 250 employees making 50,000 television sets annually.

Gold Star is part of South Korea's Lucky Group conglomerate, which reported annual worldwide sales of $4.5 billion in 1980. Gold Star says its worldwide sales were $600 million, while its overseas subsidiary, Gold Star Electronics International, had sales of $80 million in the United States. Shinkoo Huh, president of the Gold Star Company Ltd., believes that other Korean MNCs will follow his company's move to the United States. "The possibility that [others] will keep their eyes on us is pretty good," he says.[12] Consequently, to the roster of such traditional corporate giants as Jardine, Matheson & Co., Sime Darby Holdings, Swire Pacific Ltd., and others must be added new names such as Daewoo, Samsung, and Gold Star's parent, the Lucky Group.

3 *Market-rich, rapidly industrializing countries.* Building success through their large, growing domestic markets has been the favored overseas route for several Third-World countries: Brazil, Mexico, the Philippines, and, to a lesser extent, Argentina, Venezuela, and Turkey. In many instances, of course, these same nations are also resource-rich, but it is their unique ability to gain manufacturing and marketing experience at home for subsequent reexport abroad that sets them apart from the others.[13] Two leading Filipino firms illustrate this category.

☐ The colors of the management services firm of SyCip, Gorres, Velayo & Company (SGV) fly in every commerical capital in Asia. Following extended market dominance in the Philippines, the firm now maintains a multinational staff of professionals in public accounting and management services. In the Pacific Basin, SGV more than holds its own against the "Big Eight" accounting firms or, for that matter, any other professional group from the developed world.

☐ The international standing of San Miguel Corporation, a food-processing conglomerate, would not have occurred without its virtual monopoly of the Philippine beer market. Success at home quickly led to success abroad—first, through exports; then, through the sales of foreign-manufactured products. As a result, today one finds San Miguel breweries in such diverse locations as Spain, Hong Kong, and Papua, New Guinea.

There are significant differences among the three types of Third-World multinationals, but they share a common denominator: governments that are manifestly probusiness and committed to the expansion of overseas trade and investment. This feature, perhaps more than anything else, differentiates them from the rest of the pack.

But two other critical factors have also aided the rise of major corporations in the developing countries:

1 *Third-World solidarity.* The 1970s introduced a ground swell of supranationalism in the developing countries. Through such forums as the United Nations' Commission on Trade and Development, "collective self-reliance" has now become a byword of the times. To be sure, certain of the more impoverished nations still seek the fundamental human needs of nutrition, health, and education. But today, the goal of many other developing countries is a more equitable stake in the global economy.

One effect of greater Third-World unity, Louis T. Wells, Jr., notes, is a strong preference in the developing countries for corporations from like countries.[14] Regional success, it seems, tends to accompany the Third-World multinationalism. Take, for example, the recent agreements by Brazilian companies to assist Peru in the mining of its copper and Colombia its coal.

In many cases, developing countries appear to prefer investment from other like countries to investment from a major power. For one thing, such investment is less threatening. In wooing Hong Kong investors, Sri Lanka's trade minister made it clear that investors from smaller countries would receive a warmer welcome than those from the developed nations: "We favor investors from small places like Hong Kong because nobody can talk about a sell-out to imperialism in the case of a country that is as small as or smaller than we are."[15]

2 *Access to technology.* Since developing country leaders are well aware of the importance of Western technology in their own industrialization and worldwide competitiveness, it is not surprising that they are demanding access to it. In fact, a complex network of national, regional, and international institutions has evolved to serve this end.

But even without legislated transfers of technology from the developed world, the more enterprising developing countries continue to astound the world with their resourcefulness. Many Third-World companies have developed successful niches by exporting technology appropriate to labor-intensive environments. The most significant breakthroughs have been made in tropical agriculture, aquaculture, textiles, rural construction, and housing.

While most Third-World companies have avoided capital-intensive industries, a few have proved that they need not be confined to bottom-of-the-line market segments. Through technological leap-frogging, they have been able to advance quickly into complex industrial areas.

Take, for example, South Korea's spectacular entry into shipbuilding. Its Hyundai Group had very limited success in that industry prior to the ground-breaking ceremonies of its shipyards a decade ago. Less than two years later, Hyundai launched its first supertanker, the 260,000-ton *Atlantic Baron*. Today, it is able to construct thirty-five ships of various sizes simultaneously, and the 1981 turnover of the Hyundai Group was $6.7 billion. Many other examples of increasing Third-World involvement in complex industries could be cited. To name a few: Taiwan's success in electronics, Singapore's in oil-rig construction, and Brazil's in light aircraft manufacturing.[16]

Developing countries are also making up ground in sophisticated service industries. For example, take banking. Although the Third World is represented by only two banks, the Banco do Brasil and the Hong Kong & Shanghai Banking Corporation, among the world's fifty largest financial institutions, several others, particularly the OPEC banks, are going multinational.

The Arab nations of OPEC are building a new international banking system that threatens to capture control of the world's financial resources in the 1980s in the same way they took control of the world's energy resources in the 1970s. "It took the Arabs 10 years to learn how to wield their oil power, but it isn't going to take them that long to wield their money power," says a U.S. investment banker in Europe.[17] By 1981, Arab banks had recorded foreign holdings of over $350 billion, surpassing the combined holdings of the five top American banks and equaling the gross national product of *all* of South America. The Saudi Arabian Monetary Agency alone has $80-$90 billion in foreign holdings and deals directly with multinational corporations. So opportunities abound, especially at the regional level, for Third-World banks with international ambitions and resources.[18]

IMPEDIMENTS TO EXPANSION

The road to global success by the Third World is not without barriers and dangers. There are the obvious growing pains that strain the inner tissues of all countries in transition. From population control to the latest food crisis, the developing countries must confront a host of complex problems. Four important countervailing forces that merit special attention follow.

1 *Sluggish demand in the advanced nations.* The economies of the developing world depend on the health of the Western nations. Without significant improvements in the economic conditions of developed countries, which are the primary export markets for the developing countries, Third-World industrialization will be stalled — at least temporarily.

2 *Rising protectionism.* Growth in world trade means economic and political survival for most emerging nations. Without steady export gains, the Third World can expect economic stagnation and, eventually, political instability. In 1980, world trade barely budged, climbing a negligible 0.4 percent, and it declined almost 3 percent in 1981.

The General Agreement on Tariffs and Trade, the eighty-five-nation organization that oversees international commerce, attributes slowdown in world trade to the contraction in the international flow of oil as well as a rash of neomercantilism that is now gripping the world economy. There is no doubt that the import quotas imposed by the United States and the European Common Market's nontariff barriers will have serious implications for developing countries and their internationally ambitious companies.

3 *Growing public debt.* The bogeyman of the developing countries is their swelling public indebtedness, estimated at $524 billion in 1981. Unfortunately, one cannot be optimistic about an improvement in the balance-of-payments positions of the emerging nations. For the reasons just mentioned—stagflation and protectionism—the majority of developing countries should anticipate continued current account problems, requiring balance-of-payments loans. Debt servicing difficulties, in turn, will reduce the trade and investment opportunities of these nations. As a result, most emerging nations will face massive debt payments at precisely the time when their export earnings are likely to be under heavy pressures. Thus their ability to repay could be seriously threatened.

4 *Widening gap between rich and poor.* What political scientist Robert A. Scalapino of the University of California at Berkeley calls the "capital centrism problem" may outweigh all other factors in impact.[19] Simply stated, the economic and political power of most developing countries typically gravitates to the major urban centers— excluding the rural masses from adequate participation in decision making. Unless these distortions are eliminated or at least lessened, Scalapino warns, a nation's political stability will be endangered.

In their excitement to become first-class trading nations, developing nations also often sacrifice business sense for cosmetic attempts at commercial status. The Philippines' overbuilt hotel industry— typically operating at 50 percent capacity—is symptomatic of a tendency to let wishful thinking sway hardheaded business judgment. Far more serious, however, is the preoccupation in some developing countries with excessive defense spending at the expense of industrialization. (The size of the military budget for some of them approaches 35 percent of GNP.) In the end, such shortsighted nations will have neither guns nor butter.

Thus leaders in the Third World must be mindful of the tug between "head" and "heart"—between what is realistic and what is fanciful. Selectivity is the key. Given their limited resources and shifting global conditions, Third-World industrialists must carefully pick their spots if they are to survive and prosper.

IMPLICATIONS FOR AMERICANS

Despite these caveats, businesses should take the Third-World multinational seriously. This evolving force is here to stay and, on balance, its pluses outweigh its minuses.

These corporations bring important resources to the world economy. Obviously, they offer major contributions to those industries that can profit from skilled—and inexpensive—labor. Not so obvious is their resource of executive talent and the potential for "reverse takeovers," that is, instances where a developing country investor gains a controlling interest in an enterprise based in a developed nation. There are several noteworthy instances.

☐ In 1973, Hong Kong's Jardine, Matheson & Co., Ltd., doubled its net worth with two such acquisitions—Theo. H. Davies & Co., Ltd., an established Hawaii-based agribusiness company, and Reunion Properties Company, Ltd., a major British enterprise. Then in March 1982, Jardines purchased Bache Insurance Services, Inc., from the Prudential Company of America.

☐ Venezuela's Organisacion Diego Cisueros not only bought out the Venezuelan subsidiary of the International Basic Economy Corporation (IBEC) but also acquired 20 percent of the parent company. Today, "mother and daughter" companies jointly run IBEC supermarkets in Ecuador and El Salvador.

☐ The renewed takeover bid by a Malaysian group that now holds 17.5 percent of Britain's Dunlop Holdings, Ltd. Among the possible implications of this takeover is a shift of this venerable British giant's corporate headquarters from London to Kuala Lumpur.

☐ But more than any other case, the Hong Kong & Shanghai Bank's acquisition of a 51 percent controlling interest in Marine Midland Bank, the thirteenth largest in the United States, revealed this growing force of the Third-World multinational. Equally surprising was the Hong Kong-based banking company's $1.1 billion bid (albeit rejected) for Royal Bank of Scotland and its 1980 takeover of Anthony Gibbs, a London investment bank. Though its top officials originally came from England, The Bank (as it is known in the colony) is owned primarily by local Chinese investors.

The foregoing is not to suggest that the Americans gird themselves for a contemporary replay of David and Goliath. But these examples do point to the increasing competitiveness of the Third World. Nobel laureate Lawrence R. Klein of the Wharton School advises American executives that a serious challenge will be coming from the newly industrialized countries of the Third World.[20] The second Japans of the Pacific have become competitive, and several Latin American countries, including Brazil, Mexico, and Venezuela, are on the rise. This makes it all the more imperative, Klein warns, for the United States to tool up and be prepared for competition from this new source.[21]

The Challenge of State-Controlled Enterprise

American businessmen, while adjusting to the ensuing encroachments of the Third World, are now having to focus on another competitive threat: the state-controlled enterprise. These are commercial vehicles whose formal authority ultimately rests in the hands of the nation-state. More often than not, the public sector owns a majority of the firm's shares.

One long-time observer of this emerging phenomenon, Professor Douglas F. Lamont, notes that national governments around the world see that the power in the international economy comes from the production and distribution of products on a competitive basis in both domestic and overseas markets. For this reason, they have sought to copy the private sector by setting up state companies which, they believe, can make them more competitive.[22]

PERVASIVENESS PERSONIFIED

State-controlled enterprises operating outside of socialist economies are pushing vigorously into international and domestic markets. To illustrate their growing dominance:

☐ In Europe, the public sector has an ownership stake in twenty-nine of the fifty largest companies. Investment in government-owned enterprises accounts for more than 25 percent of all investment in Sweden, 50 percent in Austria, and 35 percent in Italy. The basic industries of coal, steel, and petroleum are partly or wholly nationalized in most countries. Government companies also produce automobiles, airplanes, chemicals, papers, ships, textiles, electrical and nonelectrical machinery, and electronic goods.[23]

☐ South of the border, 77 percent of the largest Latin American companies are state controlled; they account for almost three-quarters of total exports from the region.[24] As one indication of the Latins' global reach, Petrobras, the Brazilian giant, is conducting oil exploration in several Middle Eastern countries, as well as in the North Sea, Madagascar, and Colombia.

☐ Nor is the Middle East immune to this trend. Before the hostilities with Iraq, the National Iranian Oil Corporation was the third largest company domiciled outside the United States. Its British and Danish subsidiaries had been actively searching for oil, while its Indian affiliate continues to manufacture fertilizer in India.

☐ Asia, too, has witnessed a rise in its state-backed multinationals. "What stronger backing do you need than that of a rich, prospering nation?" ask the advertisements of Pernas, Malaysia's state-owned monolith. Today this conglomerate of sixty-nine companies is engaged in insurance, construction, real estate, shipping, trading, and advertising. Its chairman, Tunku Data Shahriman, points out that, while assuring private investors of a strong public commitment to their affairs, Pernas operates "strictly on a commercial basis."[25]

☐ Finally, those sources of global inspiration, West Germany and Japan, also recognize the value of building public-sector companies. In Germany, the federal government alone owns and operates some $25 billion worth of assets ranging from the largest oil company (Veba A.G.) to the largest automobile producer (Volkswagen).[26] State governments also participate in commercial ventures; for example, Hamburg, Bremen, and Bavaria share ownership with private sources in Germany's two major aerospace companies. Japanese shipbuilding, railroads, steel, electronics, and cameras were all developed by what Chalmers Johnson calls "public policy companies"—that is, mixed public and private enterprise.[27] Although most of them are privately owned, governmental influence is often substantial.

True, commercial state enterprises per se are not new. What is new, however, is their enormous explosion in recent years. Between 1957 and 1979, the number of such companies increased twelvefold, while their sales quadrupled every seven years and their assets doubled every five years. State-controlled MNCs represent approximately one-fifth of the 500 largest corporations headquartered outside the United States. A partial listing of some of the majors are found in Exhibit 4.2.[28]

For some industries the persuasiveness of the public sector is particularly profound. In financial services, four state-owned French banks—Credit Agricole, Banque Nationale de Paris, Credit Lyonnais, and Societe Generale—are found among the five largest banks outside the United States. What is more, one government giant, the Banco do Brazil, has consistently outperformed almost every other bank in the world. Tracing its roots to 1808, Banco is half the size of Bank of America; and simple extrapolation from present growth rates implies

Exhibit 4.2
Partial Listing of State-Owned Multinationals

Company	Country	Industry	1980 sales in estimated millions of dollars
Renault	France	Motor vehicles.	$18,818.9
National Coal Board	Britain	Mining—coal	8,158.6
DSM	Netherlands	Chemicals	7,514.2
British Steel	Britain	Metal refining—steel	6,772.7
British Leyland (BL)	Britain	Motor vehicles	6,690.8
Charbonnages de France	France	Chemicals, mining—coal	4,959.2
Salzgitter	Germany	Metal refining—steel, shipbuilding	4,817.5
VOEST-Alpine	Austria	Metal refining—steel	4,484.2
Italsider	Italy	Metal refining—steel	4,285.9
Statsforetag Group	Sweden	Paper and wood products, mining—iron	3,341.5
British Aerospace	Britain	Aerospace	3,309.4
Aerospatiale	France	Aerospace	3,120.1
Rolls-Royce	Britain	Aerospace	2,926.4
Zambia Industrial & Mining	Zambia	Mining—copper; food products	2,744.4
VIAG	Germany	Metal refining—aluminum	2,692.5

South African Iron & Steel Ind.	South Africa	Metal refining—steel, iron, coal	2,581.7
Alfa Romeo	Italy	Motor vehicles	2,281.4
CODELCO-CHILE	Chile	Mining—copper	2,280.8
Steel Authority of India	India	Metal refining	2,258.4
Canada Development Corp.	Canada	Chemicals	2,017.8
British Shipbuilders	Britain	Shipbuilding	1,773.5
Enterprise Miniere et Chimique	France	Mining—potash, chemicals	1,766.8
Vale do Rio Doce	Brazil	Mining—iron	1,644.3
ENSIDESA	Spain	Metal refining—steel	1,623.1
SEAT	Spain	Motor vehicles	1,611.5
GECAMINES	Zaire	Mining—copper, cobalt, zinc	1,469.9
SWEDYARDS	Sweden	Shipbuilding, building materials	1,456.5
SNECMA	France	Aerospace	1,226.9
Siderurgica Nacional	Brazil	Metal refining—steel	1,126.5
Enso-Gutzeit	Finland	Paper, pulp, and wood products	1,103.9
SEITA	France	Tobacco	1,056.0
Valmet	Finland	Industrial and farm equipment, shipbuilding	874.9
Chemie Linz	Austria	Chemicals	859.7

Source: "The 500 Largest Industrial Corporations outside the U.S.," *Fortune,* August 10, 1981, p. 207. Includes only industrial companies in which (a) government ownership comes to more than 50 percent and (b) that elected to report 1980 sales figures. Purposely excluded from this list are oil companies.

that Banco do Brazil may surpass the Bank of America in size in another ten years.[29]

Over the past decade, state-controlled airlines have increased their share of international passenger traffic from 70 percent to 85 percent. Charles C. Tillinghast, Jr., former chairman of Trans World Airlines, Inc., suggests that their success, at least in part, is due to the abilities of government-aided carriers to rationalize their services with those of other national airlines against which they compete. "The result," Tillinghast notes, "is that the national carrier in each country strongly dominates traffic moving over its gateway to or from the U.S., adding to it the feed it derives from its internal services."[30]

The American petroleum companies are also feeling the pressures of state enterprises.[31] Just a decade ago, the "Seven Sisters" controlled 70 percent of the world's oil trade. Today, the percentage is below 50 and dropping. Not all state-controlled oil companies, of course, are overnight creations. France's Societe Nationale Elf-Aquitaine and Compagnie Francaise des Petroles and Italy's Ente Nazionale Idocarburi (ENI) have always kept a tight grip on national oil tradings. But the relatively new boys on the block— Canada's Petro-Canada, Mexico's Pemex, Kuwait National Petroleum, and others—pose a serious threat to the Seven Sisters.

Petroleum and other American industries with mature technology are especially vulnerable to competition from state enterprises. Renato Mazzolini of the Columbia Business School believes that state-owned multinational corporations have access to the same technology as America while enjoying such advantages as cheaper labor or raw materials, newer plants, and large-scale government financing.[32] United States steel, rubber, and textiles could become endangered species. But most observers believe that the next major industry to come under attack is basic chemicals.[33]

Several state chemical companies in Europe are adding capacity, despite excess capacity in many sectors of the European industry and the rising stream of East-bloc chemicals into that market. Add to this the plans of the oil-producing countries, notably Saudi Arabia, to build big petrochemical complexes that will be almost totally export oriented. These events led Union Carbide chairman William Sneath to predict that by the mid-1980s companies owned or controlled by government will account for nearly 50 percent of the U.S. chemical industry's competition in export markets for petrochemicals, plastics, and fertilizers.[34]

The advance of state-controlled business, though, will not be confined exclusively to industries with mature technologies. In high-performance aircraft, once a bastion of U.S. technological supremacy, one can view the increasing vulnerability of American business to government-backed enterprise. Airbus Industrie, the state-controlled international consortium, is flying high with its A-300 Airbus; French SNAIS, run by Jacques Giscard d'Estaing, is now the third largest manufacturer of helicopters after Textron's Bell Helicopter division and United Technologies' Sikorsky Aircraft division; and Brazil's Embracer is effectively marketing its eighteen-seat Bandeirantes to interested foreign buyers. Observes George Prill, former president of Lockheed International: "[S]tate companies . . . will provide formidable competition. They produce good planes, and they can set prices at what it will take to win a share of the market and then work back to their cost."[35]

FAVORITE SON OR SPOILED CHILD?

As overseas nations assume a direct interest in their companies, U.S. business is bound to suffer. Abundant government support makes state-controlled enterprises extremely tough competitors. The need not to earn profits or to pay dividends, the low risk of financial loss or bankruptcy, monopoly power, and various hidden subsidies are just a few of their built-in advantages. In describing these favorite sons, *Fortune's* Hugh D. Menzies argues: "Governments endow them with guaranteed markets, tax breaks, and interest-free loans. In return, state-controlled companies are expected to perform such unprofitable activities as continuing to operate inefficient plants in order to protect jobs and selling abroad at a loss in order to earn foreign exchange."[36]

The alliance between business and government is not without its limitations, though state-controlled enterprises, despite the largess of their home governments, are often among the ranks of the unprofitable. In 1980, five of the ten biggest corporate losers outside the United States were government backed. Consistently problem plagued have been British Leyland, Spain's SEAT, Austria's VOEST-Alpine, and many others. One showcase of bureaucratic inefficiency is Alpha Romeo, which is reputed to lose over $1000 on every car produced at its new Alfasud plant near Naples. (In Alpha's defense, comparable private companies in Italy, like Montedison and Pirelli, are also big money losers.) As a result, Columbia's Mazzolini predicts a slowdown in government firms. Restraining forces for foreign expansion (by state-owned business) are tending to be greater than the driving forces. "Restraining forces," he adds, "tend to derive from ongoing government policies (regional development ends), while the driving forces generally stem from passing concerns (the pressures to invest in a particular country for foreign policy ends)."[37]

Limitations aside, state-controlled MNCs are expected to become a permanent force in the global industrial system. They add a new dimension to the competitive equation and offer major opportunities and challenges to private corporations around the world. U.S. businessmen should take heed. Professors Kenneth Walters and R. Joseph Monsen of the University of Washington warn that, "as nationalized companies grow in number, size and diversity around the world, and U.S. trade policy continues to ignore their heavily subsidized character, American business will increasingly face this most insidious form of unfair competition."[38] In the years ahead, look for more state-controlled companies to wage war with U.S. enterprise.

Ivan Goes International

The Russians, too, are coming. Their vehicle is that familiar institution long regarded by Moscow as the unique instrument of capitalist oppression: the global corporation.[39] Indeed, evidence is growing that industrialization and communism are no longer cultural contradictions. And for good reason.

AMPLE INCENTIVES

Motivations abound for the Kremlin to practice the art of global reach. Martha Mautner, chief of the Soviet policy division of the Bureau of Intelligence and Research in the U.S. State Department, suggests three: the need for hard currency; compatibility with Russia's political directions; and gathering intelligence.[40]

All nations in a sense are developing, and the USSR is no exception. Economic growth dominates Soviet thinking, and the Kremlin would like to build its dreams on something more tangible than its now inconvertible currency, the ruble. Thus, a major purpose of the Soviet Union's commercial expansionism is to earn the hard currencies with which to buy Western goods, technology, and managerial expertise. By setting up profit-minded corporations in the West, Russia improves its chances of securing the dollars, marks, and yen to finance industrialization back home.

That trade follows the flag is a realization that was slow in coming to the Kremlin's hierarchy. After many years, the Brezhnev regime put to rest the Stalinist dreams of autarchy and independence; in its place were substituted mutuality of interests and interdependence. The present sentiment is that communism's expansionist tendencies can only be fired by an economic force that matches Russia's military and strategic might. What better vehicle than its own version of the multinational enterprise, appropriately attuned to incorporate elements of Soviet ideology?

Moscow's multinationals also oversee a growing intelligence network. The Kremlin takes the intelligence-gathering function seriously; the Soviets' compulsive need to secure knowledge of things foreign is infamous. Some observers even suggest that a concerted effort by the USSR is now underway to close the technology gap with the West, with Soviet MNCs serving as centers of espionage.[41] Others contend that it is the Third World—especially countries such as Algeria, Turkey, Pakistan, Morocco, and El Salvador—that ranks higher on Ivan's hit list. Whatever the target, Russian enterprise constitutes a convenient organizational apparatus for eavesdropping.

One of the nearly fifty trading companies is Sovinflot, the USSR's maritime shipping ministry. It controls among its many affiliates Morflot America (Moram) Shipping, Inc., which has head-quarters in Clark, New Jersey. Sovinflot vessels serve as a reserve fleet for the Soviet navy, providing a tremendous naval capability in the event of emergency. What is more, Sovinflot, along with the other USSR trading companies, comes under the Ministry of Foreign Trade and the Soviet Chamber of Commerce. That body's first deputy chairman, Yevgeniy Petrovich Pitrovranov, is a ranking general in the KGB! (It is quite common for the senior officials of the Moscow-based parent companies to wear two hats: one commercial, the other military or intelligence.)

RUSSIA'S IMPRESSIVE GAINS

Although the intentions of Soviet companies may be suspect, their progress to date is not. Over the past decade, Moscow has tripled the number of its foreign-based operations, setting up banks, shipping lines, and insurance firms and peddling everything from oil to vodka, watches to machine tools, tractors to jet planes.[42] By 1978, the Soviets operated eighty-four worldwide firms in twenty-six countries, including ten domiciled in the United States (see Exhibit 4.3).

In keeping with the hidden undercurrent of Soviet life, none of these organizations is a household name. Soviet authority Hedrick Smith tells why: "Russians are masters of lying low, of adopting the protective coloration of conformity in order to get by with something or to pursue some special interest that would be crushed if dis-covered."[43] Consequently, the Kremlin prefers a *sub rosa* existence for its worldwide enterprises.

Despite their low profile, Soviet companies have been around for some time, and their influence is growing. One of the oldest is the Moscow Narodny Bank, which opened its first overseas branch (in

Exhibit 4.3
Partial Listing of Soviet Multinationals Active in Twenty-two Countries

Austria	Asotra: transportation. Donau Bank: commercial bank (agent of the Soviet Bank). Garant Versicherung: insurance.
Belgium	Belso: food products and textiles. Elorg-Belgique: data processing (agent of Elektronorgtekhnika). Ewa: optical instruments. Fermchimex: chemicals (agent of Soyuzkhimexport). Nafta-B: petroleum products (agent of Soyuznefteexport). Russalmaz: diamonds (agent of Soyuzpromexport). Scaldia-Volga: automobiles (agent of Avtoexport). Transworld Maritime Agency: shipping.
Canada	Belarus Equipment Ltd.: farm machinery (agent of Traktoexport). Emek Trading: turbines. Morflot Freightliners: shipping. Soccan Aircraft: airlines. Stan Canada: machine-tools.
Finland	Elorgdata: computers and computer services (agent of Elektronorgtekhnika). Konela: automotive equipment (agent of Avtoexport). Koneisto: machinery. Saima Lines: shipping. Tebeli: petroleum products (agent of Soyuznefteexport).
France	Actif-Avto: farm machinery (agent of Traktoexport). Banque Commerciale pour l'Europe du Nord: commercial bank. Fransov: seafoods. Promolease: plant. Rusbois: timber (agent of Exportles). Sagmar: shipping. Slava: watches. Sogo: chemicals (agent of Soyuzkhimexport). Stanko-France: machinery (agent of Machinoexport).
Italy	Dolpin Agenzia Marittima: shipping. Ruslegno: timber. Sovietpesca: seafoods. Sovitalmare: shipping. Stanitalia: machinery, tools.
Luxembourg	Banque Unie Est Ouest: commercial bank.
Netherlands	East West Agencies: optical instruments. Elorg: computers and computer services. Transworld Marine Agency: shipping.
Norway	Koneisto Norge: machinery. Koneia Norge Bil: automobiles.

Spain	Pesconsa: seafoods. Sovispan: commercial trading agency.
Sweden	Joint Trawler Ltd. Sweden: seafoods. Matreco Bil: automobiles (agent of Avtoexport). Scansov Transport: shipping.
Switzerland	Wozohod Handelsbank: commercial bank.
United Kingdom	Russian Wood Agency: timber (agent of Exportles). Anglo-Soviet Shipping: shipping. Black Sea & Baltic General Insurance: insurance. East West Leasing: plant. Moscow Narodny Bank: commercial bank. Nafta-GB: petroleum products (agent of Soyuznefte-export). Technical & Optical Equipment: photographic equipment. United Machinery Organisation Plant Hire: construction machinery.
West Germany	Neotype Techmashexport: machinery. Ost-West Handels-bank: commercial bank. Plodinies Aussenhandel: food and drink products. Russalmaz: diamonds. Sobren Chemihandel: chemicals. Sovag: insurance. Ueberee-schiffahrtsagentur Transnautic: shipping. Wesotra Spedition & Transport: trans-shipment and forwarding.
United States	Morflot America: shipping. Sorfracht (USA): shipping. Belarus Machinery: tractors.
Argentina	Coram South America: electrical equipment (agent of Energomashexport).
Cameroun	Cateco: automotive equipment (agent of Avtoexport).
Ethiopia	Ethos Trading Co.: electrical equipment (agent of Energomashexport).
Morocco	Marinexport: machinery (agent of Machinoexport).
Nigeria	Waatego Lagos: automotive equipment (agent of Avtoexport).
Lebanon	Moscow Narodny Bank: commercial bank.
Singapore	Moscow Narodny Bank: commercial bank.

Source: Andres Garrigo, "Growth of the Red Multinationals," *Profile*, Vol. 14, 1978, p. 9. Reprinted from *Profile*, the magazine of ITT in Europe.

London) in 1919. An important source of foreign capital, Moscow Narodny pioneered the development of the Eurodollar market. In 1981, its sometimes overly aggressive Singapore branch became the largest bank in that country, with $3.2 billion in total assets. Moreover, the bank's executives are well schooled in the social games and business tools of the capitalist. "I myself have seen the chairman of the Moscow Narodny Bank in a Rothschild dining room," reveals Samuel Pisar, the East-West expert. "I have also known him to go on fox hunts with his fellow bankers in England."[44]

Other enterprises, too, are learning the international business game. Perhaps most spectacular is the case of Nafta-B, a joint Russian-Belgian company launched in 1968 to market Soviet crude oil. By 1977, its turnover had increased 34-fold, making it at the time the second largest company in Belgium.[45]

Russian enterprise has even found its way into the U.S. market. The Belarus Machinery Company of Milwaukee, for example, is wholly owned by the USSR. Set up seven years ago to market the Soviet line of Belarus tractors in the United States, the company employs sixty-five Americans and four Russians in Milwaukee and thirty other Soviets in New York City.[46] Its fuel-efficient tractors, marketed in the $5,300 to $55,000 range, are about 10 percent cheaper than comparable American models. Having sold more than 4,000 units so far, Belarus has an eventual goal of 3 percent of the U.S. tractor market.

More ambitious is the Russian push in automobiles. Thanks to the technical assistance of the Italians, the Soviet Union now produces approximately 1.4 million cars a year. Exports account for less than one-third of the total production, and this year Soviet-built automobiles may be introduced to the American public. The Kremlin hopes that the New York-based Satra Corporation will market the Lada (a modified version of the old Fiat 124) and the four-wheel-drive Niva (a cross-country vehicle).

Satra's importation and preparation facility is under construction in Savannah, Georgia. Completion is soon expected for the $1.5 million center, where the Soviets intend eventually to employ

350 Americans. With Satra's help and, more to the point, with a 20 percent cost advantage over other domestic and foreign manufacturers, the Russians aim to sell 50,000 units a year by 1986. These goals, however, depend on continued access to the U.S. market, and, at the time of this writing, strong sentiments are emerging in the Congress to monitor the importation of Russian automobiles.

It is on the high seas that the Soviet Union poses its greatest threat to the West. In the mid-1950s, the Russians made two important commitments. First was the shift from being a continental land force to building a major maritime force in both the defense and the nondefense areas. Second was a post-Stalinist push for improved living standards for all Soviet citizens, and especially for better, higher protein diets. Shortly thereafter, Soviet ventures in ocean shipping and commercial fishing came to force.

With wind in its sails, the Russian transport fleet is now the largest and most modern in the world. Soviet shipping companies, often with the financial backing of the West, have succeeded in capturing a substantial capitalist clientele for their parent, the Soviet Ministry of Merchant Marine. Today, Russian vessels carry 97 percent of the goods between the USSR and Japan, 84 percent of USSR-British cargo, and 75 percent of the trade between the USSR and West Germany. On U.S. routes, the Soviets have increased the dollar volume of cargo destined for the United States from $38 million in 1971 to about $2 billion today.

In markets where price competition prevails, Russian carriers have undercut their competitors by as much as 40 percent. Like their counterparts in other industries, Soviet shippers enjoy all the advantages of a state-controlled enterprise: lower wages, no threat of strikes, state financing, preferential treatment in Soviet ports, and — most important in today's times — cheaper bunker fuel. Under the stewardship of a friendly Russian bear, the future of Moscow's multinationals seems assured.

IMPLICATIONS FOR THE WEST

"No crystal ball can be expected reliably to project the full consequences [of Soviet expansionism]," cautions Harvard's Raymond

Vernon.[47] Nevertheless, one can develop a partial listing of possible outcomes; and our advice to U.S. executives follows.

For starters, Westerners should take the Soviet enterprise seriously. Make no mistake, Russia's disposition is to advance its position in the global economy, with the multinational corporation serving as the engine of growth. We can expect the Kremlin to make increasing inroads in industrial niches once dominated by the Free World, including armaments, commercial fishing, strategic minerals, transportation, and transportation equipment.

Whether one sees this trend as a threat or as an opportunity is a matter of perspective. No doubt, many attractive possibilities will surface for capitalists eager to link up with Russian enterprises. In fact, the Soviet Union pioneered the so-called transideological enterprise or joint venture between East and West;[48] and it has more of these collaborative forms than any other command economy.

True, shared ventures require shared understanding—a scarce commodity in Russian relations with the West. The realities of our times reflect the Kremlin's invasion of Afghanistan, its intrusion into Polish affairs, and a cadre of related events. Without a significant softening in Soviet militancy, American industry may be hard pressed to increase its links with the East. But on balance, U.S. business should be open to the prospects for greater Western participation in Soviet enterprise.

Our public policymakers should also assess carefully Russia's global gallop. The rise of Soviet enterprise reintroduces the serious disadvantages that U.S. companies face when competing with state-owned institutions generally. Whether made in Moscow or elsewhere, government-controlled companies benefit unfairly from the support of their sponsors. One increasingly obvious fact of economic life is that U.S. corporations, like those in other competing nations, have a public or quasi-public character. In meeting the Soviet challenge, therefore, the United States government must demonstrate greater sensitivity to this special role.

Finally, a note of caution. Soviet enterprise is in its embryonic stage, and one should not be overly optimistic about the Kremlin's chances for global economic dominance. The Russian road to super-

103

power status is paved with many substantial barriers. From disappointing crop yields to the waning enthusiasm of its European allies, the Soviet Union must confront a host of complex problems—each seemingly more difficult than the last.

Only recently, for instance, the USSR published a new five-year economic plan that projects a slower rate of industrial growth than any recent plan and targets oil production for 1985 at the level originally set for 1980. This is further evidence of the vulnerability of the Soviet economy, and to many observers Russia remains an industrial basket case.[49] Repeated attempts by the Brezhnev regime to reform the state bureaucracy that controls Soviet industry have also failed. Fundamental changes in the Politburo's approach to doing business will require dismantling the centralized management system established by Josef Stalin. And Soviet leaders are far too conservative for hard-core restructuring. Then, too, commercial contacts with the West may represent a potential threat to the Russian way of life. "The possibility of ideological contagion resulting from prolonged contact with the free world has always terrified Soviet leaders," says *Fortune*'s Herbert E. Meyer. "In the end, they may be unwilling to risk the political hazards of trade."[50]

Nevertheless, the Kremlin will further its forays into foreign markets. Rather than say *"nyet"* to international business, Russian leaders will recognize increasingly the formidable force that commercialism, ideologically tempered to meet the Soviet condition, offers a nation with global ambitions.

Concluding Note

Gone are the old days. Today the emergence of the new multinationals shatters many of the former stereotypes that shrouded the business enterprise—mainly, that it was the exclusive instrumentality of capitalists from a few affluent countries. Nowadays, business at home and abroad is, as *Forbes*'s James Cook puts it, "a game any number can play."[51]

For the past one hundred years, observers have commented on the increasing competitiveness of world markets. But until the postwar emergence of Japan and West Germany, we restricted our thinking to companies based in a handful of countries. Inevitably, though, one nation's competitive dominance passes to another. Today the Japanese and Germans, tomorrow perhaps the Brazilians, the Koreans, and others. *"Plus ça change, plus c'est la même chose."*

5

Lessons at the
Enterprise Level

THE rest of the world's revival notwithstanding, what is especially troublesome for most Americans is the inability of our existing business institutions to create economic value. "During the next decade," Senator Lloyd M. Bentsen warns us, "we will have to look hard at many of our institutions. The relative economic strength and health of Germany and Japan suggest that they might have some lessons for us in terms of policies and institutions."[1] Exactly what these lessons might be is subject to question, but there are interesting methods of organizing and managing modern-day corporations taking place in far-flung corners of the world. For Americans and non-Americans alike, they merit, and are receiving, serious consideration.

Organizational Learning

To many observers, traditional American concepts of structuring the enterprise—once worthy of widespread emulation—are now considered a distant "second best." Particularly where global markets are at stake, we are seeing a rejection of the independent, stand-alone organization in favor of the collective or shared enterprise. Three such examples are state-owned monopolies, trading companies, and corporate coalitions. Each reflects the lasting imprint of Japanese and, to a lesser extent, European thinking on the future enterprise.

PUBLIC AND QUASI-PUBLIC MONOPOLIES

Encouraged by permissive legislation supporting public enterprise, the governments of many countries are building their own monopolies. Pernas, Malaysia's state-controlled conglomerate, was created in 1969 to provide business opportunities and employment for the *bumiputra* (the term for ethnic Malays that means "sons of soil"). Today this conglomerate of sixty-nine companies is engaged in insurance, construction, real estate, shipping, trading, and advertising. Pernas assures private investors of strong public commitment to their affairs in businesses ranging from mining to insurance.

The Malaysian government now owns all or part of 674 corporations and will keep such major ones as the national airline and the petroleum production company. But minority holdings in other companies are being shifted to a new creation called *Permodalan Nasional Berhad*, or the National Equity Corporation. This, in turn, will sell its own shares—in effect, a mutual fund—to indigenous Malays on nearly risk-free, high-profit terms.

"If it works," writes Robert Keatley, editor of the *Asian Wall Street Journal*, "Malaysia will have found one way to get private funds into industrial ventures without having the government itself put up the cash and run the businesses."[2] By not nationalizing everything in sight and putting a pedantic bureaucracy in charge forever, Malaysia is patterning key segments of its industry along the lines of Japan's "public policy companies"—that is, privately run enterprises with significant administrative guidance from government.[3] This tropical, resource-rich nation wants to put more and more of its wealth in private hands, particularly through the ownership of private shares, and it is trying to phase out government from positions of the economy's most modern sectors. This strategy worked for Japan and others. Hopes are running high in Malaysia and in other nations that it is well worth pursuing.

TRADING COMPANIES

To a great extent, powerful trading corporations are fueling the commercial activities of non-American businesses. The "general trading companies" (or GTCs) of South Korea, fashioned in the image of Japanese *sogo shosha*, are a good example. Their charter is quite specific: (1) to penetrate domestic and foreign markets, (2) to establish a global distribution network, and (3) to finance smaller Korean companies that act as suppliers.[4] These quasi-public monoliths have been directly responsible for the lion's share of Korea's economic success. The $5.1 billion Samsung Group, for example, maintains an active presence in twenty-nine countries — building hotels, refining sugar, and overseeing many other businesses. Since 1970 it has averaged 40 percent growth in annual revenues, and it accounts for almost 8 percent of South Korea's gross national product.

Malaysia's first Japanese-style trading company is also taking shape.[5] The company, to be called Nastra Sdn. Bhd., combines private- and public-sector monies and is expected to begin operating in 1982. The godfather of this new venture is Prime Minister Mahathir Mohamad, former minister of trade and industry. The Malaysian leader, impressed by the success of the large, multifunctional Japanese trading companies in marketing Japanese products around the world, suggested that his country could use a similar approach to find new outlets for its traditional exports and to introduce manufactured exports overseas.

Neighboring Singapore, too, is eager to establish large trading companies along Japanese lines.[6] Government and business supporters of the trading company idea argue that a significant portion of gross national product remains to justify merging small family businesses that have dominated trading in this city-state into larger, more efficient companies. But these larger trading companies will not necessarily be as expansive as their Japanese counterparts.[7]

Singapore's first venture in this area came in 1968 with the establishment of Intraco Ltd., a government-controlled enterprise. Originally conceived to help Singaporean traders deal with communist countries, the firm has since become a general trading company. Manufacturers who use Intraco's marketing services pay commissions as they would with other sales agents; now the private sector seems keenly interested in building its own version of the trading companies. Similarly, the Philippines, Mexico, Brazil, and Canada are just a few other countries seeking to pursue the same course.[8]

CORPORATE COALITIONS

Nowadays, industrialized and newly industrializing countries are reluctant to "go it alone." Their companies favor interdependence over independence. The value of building joint ventures has been recognized by enlightened executives for many years: large-scale economies, resource pooling, improved access to foreign markets, and other significant advantages of shared enterprise. With so much to gain, we can expect a rise in new forms of shared enterprise in the developed and developing nations, conglomerates with *multiple* national identities. First spotted by Howard V. Perlmutter of the Wharton School, who called them "industrial systems constellations," these alliances permit nationally oriented companies to join together to achieve a worldwide competitive advantage—without sacrificing their national identity.[9] Hence they are quite different from the single enterprise whose global strategy is managed from a single corporate headquarters.

Multinational marriage is becoming increasingly visible today. To illustrate:

☐   The PSA Group in Thailand represents a consolidation of many small-scale enterprises into one dominant force at the *national* level. With origins that go back to 1970, this constellation now claims more than twenty-five local companies. (Appropriately, Thais refer to PSA as "the management hospital.")

In much the same fashion, Bancomer S.A. became Mexico's largest private banking institution in November 1977 following the merger of thirty-seven local banks. In addition to its almost six hundred branches south of the border, this national giant is represented in New York, Tokyo, London, Madrid, and Los Angeles.

Volvo's recent merger with Beijerinvest, a wide-ranging conglomerate that is Sweden's fifth largest company, is even more energetic. The product of this union is a $10 billion coalition, the largest industrial and trading concern in Scandinavia. In doing so, it offers tremendous promise for both participants as well as the Swedish economy. Beijerinvest and Volvo will combine resources in industrial know-how, transportation, energy, food, and financial creativity. Its contribution to the nation may be even more significant. The men at the head of Volvo and Beijerinvest are two of Sweden's rare free spirits; and "there is need for their entrepreneurial zest in Northern Europe—and that's very healthy," notes one observer.[10]

☐ As one of many *regional* coalitions, the Triad Holding Corporation represents the first Arab-owned and managed conglomerate. Principal investors come from Egypt, Iran, Lebanon, Saudi Arabia, and Sudan. Included in Triad's portfolio are oil tankers in Indonesia, cattle feeding operations in Brazil, and fashion houses in Paris.

Similarly, on the heels of a United Nations study encouraging regional coalitions, the Association of South East Asian Nations is taking steps to build ASEAN multinationals. Results are expected soon in banking, trading, shipping, and fertilizer production.

On the European continent, where building coalitions are in vogue, one should also include the agreement of the Italian Banco de Roma, the French Credit Lyonnais, and the German Commerzbank to offer regional financial services.

☐ On a *global* scale, the Saudi Arabians and the Dutch established the Albank Alsaudi Alhollandi, headquartered in Jeddah. Offering worldwide banking services, this combination blends the substantial Arab influence of the Saudis with one hundred fifty years of international financial experience of the Dutch partner, Algemene Bank Nederland.

Then there is the trilateral agreement of Japan's Kawasaki Steel Corporation, Italy's Societa Finanziara Siderugia, and Brazil's Siderugia Brasileira to develop an integrated steel plant and deep-water harbor facilities in Brazil.

As in any marriage, the pressures of cohabitation are demanding, especially when leading companies representing various nations are involved. Hence the challenge of managing these coalitions is staggering.[11] In fact, one of the first cross-border mergers, the union of Britain's Dunlop Holdings Ltd. and Italy's Pirelli & Co., two major European tire makers, fell apart on April 23, 1981 — just as did Italian automaker Fiat's merger with France's Citröen in 1975. A combination of nationalism and sick home economies sank both efforts. Despite these failures, we can expect more, not less, of these traditional combinations in the years to come.

What Peter Drucker has coined "production sharing" is, in his opinion, "increasingly becoming the dominant mode of economic integration throughout the non-Communist world."[12] Take, for example, the European Common Market's rush into these transnational cartels. Since 1974, the EEC's Business Cooperation Center (popularly referred to as "the Marriage Bureau") has matched over two hundred fifty European companies in various forms of cooperation, ranging from joint ventures to technical exchanges and joint marketing.[13] Set up by a decision of the Commission of the European Communities in the summer of 1973, the Center's function, which it performs free of charge to the companies concerned, is to foster "long term reciprocal ties which go beyond the stage of purely commercial relations" — to cite the statutes. The Marriage Bureau's services are offered to all kinds of businesses whatever their legal form, financial structure, or industry, but with special emphasis on small and medium-sized firms. Initially, its efforts were confined to cooperative ventures of EEC member nations; by the end of the 1970s, however, its span of activity included Switzerland, Austria, Sweden, Israel, Canada, and a number of ASEAN countries. A network of "correspondents" was established, mainly through cooperation with various confederations of industry, but also with individual industrial and trade organizations.

Few would disagree that the Business Cooperation Center's biggest successes have been in banking. Its prodding resulted in the formation of the European Group of Banks, an unusual cooperation scheme linking ten medium-sized banks: two Belgian, two French, three Italian, one German, one Danish, and one Dutch. "The banking sector has been the object of a steady and rapid process of concentration for some time," concedes Italian Luigi Morosi, managing director of the Center.[14]

As tangible evidence of the Center's effectiveness, calls for help are growing steadily each year. Writes Mats Halvarsson of Sweden's *Veckans Affarer*: "In response to 120 requests for partners in 1979, the Center was able to set up 102 contacts, with a total of 1,737 firms expressing interest. This is an increase of about 20 percent over 1978, which also showed a higher rate of activity than 1977. As a result of the 102 contacts, 36 agreements were confirmed by the Center—a good record by any standard."[15]

The lure of cooperating rather than competing is viewed by many Europeans as the best way of reviving their persistent problems of overcapacity and unemployment. In computers, for instance, they feel that about the only way that even the big three European companies—International Computers Ltd. (ICL) in Britain, Siemens in Germany, and Companie Internationale pour L'Informatique-Honeywell Bull (CII-HB) in France—can keep up is to move toward more cooperative efforts and joint ventures either among themselves or with American or Japanese manufacturers. Says Oscar H. Rothenbuecher, a senior computer analyst with Arthur D. Little Inc.,

"Survival [for the Europeans] means one thing: getting together and cooperating."[16]

"If you look at the problem of competing with IBM, the logic of joint ventures is inescapable," declares Terrance A. Stones, director of planning for Honeywell Information Systems Ltd. in Britain.[17] "The fundamental problem," he says, "is facing up to IBM, with its $1.2 billion worth of research and development spending and its volumes that ensure low production costs."[18] Therefore, the European Community and its industrial commissioner, Etienne Dovignon, are actively encouraging the member countries to coordinate their efforts in computers, telecommunications, and microelectronics. Several of these ventures involve Japan. Germany's Siemens, for example, has entered into a reciprocal agreement with Japan's Fujitsu Ltd. Siemens is buying its largest computer from the Japanese company and, in return, is selling Fujitsu its laser printer. The Fujitsu Series M computer fits nicely into the German company's strategy of building computers that can operate on IBM software but cost less than IBM hardware. Whether Siemens's strategy and those of other European computer manufacturers will pay off remains to be seen. The Common Market, though, remains committed to these collaborative schemes, which closely parallel the postwar system of German and Japanese conglomeration.

As automakers fantasize about the prospects of a "world car," many are building similar coalitions to realize their dreams. "With the worldwide industry in a state of transition and companies facing rising cost pressures, intensified political constraints and accelerating capital requirements," writes Marina v. N. Whitman, vice-president and chief economist at General Motors Corporation, "the trend toward pooling of resources—in the form of mergers, joint ventures and cooperative agreements—will continue in the 1980s."[19] When discussions turn to the future of the car industry, Bernard Hanon, executive vice-president in charge of Renault's worldwide automobile operations, reaches similar conclusions.[20] Times are difficult, he feels, and getting even more so. Smaller companies simply cannot survive alone. Instead of today's eleven or so "decision centers" (or major car builders), by 1990 there will be no more than five or six—the result of a constant stream of mergers through this decade.

As the market for new cars becomes increasingly international, the highly competitive drive for technological and engineering advances, as well as the need for cost efficiencies from product conception through final sales, is already forcing the world's carmakers to consider new partnerships. By the final decade of this century, the rigors of worldwide competition will cause even further a wholesale consolidation of the industry. "Few companies will have the muscle to go it alone," predicts George C. Meyers, a director and former chairman of American Motors Corporation. "Cooperation is going to grow and cross oceans and national boundaries."[21]

The Japanese, with their remarkable success in automaking, have always been savvy to the changing dynamics of the industry and the importance of achieving scale economies. At a time when Japan's car companies are coming off several banner years, they are seeing the advantages of transnational mergers.[22] To cite a few examples:

☐ Honda's production agreement with BL Ltd. (formerly British Leyland), owned by the British government. Under this December 1979 arrangement, BL will be able to put a new Honda-designed car immediately into production, gaining two years over the time it would have taken BL to design and build a new, more competitive model of its own.

☐ The agreement by Alfa Romeo S.P.A. of Italy and Nissan Motor Co. of Japan to coproduce a car for Europe. In addition, Nissan agreed recently to acquire a 36 percent capital share in Spain's Motor Iberica from Massey-Ferguson of Canada for $40 million. The company has reached a similar accord with the Spanish government for cooperating in rehabilitating Empresa Nacional Autocamiones.

☐ Nissan has also agreed with Volkswagenwerk A.G. of West Germany to produce Volkswagen cars in Japan. In 1981, the two companies set up the new venture on a fifty-fifty basis with a capitalization of $30 million. Output of 60,000 cars per year is planned for 1983. At VW, top officials have not ruled out the possibility that such cooperation could lead to the production of Nissan models at their U.S. plants.

☐ The discussions between Toyota and Spain's ailing SEAT to conclude a joint marketing and technology agreement. Tokyo is making no secret of its motive in a linkup with SEAT: a base for entry into the European car market. These negotiations follow Toyota's recent arrangement with the British sportscar maker Lotus Cars for long-term cooperation and engineering, manufacturing, and "other areas where practical."

☐ The pact with PSA Peugeot-Citroën for Nissan to supply technical advice and licensing to help the French company's exports to Japan meet the country's severe new emission control standards.

☐ The deal between the Japanese motorcycle maker Yamaha and Italy's Fiat to grant licenses on new technology for reducing fuel consumption in car engines. Fiat is expected to use the technology in producing this year's models in the 1500 to 2000 c.c. range.

☐ The plans of Mitsubishi Motors Corp. to build a large plant with Hyundai Motor Co., South Korea's biggest automaker. The plant, slated for a capacity of 300,000 units a year in 1986, would produce a new front-wheel drive model with a 1.2 or 1.4 liter gasoline engine designed by Mitsubishi. Half the production is to be sold in the local market and the other half overseas. To cement its relations further into Korean soil, Mitsubishi Motors (and Mitsubishi Corp.) have been authorized to acquire 10 percent of Hyundai's stock.

Japan, of course, is well experienced in constructing conglomerates. Its infamous *zaibatsus*, disbanded at the end of World War II, were completely transformed into component companies, whose ownership has passed entirely from the original founding families to scattered shareholders.[23] These new combines are the archetypal coalition, at least at the national level. When the Hiroshima-Toyo Kogyo, maker of the Mazda, began to falter in the mid-1970s, it received considerable help from its friends.[24] The company is a member of the Sumitomo group, one of Japan's major industrial conglomerates. The group's two banks, Sumitomo Bank and Sumitomo Trust (also Toyo Kogyo's principal creditors and among its largest shareholders), came to the rescue with a thorough belt-tightening plan. By doing so, Tokyo was absolved from undertaking a governmental bail-out scheme on the order of Washington's loan program to save Chrysler.

Whether it is help within a multi- or single-industry conglomerate, Japanese automakers recognize the value of corporate coalitions—or "business relationships," as they are called in Japan.[25] We may expect collaboration on technical, marketing, and other levels to become more prevalent, especially as small companies struggle to compete with industry leaders.

Sharing the load through collaboration also prevails in Europe, where there are many current examples of transnational cooperation in the automobile industry. For example:

☐ Following abortive merger discussions with Volvo in 1977, Swedish Saab-Scania's decision to join with Italy's Lancia, a subsidiary of Fiat. Saab and Lancia, both low-volume specialty carmakers, will share the $350 million to $500 million development costs of a midsized family sedan, which each company will then customize, while sharing many basic parts. Current plans aim at an annual output of 100,000 cars by Saab by the mid-1980s; Lancia's target will be about 200,000 cars. Overall, the production-development pact will save Saab an estimated $250 million over a ten-year period.

☐ Fiat's negotiations with the French PSA Peugeot-Citroën group to produce jointly about a million medium-sized engines a year. The parts would most likely be produced in France and Italy on

117

an equal basis, and the engines would be assembled in a new plant to be built in one of the countries. The move is part of Fiat's strategy of joining forces with other European car producers to achieve economies of scale.

☐ The series of deals concluded in recent years by Renault, the state-owned French manufacturer, designed to bolster its chances of becoming a major force in the industry. By forging equity and technical links with private-sector carmakers, Renault is viewed by many as the pacesetter in building transnational pacts.[26] Included in its portfolio are the following:

   ☐ A 10 percent interest in the passenger-car business of Swedish Volvo, with the opportunity to expand its interest in Volvo Car Corporation, a subsidiary of the parent company, up to 20 percent.

   ☐ A majority stake in American Motors Corp. (AMC), a 20 percent share in Mack Trucks, a subsidiary of Signal Corp., as well as a big piece of Bendix Corporation's automotive electronics business.

   ☐ Links with the privately owned PSA Peugeot-Citröen group and Volvo to produce a six-cylinder engine in France.

   ☐ An arrangement with Volkswagen to develop jointly a new generation of fuel-efficient automatic transmissions. It is the first noticeable cooperative venture between Renault and Volkswagen, preceded only by an exchange of apprentices in a training program.

   ☐ A ten-year contract with San-Fu Motor Industrial Co. to manufacture and market a car in Taiwan. The new model will be made with some locally manufactured parts, with Renault designing the vehicle and providing technical assistance. Auto production will be increased to a level of 15,000 vehicles annually at San-Fu Motor's factories in Taichung, in central Taiwan.

   ☐ Active discussions with Hyundai, producer of the fast-selling Pony, to enter a joint venture or technical agreement to produce a line of models in South Korea beginning in 1982 or 1983.

Renault's President Bernard Vernier-Palliez noted, in concluding the Volvo deal, that the motor industry has left the first phase of independent, national producers and entered the second phase of integrated, transnational companies.[27] By forging new alliances, Renault appears well positioned to meet these challenges.

Where the U.S. automobile industry stands in this period of transition and shakeout is difficult to assess. On the surface, there would seem to be ample evidence of an American interest in forming cross-border alliances. Consider:

☐ Chrysler Corporation's linkup with PSA Peugeot-Citroën and its exclusive dealership contract with a 15 percent stake in Mitsubishi Motors Corp., one of the larger Japanese automakers.

☐ American Motors' arrangement with Renault, giving the French company access to the AMC distribution network for the Renault 5 ("Le Car") and for potential U.S. production of the R18.

☐ General Motors Corp.'s large minority share (34.2 percent) of Isuzu Motors Ltd., a small Japanese maker of cars and trucks, and small interest (5 percent) in Suzuki Motor Co., a major producer of motorcycles and minicars. GM has also agreed with Toyota, Japan's second largest company, to explore possible joint production of a small-car factory in the United States.

☐ The efforts by Ford Motor Co. to obtain a 25 percent position in Toyo Kogyo. Under this agreement, Ford will market small passenger cars developed by its Japanese partner in Southeast Asia, the Middle East, and Australia under the Ford name.

The bottom line of all these developments should almost certainly be a stepped-up pace of innovation and competition by U.S. companies in an increasingly global automotive industry. But when the epidermal tissue of America's involvement in these cartel-like affairs is pulled back, our prognosis is quite different.

119

For starters, there is the General Television case. In 1977, General Electric Company wanted to form an alliance with Japan's Hitachi Ltd. The new company, to be called General Television of America, Inc., would draw its technology from both partners and use GE's existing television manufacturing plants in Portsmouth, Virginia, and Syracuse, New York, which together employ four thousand people. Under the proposed alliance, General Television would make television sets under General Electric, Hitachi, and private labels. However, the Justice Department nixed the deal on antitrust grounds. The unfortunate epilogue: Hitachi, on its own, opened a plant near Los Angeles to manufacture nineteen-inch color television sets.[28]

Even well-structured, "safe" combinations in the U.S. must proceed with caution. France's Renault, for example, cleverly announces in its national advertising campaigns its intentions to work *with* American Motors as a coequal, not as a predatory acquirer. Its national ads claim: "*Avec* [French for 'with'], in fact, symbolizes the thinking behind our efforts, our know-how, our success. All of us at Renault are to be reckoned *avec*. Long live *avec!*"

Notwithstanding these cosmetic attempts to sidestep the long arm of U.S. antitrust law, American enterprise remains at a distinct disadvantage from its competitors. Fashioning industrial combines, which has been viewed as empire building in this country since the days of Senator Sherman, is perceived by other nations to be an essential prerequisite for economic success. Consequently, look for America to fall further behind the rest of the pack unless these new organizational vehicles spring to life in the near future.

Managerial Learning

Another prism through which the American and alternative industrial approaches can be viewed is the managerial processes or systems that enterprises from each nation chose to adopt. In former times, executives from around the world marveled at the U.S.-style management practices that had given rise to America's economic dominance. The reasons for our success varied from country to country, "but the general drift did not: The American manager was nonpareil—revered, even feared, throughout the world."[29] By the 1970s, though, foreigners were no longer awestruck over the United States and its platoons of managers and methods. A nation that had once been regarded as an invincible juggernaut became the subject of downright scorn.

To Americans and non-Americans alike, the inevitable benchmark, Japan, consistently outperforms the United States. Japanese productivity outpaced by five times the rate of U.S. productivity since World War II; it is growing at a faster rate each year. Predicasts, Inc., a Cleveland-based market research firm, projects that Japan, with its emphasis on innovation and quality control, will emerge by the early 1990s as "the indisputable world technology leader."[30] By contrast, the United States, which had the world's highest level of overall productivity in 1965, had slipped to sixth in 1975 and will fall to fourteenth by 1995—tied with Australia, the study said.

On the related matter of employee turnover, the United States cannot begin to match Japan or West Germany. It is almost taken for granted that half the graduates recruited on American campuses will have moved on to other organizations within five years.[31] One group of Harvard M.B.A.'s, in fact, has been tracked over a five-year period after graduation: 70 percent changed jobs. One out of three middle managers are estimated to have a résumé in circulation at this moment. Our penchant for high-velocity employment is, no doubt, incited by the siren songs of America's headhunters. Says Arnold R. Deutsch, chairman of his own human resources consulting firm, "For some 30 years, corporate recruiting teams have been systematically raiding St. Petersburg to staff St. Paul."[32] The result: employee turnover rates in the United States are over four times higher than in Japan. Understandably, absenteeism too is much higher in this country.

Why America's dismal record? In polls done recently by the Gallup Organization for the U.S. Chamber of Commerce, 83 percent of business leaders and 53 percent of workers at all levels agreed that employee attitudes are a major factor in explaining declining productivity and rising employee absenteeism in the United States.[33] An April 1981 poll by the *Los Angeles Times* also found that most American workers believe that they are not working as hard as they could and that they could accomplish more on the job if they tried.[34] But if our workers are turned off to their jobs, they openly admit the value of the work ethic. Another Chamber of Commerce study on industrial attitudes, for example, revealed that almost nine out of ten American employees say that it is important to work hard on their jobs and do their best.[35] The gains of hard work itself far exceed the material benefits of being employed. The *Los Angeles Times* survey confirmed that Americans are motivated by much more than just a paycheck. An "interesting job" was rated as the most important factor in achieving job satisfaction; money is only in fourth place as a means of achieving satisfaction.[36]

Creating employee interest in their jobs is what Japanese and German employers do best. In Japan's case, the real secret for its success (in relative and absolute terms) is better management, especially in personnel relations. Peter Drucker argues: "The greatest weakness of American business is people, and it is the greatest strength of the Japanese, the management of people."[37] This same thesis is shared by William G. Ouchi, a management professor at the University of California, Los Angeles. He recommends that U.S. companies pattern themselves after their Japanese peers.[38] By emphasizing long-range planning, consensus decision making, and strong worker-employer loyalty, American industry might avoid the current dilemma of high employee turnover, declining productivity, and generalized alienation. The process of converting American companies into what he calls "Type Z" concerns, he feels, would create a much-needed atmosphere of subtlety, trust, and intimacy. "What a lot of it boils down to," Ouchi explains, "is creating an environment in which people want to cooperate with each other and it is in their interest to do so."[39]

Clearly, the fast-learning nations of Asia are heeding Dr. Ouchi's advice. They are pursuing actively corporate policies that put much greater importance on personal loyalty and a host of other organizational values now alien to most American businesses. "Management philosophies in the ASEAN countries [Malaysia, Indonesia, Singapore, Taiwan, and the Philippines] reflect the same organizational values espoused by Japanese corporations," says Regina Ordonez, a professor of human behavior at the Asian Institute of Management in Manila. "[A] Malaysian chairman has more in common with the president of Mitsubishi than he does with a Sears executive from Chicago."[40]

Still, Chicago-based executives can and should follow the Japanese example. That is Professor Ouchi's major message, and he has found that several of America's most successful companies—IBM, Proctor & Gamble, and Hewlett-Packard—have Type Z traits. Akio Morita, the sixty-year-old chairman and co-founder of the Sony Corp., has similar sentiments. He thinks that the antagonism between management and labor in America is the root of its problems.[41] Herein lies one of the greatest contrasts between the United States and Japan, with its tradition of corporate paternalism and lifetime employment. Morita argues that the Japanese approach to labor-management relations is not tied to cultural eccentricity, applicable only in Japan. He says it can be transplanted in slightly watered down form to America. As evidence, he points to Sony's plants at San Diego and Dothan, Alabama, where, he says, productivity has risen steadily so that it is now very close to that of the company's factories in Japan. "The workers in San Diego and Dothan are terrific," beams Morita.[42]

THE "NEW MANAGERIAL GOSPEL"

Notwithstanding Mr. Morita's positive experiences, a host of factors have worked to betray America's economic superiority. In their McKinsey award-winning *Harvard Business Review* article, "Managing Our Way to Economic Decline," Professors Robert H.

Hayes and William J. Abernathy outline the components of this country's managerial inertia: "[G]uided by what they took to be the newest and best principles of management, American managers have increasingly directed their attention elsewhere. These new principles, despite their widespread usefulness, encourage a preference for (1) analytic detachment rather than the insight that comes from 'hands on' experience and (2) short-term cost reduction rather than long-term development of technological competitiveness. It is this new managerial gospel, we feel, that has played a major role in undermining the vigor of American industry."[43]

The apostles of this new managerial gospel are the so-called professional managers, who prize analytical detachment and methodological elegance over insight and experience. Gone, it would seem, are the entrepreneurs and innovators of Corporate America. As a result, warns John Kenneth Galbraith, "investment becomes cautious, analysis becomes a surrogate for action; innovation has an aspect of danger; the ability to adapt to changing circumstances dwindles; the future is sacrificed for the near present. Performance becomes increasingly mediocre — or worse."[44]

"These professionals, usually with financial or legal backgrounds, know little about the functions of the very business they run — the markets, technologies, production processes, and workers," says Steven Lohr of the *New York Times*.[45] Despite these apparent failings, they often occupy the executive suites of most American corporations. "Critics contend that these managers run business by the numbers, period," Lohr adds. "What is needed today, they argue, is less of the Olympian detachment of the 50th floor and more nuts-and-bolts understanding of the factory floor."[46] Yet the truth remains: only 27.2 percent of the CEOs of the 1,300 largest U.S. companies are manufacturing men.

The explanation, at least in part, lies with the citadels of capitalism — the business schools. For the past two decades, "real world" influence on their curricula has given way to cosmetic sophistication. "In the 1960s courses tended to be descriptive, not analytical, including things like plant tours," recalls Richard R. West, dean of Dartmouth's Amos Tuck School of Business Administration. "[Then] the technicians took over. While the old guys show how a company made scheduling decisions, the new approach was to build models."[47] Of course, scientific management has been under serious study in schools of business (and engineering) since Frederick W. Taylor's *Principles and Methods of Scientific Management*, published in 1911.[48] Moreover, an enormous cache of useful analytical tools and techniques has been made available to all major themes of management—from human relations to economics. But in the past decade America's centers of learning took their eye off the ball, as analytical alchemy came into being.

"What worries me," says Dr. Robert A. Frosch, president of the American Association of Engineering Societies, "is that academic research may become increasingly theoretical and diverge more and more from practice in industry. One of the great strengths of American education and industry has been the flow between the two and I would hate to see that lost."[49] Building more effective "town-gown" relations has become endangered as fashionable technology replaces old-fashioned notions of "hands-on" experience. Donald S. MacNaughton, chairman and chief executive officer of American Hospital Corporation of America, puts the problem in perspective. "It is essential to good management that this scientific flow continues and keeps pace with the ever changing nation of modern corporations," he suggests. "Nevertheless, we should avoid the danger of substituting scientific management for the art of management."[50] Perhaps no one has been a more vocal spokesman against this danger than Theodore Levitt, a leading observer of the American business scene and a highly respected professor at the Harvard Business School. "There is a tendency to subject [business] to a rapidly expanding retinue of eager sycophants equipped with new 'scientific tools' and decision-making modes, who promise to free the manager from the inescapable uncertainties, risks and traumas of running an enterprise," he warns. "'Experts' trained to the teeth in the techniques (but not necessarily the practice) of management, are enlisted to do even better what people of native shrewdness, sound good sense and abundant energy did quite beautifully before."[51]

These same traits—shrewdness, sense, and energy—the critics of American business schools argue, are in woefully short supply among today's M.B.A. students. Donald C. Carroll, dean of the Wharton School, admits that one of the most frequent complaints is that his students do not know how to work with people and that they are antisocial geniuses.[52] "[I]t is a widely held view that the M.B.A. might be part of the current problem," adds Steven Lohr of the *New York Times*. "The charge is that leading business schools . . . have been teaching how not to manage a modern American company, that they have simply taught business as business has been practiced, and not helped lead the way to necessary change."[53] Professor Burt Nanus, a professor of management at the University of Southern California, concedes that "all business schools are slipping. They're failing dismally in preparing business leaders of tomorrow.'[54] Even John H. McArthur, dean of the prestigious Harvard Business School, generally agrees that in the past too little attention has been paid at the business schools to the handling of workers, production, and international business. "I don't think these are things that we in the business schools are passing along well yet," he admits.[55]

It is axiomatic that recognition of a problem is the first step in its resolution; and on this score one can be cautiously optimistic. The business schools, perhaps more so than any other educational institution, are capable of adaptive learning, especially when the marketplace demands it. A resurgence, albeit modest, of a new pragmatism finally seems to be arriving on campus. More nuts-and-bolts courses, corporate internships, and directed practicums are just a few instances of a gradual return to reality. How far this movement will go is difficult to assess. For one thing, business school faculties are sensitive to the *sine qua non* for professional advancement: rigorous analytical research in lieu of classroom teaching. For another, M.B.A. students are intellectually titillated by the latest methodological twists as well as by prospective employers who value such learning (management consulting firms, in particular). Neither the purveyors nor the consumers of the current pabulum of schools of business are likely to be committed to an abrupt swing back to more practical approaches to learning.

Rather than being caught in the swinging pendulum confronting the business schools, executives would be well advised to examine the shortsighted measurement criteria that have become so identifiable with American industry. "Today American management is among the best educated and most professional in the world," argues Senator Bentsen, chairman of the Congressional Joint Economic Committee. "But they often operate with goals imposed by the financial community that are counter-productive to the long term interest of American competitiveness. The measure of achievement and the goals to be reached are as short term as a politician's next election."[56] Frank A. Weil, former assistant commerce secretary for industry and trade, chimes in: "[T]he managers of the powerful institutional owners of [a] company's shares don't want a whole lot of explanations. They want results now. Five years from now won't do. Their overlords—stockholders, pensioners, and policy holders—are measuring only a financial result against overall current market standards."[57]

To management expert Peter Drucker, the real villain can be easily uncovered. "[T]he pension funds, our way of capital intermediation, push companies into short-term thinking," he says. "I know a number of high-technology companies that should plow back money long-term, and know it, and don't do it because the pension funds are their source of capital. The companies have to maintain those 40-P/E ratios."[58] America's dedication to "making the numbers," especially the price-earnings ratio and earnings-per-share, came into vogue in the 1960s, recalls Harold M. Williams, former chairman of the Securities and Exchange Commission, "about the time that investment and productivity measures . . . began to turn down." "I would suggest," he continues, "that this was not coincidental."[59]

The consequences of America's overorientation to immediate results are far-reaching. They encourage generating earnings through financial gamesmanship rather than market competition; improvement of earnings by allowing plant and equipment to age or by reducing product quality; or increased dividends to bolster the stock price. This allegation, says Kenneth R. Andrews of the Harvard Business School, is "hard to document, but it is plausible enough to concern managers and students of management."[60]

Two concerned students of management are Thomas H. Naylor of Duke University and Alfred Rappaport of Northwestern University. According to Professor Naylor, America is drowning in the numbers. It is our "information overload [that] leads to a preoccupation with next year's financial performance, insufficient attention to long-term strategic planning, and an inability to cope with change."[61] For Professor Rappaport the problem is somewhat different: The need for numbers is inevitable, but we must be certain that the *right* numbers are being used. His advice? "Long term plans must be developed, and executive incentives must be linked to strategies that create economic value."[62]

The shortsightedness of Wall Street and American management and the preoccupation with quarterly financial reports are largely responsible for executives' shying away from creating economic value through long-term investments. But there is also the bias of our federal tax codes, which tend to penalize savings and investment and which fail to adjust depreciation schedules to account for replacement costs. Once again, two major societal institutions, business and government, seem out-of-sync.

Concluding Note

In the eyes of many experts, the fault behind declining U.S. power lies mainly with the inability of our corporations to adopt the policies and practices through which economic value can be increased. Nowhere is this phenomenon more visible than in the organizational and managerial limitations of U.S. industry, especially when compared with its foreign competitors. If the ruptured breach between Washington and Corporate America is a major force in our economic decline, what are the underlying reasons for its existence and what, if anything, can be done to reduce the tensions? The following chapters examine these important questions.

Part 3

The Problem Revisited

6

Beyond Arm's Length

I F AMERICAN enterprise anticipated any help from the United States
government in warding off the competitive volleys of multinationals from the industrialized and newly industrializing countries,
they were laboring under false pretenses. Precisely when a tighter
bond between U.S. business and government would have been in
order, the opposite, in fact, took place. Frosty, not friendly, relations
between America's private and public sectors dominated the 1970s,
and one might justifiably conclude that the major challenge to
American enterprise comes not from foreign sources, but from the
U.S. government.

Washington's growing displeasure with the capitalist class has
evolved slowly over time. In large part, the root causes are uniquely
American, with historical overtones that reach back to the nineteenth
century. But in large part, they also reflect the global realities of our
times, particularly the growing concern for corporate legitimacy. Both
sets of factors—national and international—prompted, and continue
to prompt, the U.S. government to reassess critically the role of
American corporations at home and abroad. The unfortunate upshot
of Washington's scrutiny is the web of restrictive laws and attitudes

that now hobbles U.S. enterprise. Let us examine the deteriorating relationship between U.S. industry and government: how it has been spawned, what forms it now takes, and why it contributes to America's decline as a global economic power.

The Basis for Dissent

Since the birth of American capitalism in the mid-nineteenth century, an aura of mutual suspicion and distrust has characterized dealings between the public and private sectors. For the past 140 years, antistatist attitudes have preoccupied the U.S. business community, just as anticorporate attacks have consumed the energies of our public officials. "The relationship between government and business in the United States can only be described as one of latent hostility," notes Harvard historian Edward S. Mason.[1] "It is clear to [even] the most obtuse observer that there is much more distrust between government and business leadership in the U.S., than, say, in Britain, France, or the Netherlands."[2] To former Treasury Secretary George P. Schultz, this latent hostility underlies "the abrasive interface" that prevents U.S. government and business leaders from meeting the full force of foreign competition in some collective fashion.[3]

What are the historical reasons for the abrasions between the dominant stakeholders in American economic society, and why are they so deeply ingrained in the American psyche? Several important forces are responsible for the disproportionately higher level of government-business distrust found in the United States than in its global competitors.

First, and perhaps foremost, the U.S. government has played only a secondary role in the evolution of the American economy. As the basis for economic growth moved from trade and agricultural exports to industry, the emerging industrial elites began to outgrow the need for governmental aid and assistance. By the mid-1840s private capital was strong enough to demand successfully that the public sector reduce its involvements in business matters. True, the federal government did play a vital role in America's industrial growth after the Civil War through its subsidy of railroad construction, enactment of protective domestic tariffs, and other measures. But what distinguished Washington's efforts to aid U.S. commerce was the limited interest by business in the collaborative approach to economics. One observer of the times concluded: "After the Civil War . . . it became clear that capitalism was now strong enough to get along without more active assistance from government than it already enjoyed. Equally important, it began to appear that in a partnership between government and business the danger of gratuitous political interference was becoming too serious to justify the risk."[4]

A key difference between the U.S. business-government interests and those of our competitors, Berkeley Professor David Vogel points out, is that "American capitalists faced none of the obstacles that in most European nations made a strong state critical to industrialization. There was no aristocracy to overthrow, no foreign armies to mobilize against, and, most importantly, only one nation (Great Britain) had previously industrialized with which to compete."[5] This fundamentally passive role of the U.S. government, Vogel adds, "[stands] in marked contrast to the more pioneering and active efforts of the state in shaping industrial development in most other capitalist — and all socialist — nations."[6]

Japan is one case in point. Only with the help of an activist government was it able to emerge from a feudal to an industrial society. Following the turmoil of the early Meiji period, the dominant Japanese pattern of catching up with the rest of the world rested upon "central government planning and guidance, close government-business cooperation, and the rapid creation of large, private institutions through centralized capital accumulation and formalized training programs."[7] Japan, Germany, and other "late modernizers" (to use Richard Dore's description) had no other choice: a powerful government was essential to economic prosperity. But the American people reached far different conclusions. For them, the private sector controlled the nation's economic destiny, with government relegated to the role of an understudy. "To a far greater extent than in any other capitalist nation (with the partial exception of England)," says David Vogel, "the American bourgeoisie succeeded in creating the industrial system with its own initiative."[8]

Keeping government on the sidelines was very much in keeping with the American spirit of individualism and egalitarianism. Looking back, George Cabot Lodge explains: "The founding fathers of the United States, following the Lockean ideology, rejected the authoritarianism of eighteenth-century Europe, preferring the decentralization, dispersion, and division of power of an earlier period. Fundamentally suspicious of government, Americans employed Lockean thought almost as a religion to justify the most extreme divorce of economic activity from political controls, a divorce which has continued to trouble us up to the present day."[9] No doubt America's wide open spaces, its expansive geography, and sparse population also encouraged the aggresively competitive individualism that was needed to endure the hardships of agrarian living in the first one hundred years of the Republic. Adulation of the individual seemed well matched to a nation in which human resources were scarce and natural resources abundant. Values emphasizing individual fulfillment outweighed in importance alternative notions of cooperation, harmony, and community. Ideologically speaking, Americans were well suited to construct arm's-length barriers between business and government and to minimize the contributions of the central state.

Naturally, the primacy of the private sector in American society has been called into question on many occasions. The U.S. government, at different points in its history, has attempted to reject its stepchild status for a more active, interventionist role. Whether the outcome was specific legislation to control the "robber barons" or to create a new administrative agency to protect consumers, widespread populist perceptions of corporate misbehavior brought calls for increasing government regulation of business. These attacks on

Corporate America have typically taken place when its political influence has been weakest, and antibusiness pressures strongest.

The New Deal was such a period. To Berkeley's Vogel and other economic historians, it represented "a major discontinuity in the development of American capitalism" as government's power grew relative to that of business.[10] On balance, however, these discontinuities were rare. The great majority of our citizens regarded those in the public sector as "newcomers to American institutional life, whose late arrival testifies to their inexperience and irrelevance to economic development."[11]

It is one thing for America's public servants to be viewed by their constituents as newcomers; it is quite another to be perceived as marginally competent. A second cause of the ideological gap between government and business is the perceived mediocrity of the U.S. civil service. From its seat on the sidelines, government has consistently seen the best and the brightest snatched from its bosom by big business. Alexis de Tocqueville wrote: "When public employments are few in number, ill-paid, and precarious, whilst the different lines of business are numerous and lucrative, it is to business, and not to official duties, that the new and eager . . . turn."[12] Similarly, Amherst historian Henry Steele Commager has argued that one of the greatest tragedies of the American dream is its inability to funnel the cream of its youth into positions of public service and responsibility.[13]

Admittedly, the New Deal brought with it a partial rejuvenation of status of public administrators in the United States. Today, opportunities abound for university graduates interested in careers in government at salary ranges that often outpace those in industry (particularly at the entry and mid-career levels). Still, the problem persists: when presented with two opportunities (one in business, the other in government), most of America's best graduates opt for the former.

In my discussions with the deans of America's leading management schools, those offering master's degrees in both business and public administration, the overwhelming preference of their graduates was for the M.B.A degree, and the career prospects that go with it. One dean confided: "In the beginning of their second year, our prospective grads begin their job interviews. It's a period of intense disillusionment for our M.P.A. candidates. When confronted with job offers from Citicorp or the City of New York; TWA or TVA; IBM or the IRS—it becomes no contest. Industry invariably wins!"[14] Similar stories are being echoed on other campuses across the nation.

One noticeable exception is international affairs. For some time, the U.S. Foreign Service has been able to attract outstanding young men and women from prestigious sources, such as the Fletcher School of Law and Diplomacy at Tufts University, Princeton's Woodrow Wilson School, and Johns Hopkins's School of Advanced International Studies. Despite intensive competition from U.S. multinationals, the Foreign Service more than holds its own in recruiting internationally oriented graduates from these first-rate programs. More often than not, however, the federal government comes out second best in the search for talented careerists.

Unlike Japan, West Germany, Sweden, and France, the United States is disinclined to build a bureaucratic elite. Harvard's Ezra F. Vogel reminds us that America's bureaucrats "are not meritocratically selected, professionally trained, or subject to career discipline."[15] To a fault, we have encouraged mediocrity over merit, amateurism over professionalism, and frozen motivations over inspired ambitions.

Missing, too, are meaningful personnel interchanges between government and business at the leadership level. Dual careers, while attractive in principle, are a rarity in practice. Business remains "the fast track," and few managers are prepared to leave it in their mid-careers. Similarly, corporations are inclined to discount the experience of those bureaucrats interested in short- or medium-term employment in industry. This imbalance in opportunity and esteem, skewed in favor of the private sector, heightens the hostilities that exist in American society.

Third, the disparities *within* America's industrial and political communities also aggravate business-government tensions. Detlev F. Vagts of Harvard Law School contends that "the United States business community, by virtue of its dispersion, the variety of its activity, and the variety of the sizes of firms involved, is not a unity; different elements of the business community are quick to suspect others of overreaching by means of preferential government contracts."[16] David Vogel describes American industry as the most fragmented in the capitalist world. "The business community," he adds, "is largely a community in name only; its internal structures of authority remain remarkably decentralized; investment decisions are made by firms or industries relatively independent of each other . . . [and] even industry-wide organizations are not particularly important."[17]

While Japanese and European business groups present a united front to their governments through trade associations and related interest groups, American industry remains fragmented. Here, a lack of solidarity among businessmen contributes to industry's inability to generate its own political leadership. In such a vacuum, uncertainty abounds. Paradoxically, clarifying legislation—and all the formalities that go with it—becomes vital to the economy. "Capitalism works," the late Arthur M. Okun wrote, "only because the government authorizes the posting of millions of 'keep-off' signs—not merely to thwart trespassing and theft in a narrow sense, but to establish ownership; to maintain trademarks, patents, franchises, and copyrights; and to clarify who has the right to sell any particular asset to someone else."[18] If our goals were truly to maximize liberty by reducing the role of the state—if we really wanted laissez-faire—we would have a wasteland of chaos rather than a marketplace of economic activity. Under the American way, successful businessmen and public officials owe each other a great deal.

Despite the pressures for collaboration, the shortsighted and parochial attitudes of America's splintered business community cause Washington to respond in an impersonal, legalistic, and highly formalized fashion. Harvard's Vagts explains: "There is a strong sense, shared by many, that the United States style (of dealing with the corporations that constitute the large business community) is one of impersonality, openness, and legalism. This is true, at least, by comparison with other countries."[19]

But even Washington finds it difficult to convey a unified image to the corporate world. Unlike most other industrialized nations, the United States has no tradition of a strong autocratic state or of a bureaucracy independent of popular pressures. Here, decentralization is king. American bureaucrats are anything but buffered from the political process, and those governmental agencies vested with economic responsibilities must always look over their shoulders at the Congress.

In Japan, on the other hand, the top politicians have little leverage over the bureaucracy. "The key decisions," says Ezra Vogel, "are made by the permanent bureaucrats rather than by politicians of the Diet and the cabinet. Not only is the bureaucracy much more powerful than in the American system, but other parts of the government, like the judiciary and local government, are much weaker."[20] Not so in the United States. By the 1930s, interest-group pluralism had become the pervasive means of influencing the directions of the nation, the priorities it sets, and its definition of goals and needs. "In normal times, when overwhelming crises did not command differently," writes George Lodge, "government resembled a giant organ responding to whatever collection of interest groups trampled most heavily on the keys."[21]

The United States, in opting for a special-interest democracy, became prey to the perils of political ad hocery. Rather than suffer from the whims of elected officials, growing numbers of civil servants became disenfranchised from any overriding sense of national interest. This, in turn, nurtured a "cover-your-assets" mentality by those in government. And quite understandably, America's civil servants have preferred to embrace legalism, impersonalism, and formality when confronting their peers in industry. Many in public service feel that proximity with the capitalist class breeds contempt. It is to be avoided at all costs.

A fourth factor in explaining the tensions between the federal government and the U.S. business community is their collective ambivalence of the importance of world markets. Historically, our leaders in industry and government have been preoccupied with the affluent domestic economy — to the virtual exclusion of foreign opportunities. After all, the United States from 1850 onward represented the richest market in the world. Therefore, it was only logical that it should receive the highest priority of American enterprise. Besides, by focusing on the market they knew best, U.S. businessmen gained an added benefit: they could remove themselves further from the need to call upon the public sector for assistance.

Washington, for its part, yielded to industry's narrowly defined economic map. Unlimited natural resources, boundless growth, and plentiful jobs seemed to be synonymous with the prosperous American marketplace. So the federal government pursued a course of economic independence, bordering on outright autarchy. Our laws (from antitrust to taxation) acquired distinctly domestic overtones, and the commercial arm of government concentrated primarily on the home country.

A much different scenario evolved elsewhere. Japan, Sweden, Switzerland, and most other European nations, plagued by the insufficiencies of their local economies, have had to adopt "export-or-die" strategies. For them, importing raw materials, adding value, and exporting finished products became the name of the game. Government and business simply had to coalesce if foreign exchange were to be earned. These countries have recognized the critical role that a benevolent government plays in aiding its industry to secure a foothold in foreign markets.

It is their long-standing recognition of world polity and the fundamental trend toward economic integration that set Japan and the others apart from the United States. To Peter Drucker, the only effective economic policies in the post-World War II period have been those that accepted the dominance of the world economy. "Japan and Germany," he argues, "emerged as the most successful governmental managers of the economy, precisely because they base themselves on the novel premise that the national economic policy begins with a careful assessment of the world economy. Japan and Germany tried to manage supply to fit the demands of the world economy; they succeeded. The United States (and Britain) tried to manage demand to fit domestic political gains; they failed."[22]

Throughout its history, America has understated global economic objectives as well as the need for a nexus between the private and public sectors where international trade is concerned. Hence, one paradox of American history is that our national stock of wealth and power so blinded us as to sidestep the growing realities of economic interdependence. We have suffered from the home field disadvantage. Our preoccupation with the local terrain has contributed, and continues to contribute, to the sorry state of U.S. business-government affairs.

To summarize so far, four factors are primarily responsible for the weak links between business and government in the United States. They are: (1) the limited role of the central state in America's economic development, (2) the second-class status of its civil servants, (3) the disunity within the private and public sectors, and (4) a lust for the domestic market at the expense of foreign opportunities. These forces deeply affect the nature and conduct of current dealings between the federal government and American business, and they limit the range of possible policy options available to future generations. Perhaps more important, these phenomena also reflect the overriding historical commitment of the American people to democratic capitalism.

The Ethos of Capitalism

"Ever distant frontiers and ever brighter tomorrows," says *Time* editor George M. Taber, "created a nation of optimists, who believed that a rising tide lifts all boats. This was the U.S. social contract."[23] Although capitalism has always been regarded as raw and risky, most Americans accepted the system because it held out the promise that hard work and talent would lead to high rewards. While not everybody was created economically equal, everybody had a full and free opportunity to prosper. Capitalism's latest disciple, George Gilder, argues: "Capitalist production entails faith—in one's neighbor, in one's society, and in the compensatory logic of the cosmos. Search and you shall find, give and you will be given unto, supply creates its own demand. It is this cosmology, this sequential logic, that essentially distinguishes the free from the socialist economy."[24]

Even the critics of earlier decades conceded a grudging admiration for the extraordinary complex and productive economic machinery that the robber barons had fashioned in their transformation of American society. Though often critical of corporate power, both the socialists and the progressives assumed the usefulness of the essential purpose and promise of the private enterprise system, namely, a perpetual rise of per capita income. Faith in the future became an important tenet of American capitalism, and the promise of potential prosperity enabled the corporation to increase its power and privilege. Writes David Vogel: "By identifying its purposes with those of the society as a whole (namely, relatively high wages and a wide choice of consumer goods), business has been remarkably successful in presenting its autonomy; the public has been afraid to tamper too much with corporate prerogatives, lest it 'kill the goose that lays the golden egg.'"[25]

Few question the staying power of the capitalist goose. It has survived wars, slumps, and economic booms; on balance, the market system has exhibited a phenomenal ability to provide what consumers demand. Rather than a government planner dictating what a society should produce, consumers themselves decide what they buy. They vote in the marketplace. These votes, on occasion, can be manipulated by the modern-day corporation—but the risks are low when compared to the alternative: an interventionist state. Quips Ben Heineman, president of Northwest Industries: "Capitalism makes mistakes like oil spills, but they are compartmentalized and hence limited. When government makes a mistake, it is a big one, like the Post Office."[26]

By relying on the maximum use of free markets and the minimum of government controls, American capitalism produced long spells of economic progress consistent with the values of an egalitarian society. Indeed, every democracy practices some version of capitalism. Capitalism may flourish without democracy, but democracy apart from capitalism is very difficult to achieve. Between capitalism and democracy there is an underlying mutual reinforcement, an internal harmony. The reason is clear: political freedom is impossible without economic freedom. British poet Hilaire Belloc expressed it well: "The control of the production of wealth is the control of human life itself."[27]

The economic freedom on which capitalism rests is itself a form of liberty, as Milton Friedman and others have emphasized. Yet economic freedom has another equally important dimension. "By imposing a limit on the power of the state," Norman Podohertz writes, "it serves as a necessary condition for the establishment of political liberty."[28] More than perhaps any other contemporary society, the United States recognizes the payoff of linking political liberty with the open market system. Comments theologian Michael Novak: "No other system has so quickly and universally raised the levels of health, longevity, and income."[29] Fellow conservative Irving Kristol pipes in: "[Capitalism] really does work. . . . It does improve people's material standard of living, and it does give each person the opportunity to exercise a more meaningful freedom of choice in the shaping of his life."[30] Even Robert Heilbroner, one of democratic capitalism's toughest critics, concedes: "History has shown capitalism to be an extraordinarily resilient, persisting and tenacious system, perhaps because its driving force is dispersed among so many of its population rather than concentrated in a government elite."[31]

By maximizing business and minimizing government, Americans sought to exploit the spirit of self-reliance over the forces of dependency. This "reverence for the limited state" affected our attitudes up to and including the highest levels of government. Such thinking swept President Reagan into office. Even his soundly defeated predecessor, Jimmy Carter, openly professed an almost minimalist role for government. In his 1978 State of the Union Message, President Carter said: "Government cannot solve our problems. It can't set our goals. It cannot define our vision. Government cannot eliminate poverty, or provide a bountiful economy, or reduce inflation, or save our cities, or cure illiteracy, or provide energy."[32] These remarks closely parallel those made by Herbert Hoover in the depths of the Great Depression: "The sole function of government is to bring about a condition of affairs favorable to the beneficial development of private enterprise."[33]

Our presidents are neither blind to the imperfections of democratic capitalism nor enamored with false dreams of a perfect, frictionless, and self-equilibrating system that allocates scarce resources in an optimal direction. Rather they are partial to the proven effectiveness of "an economic order built upon respect for the decisions of the individual in the marketplace, upon rights to property which the state may not abridge; and upon limiting the activities of the central state."[34] Their constituents, too, consistently choose the forces of a market economy over those of an activist state. The reason is simple: the great majority of our citizens appreciate the proven track record of the private sector. Big business has provided material prosperity for most Americans without onerous social costs. Therefore, the keys to America's economic car have been, and continue to be, entrusted to the private sector, with Washington relegated to the back seat. But the shortcomings of such a system are the strained relations between U.S. industry and government that today extend far beyond arm's length. Nowhere are the tensions more deeply felt than in our worldwide companies.

7

Multinationals under Attack

"**T**HE United States can't sit around in striped pants drinking pink gin. The State Department has the notion that business is, somehow, less than honorable. This is wrong."[1] These remarks, made by former U.S. Senator Jacob Javits, suggest that America's abrasive interface carries over to the international arena. In his research, Detlev Vagts found that "the supervision of United States business activities abroad has followed our domestic pattern of arm's length formality."[2] Berkeley's David Vogel reached similar conclusions: "The relative distance between business and the U.S. government abroad . . . projects the historic structure of American business-state relations on an international scale."[3]

First, Collaboration

In former times, the proximity between the U.S. government (the State Department, particularly) and American companies operating abroad was quite close. It has widened, however, over time. One student of this ebb and flow is Professor Richard D. Robinson of the

Massachusetts Institute of Technology. Beginning in the mid-nine-teenth century, he points out, a "colonial-extraterritorial system" emerged where the primary aim of Western enterprise was political domination, not profits.[4] Washington viewed political socialization of the indigenous masses as not only a proper but also a legitimate role for U.S. firms doing business overseas. Consequently, American expatriates in both business and government were never closer than in this "exploitative era" of international business.

Under the so-called open door policy, the State Department attempted to provide commercial equality for American concerns in overseas markets — first in China but later extending to a full range of countries, from Kuwait to Guatemala. Presidential calls for diplo-matic assistance to U.S. investors were most explicit. Take, for instance, President Taft's statements on the subject: "The diplomacy of the present administration has sought to respond to modern ideas of commercial intercourse. This [open door] policy has been charac-terized as substituting dollars for bullets. . . . *It is an effort frankly directed to the increase of American traders upon the axiomatic principle that the Government of the United States shall extend all proper support to every legitimate and beneficial American enterprise abroad*"[5] (italics added). The open door policy was, in the words of Professor W. A. Williams, "a brilliant strategic stroke, which led to the gradual extension of American economic and political power throughout the world."[6] It represented the United States' core strategy of commercial expansion in the nineteenth and early twentieth centuries.

Then, Independence

The love-in that ensued between U.S. business and government abroad persisted up to the beginning of World War I, when the political sanctions once bestowed on American firms by the home government were slowly withdrawn. Without the carte blanche of Washington, U.S. concerns worked to consolidate their positions overseas by means of long-term concessionary agreements with the nations of Asia, Africa, and Latin America. These contracts took many forms. Some were industry-specific, designed to develop particular sectors with U.S. aid: to name a few, the airline rights granted to Pan American Airways for most South American routes, Firestone's rubber concessions in Liberia, and Aramco's exclusive franchise for Saudi Arabian crude oil. Other concessions were designed to prevent rival nations from gaining a foothold in important markets. For example, U.S. multinationals, with the help of the State Department, were able to deter the Soviet Union from acquiring an undue influence in Iranian oil fields as well as to thwart Germany's plans to exploit Panama and Liberia for military reasons. Still other arrangements sought to promote American investments in high-priority areas, such as China, Indonesia, and Kuwait. In each instance, the United States government supported American interests, but in a much more subtle, indirect fashion than that in earlier times.

The "concessionary era" ended at the conclusion of World War II. The harsh realities of Cold War politics and rising nationalism indicated that a very different profile of business-government dealings was in order. No longer could American enterprise live under the protective umbrella of the U.S. government. Official intervention on its behalf was awkward and often ran counter to the broader political objectives of Washington. Says Professor Robinson: "[American] enterprise stood in a precarious position because of its past association with foreign political interests and its exercise of political power within concession areas, which was now seen as an infringement of sovereignty. It was caught squarely between long-run, nonWestern national interests . . . and the Cold War political policies of [the U.S. government]."[7] Corporate executives, mindful of these countervailing pressures, went out of their way to disassociate themselves from government officials at home and abroad. And it became standard policy of at least some American managements, Robinson recalls, "to avoid any relationship at all with United States embassies in countries where they were doing business."[8]

Our diplomats, for their part, seemed equally content to minimize their contacts with the business community. In his exhaustive study of diplomatic assistance to private investors, J. Gilles Wetter found that after World War II "the United States Government would in no circumstances become involved in the commercial aspects of contractual negotiations between an American investor and a foreign government, . . . [and there was] a general reluctance by the State Department to do more than provide [background] information and introductions [to the expatriate businessmen]."[9] During this postwar period of rising nationalism, Wetter also observed that "the State Department . . . nearly always desired to maintain a distance between the Government of the United States and private American corporations or financial interests, no matter who those have been. This attitude has found expression in a variety of policies and doctrines which have been implemented with remarkable consistency."[10]

This same attitude persists today. "Our multinational corporations get no Brownie points from the State Department for getting a piece of the action for the U.S.," grumbles Walter E. Hoadley, the Bank of America's highly respected economist.[11] Similarly, the head of one of the largest American banks in Tokyo quips, "You learn from experience not to call for help from our government. You just don't waste your time."[12]

Everything is relative, including the level of national cooperation between commercial attachés and corporate expatriates. When compared with its major industrial competitors, the United States performs well below par in this most important dimension. American corporations on many occasions have been placed at a disadvantage as the State Department withheld public support from their projects, which, as a matter of course, have been offered to Japanese, German, or French companies by their governments.[13]

The Crisis of Legitimacy

Whatever its shortcomings, the U.S. doctrine of arm's-length formality in international economic affairs seemed ideally suited for the fifties and sixties. Immediately following World War II, multinational corporations from the industrialized countries benefited from the support of government. MNCs, the ultimate instruments of capitalism, provided the finances, personnel, and technology so essential for nation building at the time. Former Treasury Secretary William E. Simon recalls that "U.S. policy on balance [could] not be construed as other than benign towards . . . U.S. investment abroad."[14] Peter Gabriel, a leading consultant on international business, agrees: "The continuous spread of the multinational enterprise was facilitated by a highly favorable ideological climate. In home countries of the multinational corporation, challenges to the concept and power of the large corporation were still [in the 1950s and early 1960s] relatively muted and ineffective. The notion of corporate social responsibility could still be preempted by public relations gestures and had yet to constrain corporate action to any significant degree."[15] Moreover, Gabriel adds, "the view generally prevailed that the influence of multinational corporations on economic growth as conventionally defined was positive."[16]

A far different view of corporate multinationalism began to emerge in the 1970s. A series of critical incidents, highly publicized in the world media, suggested that societal control over the MNC had become an issue. These events, which ranged from Lockheed's unauthorized payments to ranking Japanese officials to ITT's alleged attempts to overthrow the Allende government in Chile, won front-page attention. Related cases concerning U.S. investments in South Africa, windfall profits, and exported job opportunities also captured the interest of John and Jane Doe. One thing became clear: the era of unfettered expansion and ideological accommodation of MNCs by government had ended.[17]

While trying to meet the expectations of their citizenry, political leaders began to focus their efforts on gaining the benefits of corporate multinationalism without its costs. Acting collectively, nation-states and other constituent groups heightened their surveillance of the activities of global companies. The results included:

☐ The multilateral codes of conduct for MNCs approved in 1976 by the Organization for Economic Cooperation and Development.

☐ The development of related efforts by the International Labor Organization, the United Nations Committee on Trade and

Development, the Organization of American States, and many other groups.

☐ The continuing North-South dialogue between the rich and poor nations concerning the role of private investment in the Third World.

☐ The creation of the United Nation's Center for Transnational Corporations to monitor global enterprise.

☐ The increasing interest in commodity cartels (especially OPEC) as a countervailing force against MNCs.

From the World Council of Churches to the AFL-CIO, the stakeholder network confronting the multinational enterprise assumed monumental proportions in the 1970s. In their ten-year survey of 650 incidents involving five MNCs and their opponents, Professors Thomas N. Gladwin and Ingo Walter identified no less than 100 special-interest groups, each fully capable of playing havoc.[18] Mounting outside pressures such as these transformed the nature of U.S. business-government relations as well as the core mission of the global enterprise.

"The question of power and who will make the final decision in a business-government dialogue," Nancy Needham Wardell says, "is one which is tied to the more philosophic question of legitimacy and purpose of corporations as we have known them. As more critics question the role of corporations, their taken-for-granted legitimacy will become less secure."[19] No longer could our multinationals concentrate exclusively on viability objectives, as measured by the usual financial indices: profits, sales revenues, market share, and return on investment or assets managed. As Boston University's Peter L. Berger puts it: "From a sociological point of view, business must learn to speak a new language. It knows economics and politics; now it must address meaning and value."[20]

By the 1970s, the concept of legitimacy, the essence of "meaning" and "value," made its way into the corporate lexicon. In addition to being economic animals, capitalists acquired new perceptions of the sociopolitical demands of the times. Since legitimacy is confirmed not by management, but rather by outsiders, the success of MNCs in many parts of the world came to be determined as much for legitimacy reasons as for viability. While previously a company was considered to be legitimate if it were viable, by the 1970s it had to demonstrate its legitimacy to stakeholder groups with the power to influence its viability.[21] For American multinationals, no stakeholder loomed larger than Washington.

Costly Canons

The worldwide concern for legitimacy had a particularly profound effect in the United States. Political leaders, for the first time since World War II, called to question the role of the American corporation. Their former image of business as an institution that reaped domestic and world markets and distributed the fruits of technology and employment in a rational and efficient manner gave way to a far less flattering one. In many quarters of government, U.S. multinational enterprise became the whipping boy of the seventies.

In keeping with the American character, we turned to the law to hold big business in check. From product safety to financial reporting, our legislators were hell-bent on commercial canonization. One surefire index of America's rekindled propensity for lawmaking was the whopping 200 percent increase in the number of pages in the *Federal Register* during the first half of the 1970s.

Ours is a "law-drenched age," Jethro K. Lieberman explains in his book *The Litigious Society*.[22] Similarly, Stanford Law School dean Thomas Ehrlich describes the virtual impossibility in moving the economy forward "without running into a law, regulation, or a legal hassle."[23] Robert B. Reich, former director of policy planning for the Federal Trade Commission, claims that business and government have grown accustomed to communicating with one another through a formalized legal process that, by its very design, serves to exaggerate points of difference and to discourage creative problem solving. Our emissaries, he believes, are lawyers who, by nature and training, seek to minimize risk and avoid trouble.[24]

These emissaries, six hundred thousand strong, are well trained in the art of confrontation. They are the standard-bearers of the so-called new class of special-interest groups, academics, and bureaucrats that launched an ongoing public audit of U.S. business in the seventies. So pervasive is their scrutiny that former Treasury Secretary William E. Simon laments: "We are slowly but surely being shoved onto the garbage pile of history by ignorant, and worse, hypocritical politicians."[25] And no wonder. Consider the knights of the Potomac's growing reach.

☐ Oversight powers of the federal bureaucracy have increased from four areas in the 1950s (antitrust, financial institutions, transportation, and communications) to over eighty specialized functions today.

☐ With more duties come more people. The head count required to staff just four regulatory agencies (the Equal Employment Opportunity Commission, the Environmental Protection Agency, the Occupational Safety and Health Administration, and the Consumer Protection and Safety Commission) exploded over 300 percent in the past decade.

☐ Federal paperwork, too, grew by leaps and bounds. Its costs could approximate 5 percent of the GNP by 1985.

☐ The cost of coping with U.S. government regulations, of course, ran much higher. The total tab, variously estimated at between $50 billion to $150 billion a year, is now roughly equal to American industry's annual outlays on plant and equipment.

In the costly and time-consuming process of compliance, a "second managerial revolution" transferred corporate decision-making powers from private hands to a vast cadre of government planners and regulators. Worse yet, the recipients of these newly acquired powers were generally insensitive to the needs of American industry. "Bureaucratic imperialism" (to borrow George A. Steiner's phrase) set in, with the reins of commerce being held by an "arbitrary, authoritarian, arrogant, and uncompromising" public sector.[26]

The cumulative impact of this dizzying array of governmental barriers to free enterprise has been counterproductive. The irony of our times, President Reagan's senior economic adviser Murray Weidenbaum points out, is that greater government intervention into economic affairs "has tended to minimize, rather than maximize, the achievement of the basic social objectives"[27] for which it was intended. The problems of an increasingly regulated society seriously affect our international business capability.

Much maligned in congressional circles, the global corporation takes on a public or quasi-public character in most other industrialized countries. Not so, however, in the United States where a plethora of unnecessary restrictions handicap American multinational corporations. Some of the most inhibiting laws are described below.

1. THE FOREIGN CORRUPT PRACTICES ACT

In response to the Lockheed scandal and related incidents, the Congress passed the Foreign Corrupt Practices Act (FCPA) in 1977. This statute makes it a criminal offense for any corporation or its employees or agents to make improper payments to foreigners to win business or influence the legislative process overseas. Levies of up to $1 million may be imposed on corporate violators; individuals may be fined up to $10,000 and be imprisoned for as long as five years.

Besides running the risk of severe penalties, U.S. multinationals are confronted with many ambiguities over what actually constitutes an illegal payment under the FCPA. In its lengthy position paper, the Asia Pacific Chamber of Commerce, an arm of the U.S. Chamber, listed numerous practices that fear of the law had led some American companies to forego, even though they are common and sometimes necessary in doing business overseas.[28] They included:

☐ Offering an annual tip to the postman.

☐ Paying immigration officials "to perform their normal duty" and issue visas.

☐ Providing gratuities to expedite customs clearance or the return of bonds posted for customs purposes.

☐ Hiring off-duty policemen to direct traffic.

☐ Supplying gasoline to police departments so they can adequately patrol American-owned plants.

☐ Reimbursing the travel expenses of government officials to make inspections or do other official business.

☐ Hiring officials as consultants in their off-duty hours.

☐ Giving a wedding present to the daughter of a high official.

☐ Writing equipment specifications for a government agency without charging a fee.

☐ Covering the expenses of a government employee who attends a company training course.

☐ Paying a finder's fee to an agent who obtains a government contract.

Some of these things may be legal under the act, the position paper said, but in every case the payments were stopped because the businessman lacked the guidance to know with any certainty whether he was breaking the law.

Only recently has the Justice Department adopted new procedures to review overseas payments and to advise companies in advance whether particular payments would violate the FCPA. Unfortunately, there is no right of appeal for MNCs. Also, the Securities and Exchange Commission, which shares enforcement responsibilities for FCPA with the Justice Department, has chosen not to participate in the guidelines-setting process. Nor will a review decision made by the Justice Department bind the SEC. Therefore, companies attempting to comply with the statute in good faith face the distinct possibility of receiving mixed signals from separate units of the U.S. government.

These shortcomings and others prompted a special White House task force under President Carter to call for the immediate weakening and eventual abandonment of key provisions in the FCPA. Concluding that the law was costing the United States $1 billion a year in lost trade, the panel (officially called the Export Disincentive Task Force) recommended the removal of the Securities and Exchange Commission from enforcement responsibilities and proposed that Washington encourage the resumption of facilitative payments. The report also criticized the federal government for moralizing, for prying into transactions outside U.S. jurisdiction, and for needlessly creating political problems.

Proponents of FCPA, arguing that the panel's proposals would effectively emasculate the law, have blocked the Congress from making any significant amendments in the law. At the time of this writing, however, the Reagan administration is considering presenting similar legislation that would decriminalize payoffs abroad. In November 1981, the Senate voted to amend the FCPA. Senators not only changed its name but also eliminated some of what they considered vague and ambiguous provisions outlawing bribery of foreign officials by U.S. corporations. This new legislation, to be called the Business Practices and Records Act, is now under review by the House of Representatives.[29] We may expect Congress to take a fresh look at the payoff and cumbersome accounting sections of the act. In the interim, though, American MNCs continue to operate at a serious competitive disadvantage.

2. TAXATION

Only two countries in the world, the United States and the Philippines, tax the worldwide earnings of their citizens. Prior to

1976, American residents abroad could exclude the first $25,000 of overseas income, but the 1976 Reform Act lowered this exclusion to $15,000. The result: a greater tax bill for U.S. multinationals employing Americans abroad.

In congressional hearings on the subject, a U.S. company testified that it has based its bid on a contract in Saudi Arabia on the need to use Americans in key positions. The Saudi government asked that the bid be resubmitted using non-American personnel because of savings in labor costs. Eventually, sixty-two non-Americans were hired for the work. The problem was that the cost to the Saudis of using Americans amounted to an additional $10,000 to $12,000 a year per person, largely because of U.S. tax treatment of its citizens working abroad.

In the competitive world of international commerce, this resulted in lost contracts for U.S.-produced goods and services or lost jobs for American workers. According to one study by an independent consulting organization, the number of Americans employed abroad by 306 U.S. companies decreased by 38.6 percent between June 1979 and June 1980. Yet we continued to ignore this problem at our own peril.

Fortunately, the White House introduced successful tax reforms, which went into effect on January 1, 1982. Americans can now exclude U.S. income taxes up to $75,000 of income earned abroad. These exclusions will rise by $5,000 a year until they reach $95,000 in 1986. Expatriates may also be able to exclude some of their foreign housing costs from American taxes, provided they meet certain qualifications. Despite the positive aspects of these recent gains, U.S. expatriates still suffer when compared to their foreign counterparts.[30]

3. ANTITRUST POLICY

Government trustbusters also impede American companies operating abroad. Frequently, antimerger litigation is aimed not only at protecting competition in a specific market but also at combating bigness itself. As mentioned earlier, Japan, West Germany, and many other nations believe that size improves competitive efficiencies, especially where international markets are concerned. The exact opposite is true in the United States, where bigness is supposed to inhibit competition.

On the issue of market definition, the relevant provisions of the Sherman and Clayton acts work to the special disadvantage of U.S. multinationals. The focus is exclusively on closed or national markets, with no recognition of the interdependent, open economies in which today's companies operate. "The real antitrust arena is a global one," says former Senator Adlai E. Stevenson. "We should be moving to develop international (not domestic) antitrust codes."[31] In addition, the public institutions that are charged with monitoring U.S. business abroad—namely, the Justice Department and the Federal Commission—have an undeniably domestic focus. "We have the anomaly," writes Nancy Needham Wardell, "of the State Department pushing for internationalism and interdependence on the one hand (as opposed to isolation) and, on the other hand, the Justice Department bringing antitrust suits against such vigorous and successful international competitors as IBM and basing the suit strictly on domestic data. Since Secretary of Commerce Peter Peterson left the Department, there has been no subsequent analysis of United States industry in an international context; and there was not much before him."[32] For the time being at least, American multinationals must cope with an antiquated antitrust code.

Non-American firms can put together a consortium of bidders that can be more competitive than a single company bidding alone. But U.S. companies cannot. They are further constrained by other antitrust laws from pooling their resources to form comparable coalitions. Responding to rising criticism, the Justice Department has promised to give expeditious treatment to requests from U.S. companies for guidance on whether their proposed foreign joint ventures violate antitrust laws. The department reportedly will issue its preliminary opinion within thirty days from the date that it receives all relevant data concerning the proposed bid. One hopes that foreign firms will not walk away with the business during the review period.

4. ANTIBOYCOTT PROVISIONS

In response to the Arab League's sanctions against Israel, the U.S. Congress amended the Export Administration Act in 1977 and later in 1979 to prohibit U.S.-based companies from doing business with those Arab countries observing the anti-Israeli boycott. Violators of the law are subject to civil fines. One case in point: the Commerce Department required Minnesota Mining and Manufacturing Company and nine of its subsidiaries to hand over $137,500 for providing their Middle Eastern customers with information in support of the Arab boycott of Israel.

In addition, the Nuclear Proliferation Treaty limits American exports of nuclear reactors and material to countries that might produce a bomb. Only after much heated debate did the Congress agree to extend existing U.S. supply agreements with India for fissionable material. Quite understandably, many potential customers abroad (South Korea, for instance) have turned to non-American companies for their nuclear needs.

Even the environmentalists are enjoying the benefits of anti-boycott legislation. At their urging, statutes have been enacted to prevent U.S. firms from securing Export-Import Bank credits for any overseas projects that do not measure up to the National Environmental Policy Act, which sets rigorous standards for the domestic market. Also carefully scrutinized are the human rights violators. Current legislation limits American companies from doing business in those countries considered to be denying basic human rights. Among those nations so branded are South Africa, Uruguay, Chile, and most communist countries. The vagaries of these restrictions are so manifest that most U.S. multinationals are not taking any chances. They are foregoing business opportunities in many important areas of the world.

Equally confusing is the manner in which these laws are implemented. Frequently, it is an on-again, off-again proposition. Foreign countries appear, disappear, and then reappear on Washington's hit list. This is "light switch diplomacy" (to use the apt description of former Treasury Secretary George P. Schultz) at its very worst.[13] Allis-Chalmers Corp. is one of many companies that have felt Washington's uneven hand. In the late 1970s, it wanted to export $268 million worth of turbine generators to Argentina. Initially, the State Department barred the sale, invoking the human rights provision of the Export-Import Bank Act. Several months later, the ban was rescinded. Such stops and starts (in this case, to the eventual benefit of Allis-Chalmers) make it most difficult for American companies to provide the long-term commitments so essential to international trade. Increasingly, foreign customers are questioning the reliability of U.S. multinationals.

5. TRADE RESTRICTIONS

A series of regulations governing foreign trade and investment hamper the American business community. An amendment to the 1974 Trade Act, sponsored by Senator Henry Jackson (D.-Washington) and Representative Charles Vanik (D.-Ohio), affects U.S. MNCs interested in doing business with the Soviet Union. Designed to retaliate against the Soviets' restrictive emigration policies, the Jackson-Vanik amendment bars most-favored-nation tariff treatment for the USSR. Made unavailable, too, are Export-Import Bank credits that would ordinarily promote the sale of American wares to Russia.

Sperry Rand Corp. is among the many U.S. multinationals that have been stung by these provisions. The firm had spent two years negotiating for an export license to sell a $6.8 million computer system to Tass, the Soviet news agency. The license was denied because, in the view of the Carter administration, the sale was "inconsistent with the foreign policy of the United States."

More stringent U.S. trade sanctions against the Soviet Union began in January 1980, after Russian troops invaded Afghanistan.

161

In their wake, the Carterites revoked a license held by Dresser Industries Inc. of Dallas for the export of oil field technology to the Kremlin—despite the fact that this massive project on the Volga River was, approximately, 90 percent complete. No one was more taken aback by Carter's decision than Dresser President James V. James, who called the move "sheer idiocy."[34] At this stage, he figures, the Russians can probably finish the plant themselves or get another company from another country to do it.

Mr. James's prophecy is right on target. Foreign concerns are waiting in the wings of Moscow and other commercial capitals to assume the abrogated contracts of their U.S. competitors. For example, Komatsu Seisakujo of Japan has reportedly taken over Caterpillar Tractor's $80 million East-West gas pipeline deal with Moscow because of President Reagan's economic sanctions against the Soviet Union. With the full backing of their home governments, Komatsu and other rivals of America are buffered by the attitude that international business is an essential source of foreign exchange for them; permissive, rather than restrictive, laws and attitudes support their expansion overseas.

Still, the Reagan administration continues to push U.S. companies to moderate their exports of medium- and high-technology goods to the Soviet Union. Self-styled "pragmatists," led by Secretary of State Alexander M. Haig, Jr., have sought a go-slow approach, arguing that tighter trade links with the East are not in this country's best interests.[35] The Reaganites are about to take the first visible step in their long-awaited crackdown on exports of sophisticated equipment and technology to the Soviet Union. For some time, Ingersoll-Rand Co. has discreetly been sounding out the administration about what the likely response would be to a request for a license to sell components for a proposed second assembly line at Russia's Kama River heavy truck plant. The answer: Don't bother, because any such application will be turned down under a new policy of restricting such sales to the Soviets.[36]

The implications of these restrictions are staggering. Warns Raymond A. Kathe, a Tokyo-based senior vice-president and a thirty-five-year veteran of international business: "The Germans, the Japanese, the French, and the British—all of whom are advancing in Asia and elsewhere—are not bothered by antibribery and antiboycott laws, by environmental pressure, or by having to pay taxes on income earned overseas. All these countries are laughing all the way to the bank."[37]

Nowhere is the laughter louder than in international business circles. By doing little to help, by sitting around in striped pants drinking pink gin, Washington adds to the competitive disadvantage of U.S. firms at home and abroad. The consequences are impossible to quantify, but the tab to the American people runs high. From bailout loans to the failing Chrysler Corporation to nontariff barriers restricting consumer choices, the economic consequences of our arms'-length ideology are enormous.

Thomas Jefferson once suggested that a little revolution now and then was a good thing. Short of revolution, Americans must move their economy ahead. The most actionable domain is a progressive change in governmental regulation and attitude. Restrictive legislation and thinking must give way to those accommodating American business interests. There is no better starting place than removing the web of unnecessary restrictions that handcuff U.S. multinational corporations.

Part 4

Prospects for Change

8

Ideology Revisited: America Looks Ahead

Pᴿᴱˢᴵᴰᴱᴺᵀ Ronald Reagan senses that a once-great nation is in trouble. From rising unemployment to continuing balance-of-payments deficits, every indicator points to greater trouble ahead. The solution? The answer depends on one's diagnosis of the problem —and these have spanned the entire spectrum from weak national leadership to a bad case of "the British disease." There is, however, one common theme to virtually every critique of the present dilemma: the failure of U.S. business, government, and labor to build a national consensus. This failure stands in sharp contrast to America's competitors from the industrialized and newly industrializing countries, where government and unions are manifestly pro-business and committed to enterprise growth and development.

To the Carterites, the Rx for curing America's economic ills was contained in their heady catchword "reindustrialization." While somewhat vague and imprecise, it did point to the need for greater collaboration between business and government if the U.S. economy were to move ahead. Even Mr. Reagan concedes the merits of more simpatico between industry and government, although the Republican prescription calls for sharply curtailing government's role in the

167

economy. "Revitalization" is the present administration's favorite buzzword; and the President acknowledges that "both business and government will have to lay aside old hostilities and assume a new spirit of cooperation and shared responsibility."[1]

Notwithstanding the inevitable dose of presidential poppycock, are the American people, particularly the economy's kingmakers, truly eager to reshape public policy? Do elected officials at the national and state level sense the need to redefine government's role in the market system? Are the attitudes of our legislators and regulators different from those of the leaders of business and organized labor? To what extent are America's leaders committed to a major change in economic ideology?

To answer these questions, I polled influential Americans, including chief executive officers of U.S. corporations, U.S. senators and congressmen, federal bureaucrats, state legislators, and labor leaders. This project began in 1979 at the request of U.S. Senator Spark M. Matsunaga and ended three years later with almost fifteen hundred respondents. The survey focused on three possible scenarios of the socioeconomic future of the United States. Respondents were asked to identify which one they (1) prefer, (2) expect to dominate over the 1980s, and (3) feel would be most effective in solving America's problems of the present decade. (See Appendix One for an elaboration of the research methodology.)

Each scenario appears in Exhibit 8.1, but to recap briefly:

☐ Scenario I describes the regulated free enterprise system or mixed economy now in effect in the United States. It represents the status quo in which, more often than not, either adversarial or arm's-length sentiments accompany dealings between business, government, and labor.

☐ Scenario II can be summed up, to use Ezra F. Vogel's term, as "guided free enterprise."[2] Consensual attitudes dominate relations among business, government, and labor—their cooperation forging a new, economic partnership, often referred to as "America, Inc." (Japan and West Germany rely heavily on this type of an approach.)

Exhibit 8.1
The Scenarios

I. Regulated free enterprise

The United States elects to pursue its present ideology of regulated free enterprise. Privately controlled markets, subject to limited government regulation, are retained. Free market competition, profit incentives, technological change, and collective bargaining are essential elements of a system that has made the United States the world's most important economic power. This system, it is argued, must continue.

Under this scenario, government maintains its watchdog, often adversary role over business affairs — providing necessary direction in such critical areas as trade, monetary, antitrust, and environmental matters. Frequently, the public sector is oriented more to regulate than to assist the private sector. At best, the business-government relationship is at arm's length. Public ownership of the enterprise is rare, and dual careers in business and government continue to be the exception.

II. Guided free enterprise

Following the lessons of "Japan, Inc.," the United States elects to adopt a system of guided free enterprise, with government playing an increasingly important role in the direction of the American economy. An informal but directed interdependence is created among business, government, and labor, and a strong coalition among the three emerges.

Under this scenario, the adversary posture between business and government is replaced by a collaborative approach to economic affairs. Public opinion supports government's assuming a more visible hand in business. There are more forms of shared ownership of the enterprise by business and government, with dual careers in business and government on the rise.

III. Centrally planned economy

The United States elects to move toward a centrally planned economy with government acquiring primary control over the economic system. Government begins to replace market forces and pluralistic collective bargaining. As the economy becomes more complex, such a

169

transformation — it is argued — is inevitable. Managed capitalism or modified socialism is the by-product.

Under this scenario, government assumes major control over the decisions of private enterprise. New regulatory and administrative agencies emerge. Widespread public ownership of enterprise takes place, and the distinction between what is a private or public company is blurred. Dual careers in the private and public sectors are commonplace, with government often recognized as the fast track.

Note: Originally, I pretested seven scenarios ranging from laissez-faire free enterprise to economic totalitarianism. Those futures receiving less than 2 percent responses were eliminated from this study.

☐ Scenario III describes a system in which government takes the lead. Central planning of U.S. economic affairs prevails to result in what has variously been called managed capitalism, modified socialism, or a command economy. (Sweden and Yugoslavia possess many of the elements of this particular option.)

The most important findings are the following:

☐ Almost three-fourths of the surveyed participants *prefer* Scenario I or regulated free enterprise. The notion of an "America, Inc.," appeals to only one out of every four respondents; and less than 4 percent favor a centrally planned economy.

☐ When asked to predict which scenario will *dominate* the American scene in this decade, 60 percent of those polled anticipate that the regulated free enterprise system will prevail; 29 percent and 11 percent place their bets on Scenarios II and III, respectively.

☐ A distinct majority (61 percent) rank Scenario I as *most effective* in solving the country's economic problems. One-third choose Scenario II, and a small minority (5 percent) opt for a command economy as the best vehicle for resolving this nation's difficulties.

☐ Opinions vary considerably among the six respondent groups: chief executive officers of U.S. corporations, mid-level managers, U.S. senators and congressmen, state legislators, federal bureaucrats, and labor leaders. Predictably, the sharpest differences are between CEOs and labor leaders. While 86 percent of America's top corporate executives cite Scenario I as most effective in solving future problems, nearly half of the labor executives favor an "America, Inc."

☐ Age also appears to be an especially important determinant of ideological preferences. While the allegiances of older Americans are more closely allied with the mixed economy now in place, younger Americans are much more open to the merits of Scenario II. For example, some 42 percent of the thirty-five and under group think it would be most effective compared to just a quarter of the fifty-six and older group.

These highlights, while interesting, are of limited value in fully explaining the nature and extent of America's commitment to a possible new economic ideology.[3] What follows is a more detailed analysis of the preferences of U.S. business, government, and labor as well as the underlying reasons for their choices.

A House United . . .

"If our principal economic participants can get together to take collective action and provide leadership, we can stop our economic slide in the shortest amount of time and with the least amount of pain."[4] This exhortation to cooperate was spoken recently by William H. Batten, chairman of the New York Stock Exchange. If the leader of capitalism's inner sanctum is prepared to do business with government and labor, one would expect other key managers of the economy to be similarly united in their search for new directions.

Indeed, our survey uncovers a certain amount of unity: the overall vote of confidence in the present ideology. It is first in both

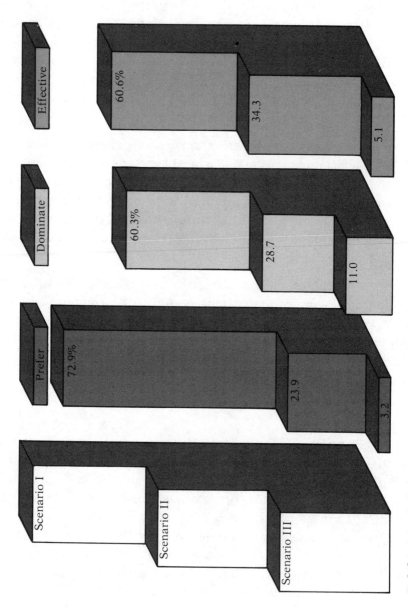

Exhibit 8.2 U.S. business-government survey: overall response to scenarios.

the hearts and the minds of the participants sampled. The following comments illustrate its wide-ranging support:

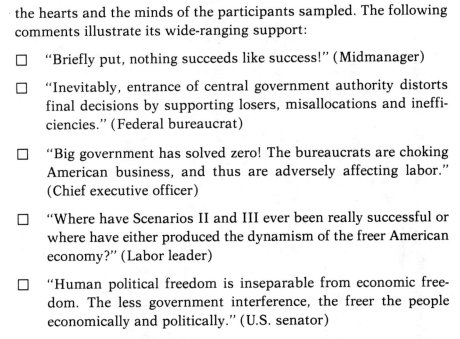

- ☐ "Briefly put, nothing succeeds like success!" (Midmanager)

- ☐ "Inevitably, entrance of central government authority distorts final decisions by supporting losers, misallocations and inefficiencies." (Federal bureaucrat)

- ☐ "Big government has solved zero! The bureaucrats are choking American business, and thus are adversely affecting labor." (Chief executive officer)

- ☐ "Where have Scenarios II and III ever been really successful or where have either produced the dynamism of the freer American economy?" (Labor leader)

- ☐ "Human political freedom is inseparable from economic freedom. The less government interference, the freer the people economically and politically." (U.S. senator)

As Exhibit 8.3 attests, proponents of the mixed economy believe it to be the best deterrent against further encroachments in business affairs by a bumbling public sector. Many cite the demonstrated accomplishments of the present approach; others suggest that the admittedly successful Japanese or German models are "culture-bound" and hence inappropriate for the United States; and some contend that the erosion of our economic privatism—in their opinion, synonymous with Scenarios II and III—will mean the loss of political liberty.

When James O'Toole of the Center for Futures Research at the University of Southern California queried thirty-nine influential decision makers and twenty leading scholars on comparable scenarios, he reached much the same conclusions. "As a nation, Americans seem to have moved too far toward the security of equality to turn back to total freedom. But it is nevertheless essential to recognize that the dream of the free market remains enticing for most Americans."[5] Conversely, O'Toole found the "America, Inc.," model

Exhibit 8.3
Central Reasons Scenarios Considered Most Effective for the 1980s (in Decreasing Order of Importance)

Scenario I	Scenario II	Scenario III
1. "Government's involvement in the private sector has been consistently shoddy."	1. "The United States must play by the same ground rules in the international market-place."	1. "Collective national planning is a must in today's world."
2. "We need to stem the tide of big government."	2. "The traditional approach— Scenario I—has failed miserably."	2. "This approach best controls intractable multinational corporations."
3. "The free enterprise system has a proven track record."	3. "Conflict between business, government, and labor is the root cause of the present American dilemma."	3. "Scenario III is simply more expedient."
4. "Scenarios II and III are ideologically alien to the United States."	4. "Collaboration alone can redirect our divergent economic actions."	4. "Nationalized efforts are needed to win world markets."
5. "Economic freedom must be preserved if our political liberties are to survive."	5. "Global interdependence requires a consensual approach."	5. "Centralized national approaches can best safeguard the allocation of scarce natural resources."

to be unattractive to most Americans. "The rejection of cooperation between business and government," he suggests, "seems to be based on the ground that, while the adversary system is ulcer producing, it is nevertheless a necessary complement to democratic pluralism."[6]

Management pundit Peter Drucker uses even stronger language: "In thinking about such things [consensus building], we are not using our strength. Our strength in industry is precisely that we have a much better business climate because it is an adversary system."[7] The thought of replacing our present arm's-length ideology with alternatives that tend to blur the demarcation lines between the private and public sectors is shocking to some Americans and infuriating to others. On the one hand, the majority wants to call a truce to the private-public sector war; on the other, it will not easily surrender its adversarial armament. Max Ways, former editor of *Fortune*, typifies the American paradox. The relation between stakeholders, he readily concedes, "should be much closer and more effective than it now is. But partnership? No thank you."[8]

. . . Or House Divided?

The advocates of Scenario I might take comfort in the consensus behind their ideological position were it not for the prominent counterpoint that underlies the main theme of the survey. If there is a consensus, it is at best a "splintered consensus." And the splinters begin right in the ranks of Scenario I supporters. As elucidated in open-ended comments solicited as a follow-up to the survey (see Appendix Two), many of its proponents see shortcomings in Scenario I and the need to analyze the pluses and minuses of Scenario II more carefully.

One staunch advocate of Scenario 1 concedes, "'America, Inc.,' is a concept well worth pursuing. It's probably only a matter of time before it becomes a reality." Many respondents, especially captains of U.S. industry, say that despite its somewhat alien overtones,

Scenario II would have been their preferred choice if the timetable for its being in place were the 1990s, not the 1980s. In fact, a full third of the respondents favoring Scenario I go so far as to predict that "America, Inc.," will, in fact, become dominant by the end of the current decade.

Invariably, the proponents of the collaborative approach feel that it alone offers the best chance of removing the United States from the unequal combat that it now faces in world markets. By pulling the key forces of economic society together, American multinationals would be better positioned to regain their foreign and domestic customers. As one member of Congress told me: "If the U.S. is to meet its international competitors in the 1980s and beyond, it will take the cooperation of business, labor, consumers, and government to realize that they must work together."

Closer scrutiny of the survey findings uncovers other splinters in the vote for the status quo. Among the more significant are the following:

☐ Chief executive officers of major U.S. corporations are the staunchest supporters of the free enterprise system. For the great majority, Scenario I is both the preferred and the most effective alternative; yet 40 percent of the survey's CEOs predict a drift toward an interventionist government. As one company president laments, "Today's economic and political malaise is the result of the tyranny of well-intentioned and aggressive political elites with a tendency toward Scenarios II and III."

☐ While sharing their bosses' pessimism over the fate of the present ideology, midmanagers in American industry are much less committed to the status quo. In the words of one junior executive, "Our present system is a poorly coordinated crapshoot!" One-half of our midmanagement sample feels that another approach—notably "America, Inc."—would be better for economic problem solving.

☐ The public sector—U.S. senators and congressmen, state legislators, and federal bureaucrats—exhibits choices quite similar

■ Which scenario do you prefer?

▨ Which scenario in the United States will dominate?

▨ Which scenario will be most effective?

	CEO's	Midmanagers	Senators and congressmen	State legislators	U.S. bureaucrats	Labor leaders	TOTALS
Scenario I	91.4%	73.5%	74.8%	71.6%	68.1%	46.8%	72.9%
	60.5	50.0	73.8	52.2	75.5	50.7	60.3
	86.0	50.6	68.0	60.7	55.3	34.3	60.6
Scenario II	8.6	24.7	24.4	22.0	30.8	40.4	23.9
	23.8	33.5	22.1	35.7	22.4	37.2	28.7
	14.0	44.7	28.7	31.4	43.6	47.1	34.3
Scenario III	0.0	1.8	0.8	6.4	1.1	12.8	3.2
	15.7	16.5	4.1	12.1	2.1	12.1	11.0
	0.0	4.7	3.3	7.9	1.1	18.6	5.1

Exhibit 8.4 U.S. business-government survey: by participant group.

to those of mid-level managers. Surprisingly, however, policy-makers in Washington are the most bullish of all groups on the likelihood that the mixed economy will be dominant throughout the decade. And members of the U.S. Congress are second only to CEOs in recognizing the effectiveness of the present approach.

☐ Organized labor, while preferring Scenario I by a slight margin, is the only sector to single out "America, Inc.," for its effective-ness. Indeed, one-half of the labor leaders sampled view the demise of the present ideology as not only inevitable but also healthy. "Business at present has been unable to smell the roses," bemoans one union official. "In order to protect the rights of all people, the government will have to step into the arena with its full power."

For a graphic representation of the splintered consensus, see Exhibit 8.5. It shows the similarities and differences of each group. As a guide, note that:

☐ The closer together the vector arrows, the stronger the correlation between responses to the "prefer," "dominate," and "effective" questions.

☐ The nearer a respondent group is to the head of an arrow, the greater its association with the attributes of that vector.

☐ The greater the correlation of responses of different groups, the closer together are their plot points.

Observe, for instance, that respondents' preferences are very closely linked with their selections of the most effective scenario. But when choosing which ideology is likely to dominate the 1980s, individuals are likely to make a different selection. This is consistent with our earlier findings of high scores on Scenario I on preference and effectiveness and low scores on dominance, especially for businessmen.

Note, too, that CEOs and labor leaders stand at opposite ends of the business-government spectrum. As Appendix Three indicates,

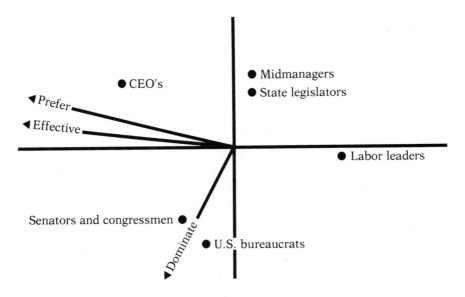

Exhibit 8.5 Multidimensional mapping: U.S. business-government survey.

their differences are statistically significant at the 0.05 and 0.01 levels; only slightly less so are their perceptions when compared with those of each and every other responding group. (There are, however, few significant differences at the 0.05 level between mid-managers, U.S. senators and congressmen, state legislators, and federal bureaucrats.)

Of all groups, captains of American industry express the least discord over which ideology is preferable and effective. Conversely, organized labor is neither harmonized with itself nor with the other respondents. Its plot point is virtually off the map. Public policy-makers at the federal level, whether elected or appointed, see eye-to-eye, particularly over which ideology is likely to dominate the years ahead. Contrary to what might be inferred from their public state-ments, congressmen and bureaucrats are optimistic about the future viability of the free enterprise system. Finally, midmanagers' views closely resemble those of state legislators. This association is most apparent in their choices of the preferred and effective scenarios.

A Matter of Time

The results suggest that a national consensus will remain elusive unless the divergent philosophies of America's leadership—especially business and labor—are laid aside in the interest of cooperation. Or, as Congressman Cecil Heftel, a former business executive, urges, "Labor, management, and government must be willing to abandon some outworn ideas and start afresh."[9]

Just how eager the present generation of Americans are to think and act collectively remains to be seen. On the basis of my discussions with leaders from across this nation, I am unconvinced of any deep-seated commitment to the partnership approach of an alternative ideology—at least in the short run. Moreover, the most significant finding of my research is the consensus, albeit splintered, of the American people for our mixed, oftentimes adversarial economy. Simply stated, the regulated free enterprise system will remain synonymous with "the American way" for the balance of this decade. For future generations, however, the present ideology may very well be endangered. If "new social contracts" are to be forged, it may simply be a matter of time, of evolution not revolution.

As Exhibit 8.6 indicates, Americans' interest in Scenario I increases directly with age. Younger people from all walks of life are more willing to explore alternative ideologies, and the consensual model of Scenario II has considerable appeal to them. It also seems probable that the differences, at least in part, in responses from chief executives and midmanagers in U.S. industry are age related. The latter generally are younger and tend to be buffered from the frustrations that top management faces in dealing with regulatory and legislative affairs. Thus, CEOs are apt to be more wary of getting government more involved in business affairs.

Will younger Americans act to put the building blocks of the consensual model in place? Or will they become more resistant to ideological change as time passes?. Will the next round of CEOs pursue the inclinations of their youth? Or will they, like their predecessors, cling to the more comfortable rubric of the past? The

◼ Which scenario do you prefer?
▭ Which scenario in the United States will dominate?
◼ Which scenario will be most effective?

	35 or younger	36 to 45	46 to 55	56 or older	TOTAL
Scenario I	67.8%	71.7%	73.4%	80.8%	72.9%
	57.2	58.0	58.5	62.1	60.3
	49.7	60.3	64.5	71.4	60.6
Scenario II	26.4	23.4	24.3	17.6	23.9
	33.5	32.9	26.9	24.3	28.7
	42.2	34.4	30.2	25.0	34.3
Scenario III	5.8	4.9	2.3	1.6	3.2
	9.3	9.1	14.6	13.6	11.0
	8.1	5.3	5.3	3.6	5.1

Exhibit 8.6   U.S. business-government survey: response by age.

answers to these questions will not come easily. For greater insight
to the prospects, one must examine the core elements, now absent
from the American scene, that would be needed to accommodate a
transition to alternative ideologies. The next chapter analyzes the
prerequisites for a commercial partnership in the United States—and
the odds against their being incorporated into America's industrial
policies of the eighties.

9

The Case of the Missing Institutions

T HERE is mounting evidence that the headbutting between business, government, and labor does not serve America's best interests. Given our contentious political and economic system, provocative proposals of revitalizing the United States along more planned, consensual lines are much ballyhooed as the answer to the "sick man" syndrome. That the problem is openly acknowledged and people are looking to solve it is a hopeful sign. But the prescription to America's economic ills will not be found in chic new labels that beg for a partnership where none exists. Verbal acrobatics alone cannot, and will not, substitute for the inherent deficiencies in U.S. economic culture. "It is far easier," warns the *New York Times*, "to reindustrialize political rhetoric than to reindustrialize America."[1]

The verdict of contemporary America is not to cast aside its seemingly slapdash, adversarial system and replace it with the more unified approach of Japan, West Germany, and the newly industrializing countries. True, many of our countrymen are openly bullish on Japan, Germany, and their clones and somewhat somber on the United States. They believe, though, that the main ingredients for stakeholder collaboration are now missing from the American scene—a condition which, if left unresolved, could continue for some time.

183

Time after time, thoughtful Americans voiced their skepticism that the United States could or would be willing to adopt the cultural virtues needed to build an organic economy. They argued that the Japanese or German models, admirable as they are, cannot be assimilated into a nation which must instead look for industrial revival in its own traditions: an open society blending Yankee ingenuity, rugged individualism, egalitarianism, legal idealism, and a competitive spirit.

Notwithstanding the sharp cultural differences between the United States and, say, Japan, our people sense the need to restore some of the institutional underpinnings of a consensual society— many of which have been rejected by this nation throughout the course of modern history. In the words of one state senator: "It is a case of missing institutions, extending far beyond just culture, that prevents this nation from fully pursuing the lessons of Japan and the others."

What are these missing institutions, and what is the likelihood of their restoration? At a minimum, they include: (1) a propensity for national economic planning, (2) an elite civil service, and (3) an ethic of collaboration. Without some semblance of these elements, any serious attempts to form an "America, Inc.," will fall far short of the mark. Let us consider the status of each of these dimensions in the United States.

National Economic Planning

Countries with an explicit industrial plan or policy attempt to come to grips with conclusions about which industries are to be encouraged, which industries ought to be allowed to go along as they are, and which industries should be discouraged. This is bound to offend those sectors not targeted as "winners"; yet countries intent on setting economic priorities have enough moxie to shunt aside the political protests of the "losers." Having successfully passed the first test of industrial strategizing, distinguishing between "sunrise" and "sunset" industries, national planners then deploy those policy instruments available to any modern government: tax incentives, credit policies, loan guarantees, and regulations, permissive or restrictive.

When it works, an industrial policy or plan expresses the collective awareness of all vital forces in the country. To Harvard Business School professors Robert A. Leone and Stephen P. Bradley, it "is the sum of a nation's efforts to shape business activity and influence economic growth. Its proper concern is not transitory issues of industrial well-being but the long-term structural integrity of a nation's industrial base. It is a government's version of a company's long-term strategy."[2] Such an instrument, therefore, reflects the economic gestalt of a nation. Japan has one—a formal economic plan; West Germany has a medium-term fiscal plan; the United States has zero. One wonders: Can the United States compete effectively without a formalized industrial strategy?

To a growing number of Americans, the answer is no. In a recent survey conducted by The Garth Group, 83 percent of our citizens believe that we need a national plan to mobilize our resources and to make American business more competitive with the rest of the world.[3] Among those in industry who strongly support national economic planning are such prominent board chairmen as W. Michael Blumenthal of Burroughs, Fletcher Byrom of Koppers, and Thornton Bradshaw of RCA.

"I advocate . . . national planning as a means of saving the very market system so often considered to be inconsistent with it," says Bradshaw. "If we examine our mixed economy carefully and realistically, we must concede that we have long been engaged in national planning."[4] But, he adds: "We have been doing it inadequately. It deserves to be done better."[5] Without a coherent industrial plan, U.S. companies find themselves waged in unequal combat. This, at least, is the opinion of John F. Cunningham, executive vice-president of Wang Laboratories, Inc. "A free enterprise American computer industry is now facing a strategic attack from Japan, Inc.," he warns.[6] "[There is] a need for immediate cooperation between the

American government and computer industry to formulate effective noninterventionist [industrial] policies."[7]

Academics, too, support some scheme of industrial planning. "It is my view that we have no choice but to move toward sectoral planning," contends Walter W. Rostow of the University of Texas.[8] "Government must lead the way, first by developing new forms of collaboration between public and private enterprise and then by stimulating investment in key supply sectors: energy and energy-conservation, raw materials, agriculture, and research and development."[9] Peter Drucker agrees in principle, but with a different focus. What is needed, he contends, is "redundancy planning," where new forms of social planning are developed to protect the obsolete workers and their companies.[10] Finally, Amitai Etzioni, the word-smith of "reindustrialization," argues that "rebuilding America's industrial capacity cannot be achieved by a government policy that is merely passive. There are too many decades of neglect and misdirection to compensate for."[11]

To the Carterites, their term of office seemed destined to compensate for this alleged neglect and misdirection. Under the heady influence of reindustrialization, they became intoxicated with the merits of national economic planning. Whether it was the passage of Humphrey-Hawkins (or Full Employment and Balanced Growth Act of 1977) or Senator Edward Kennedy's call for a reindustrialization corporation to promote new investment in business and technology, the Carter years attempted to forge some of the elements of a national industrial policy. The President personally took the lead in establishing the U.S. Synthetic Fuels Corporation; he authorized $1.5 billion in federal loan guarantees to the failing Chrysler Corporation; he supported an industrial financing bank for high-technology companies; and, perhaps most important, he conceived an Economic Revitalization Board, composed of representatives from business, government, and labor, to pursue a consensus-oriented industrial policy.

These very efforts, the critics claimed, underscore the central danger of national planning: greater government intrusion in the economic affairs of the nation. Conservative "marketeers" wondered if the Carter plan to reindustrialize the United States was not simply another step to state capitalism. Instead of backing the winners and slapping the losers, the plan seemed to have the opposite effect. The ailing auto industry, for instance, was targeted as the starting point for renewing the economy.[12] Washington's generous aid package included relief from federal regulations (notably on high-altitude emission standards and protection of autoworkers from toxic lead and arsenic), rollbacks of foreign imports, special Small Business Administration loans to dealers, and direct payments to local communities hurt by the slump in car production. Enamored by government's concessions to the automakers, other sick industries (steel, textiles, and shoes) also clamored for Mr. Carter's "multi-agency, tripartite plan" for getting U.S. industry back on its feet.

"Why doesn't America channel its capital and attention to dynamic, young industries rather than to dying ones?" we wondered. Rather than modernizing our industrial capabilities in healthy sectors, the Carter approach appeared to many as "lemon socialism"—with sick, possibly incurable, industries receiving the lion's share of Washington's largess. The main focus, it seemed at the time, was to save, not squeeze, the lemons—the obsolete jobs and companies already well on the way to bankruptcy because of their failure to compete in world markets. Commentators of the times often characterized the Carter strategy as a grand bailout. "It's a page not out of the Japanese book," the *Washington Post* insisted, "but out of the British book. It's bad for consumers, bad for the nation, bad for industry itself."[13]

Prolonging the agony of America's sunset industries ought to be the antithesis of indicative planning. Not so in the United States if the Carter years are symptomatic of our inability to prioritize key industrial sectors. To many experts, this lies at the heart of America's difficulties in developing a coherent industrial plan. "It's pretty clear that if we are going to have an industrial policy in the United States," says Harvard's Otto Eckstein, "it will back the losers, not winners."[14] His business school colleague Bruce R. Scott agrees: "U.S. planning could lead to more government support for losers, as it has in France. In the United States, as elsewhere, politics is likely to dominate economics in the crunch."[15]

It is axiomatic that the tougher the politics, the better the economics—at least where national planning is concerned. Realistically speaking, though, it is unlikely that the U.S. government has the wherewithal to differentiate sunrise from sunset industries. Senator William V. Roth, Jr., told me that in our special-interest society it would be political suicide for Congress to attempt to target winners and losers; nor does he believe that the American people are prepared to hand over this most difficult assignment to the federal bureaucracy.[16] High-level participants from business, government, and labor attending a 1980 Harvard University Conference on U.S. Competitiveness were also unwilling to endorse the concept of industrial planning because of these same factors.

Aside from a minority of key industrialists, the business community particularly remains unconvinced of the merits of national economic planning. To be sure, enlightened executives (including those cited earlier in this chapter) recognize the value of and need for strategic planning in any complex social system. Many have carved out elaborate niches in their own companies to this end. But corporate planning is one thing; national planning is quite another. Industrial leaders almost uniformly perceive economywide planning to be an exercise in futility. According to one recent survey, approximately one-half of American CEOs feel that national planning could actually lead to economic problems of *greater* severity than those currently experienced without it.[17] "Without their [CEOs'] full-hearted support," the report concluded, "it would be difficult to successfully implement national economic planning."[18]

President Reagan understands the reluctance of big business to entrust the public sector with new responsibilities for providing economic direction. His administration is clearly less inclined to intervene in the economy on behalf of special regions or industries than the previous administration was. The White House views the concept of Carter-like subsidies as running against the national grain. Predictably, President Carter's tripartite committees have been dropped, although the Reaganites believe that tax incentives to encourage investment and employment in declining urban areas are perfectly appropriate. We can expect the administration to continue its use of the tax code to achieve social and economic policy objectives because, according to University of Michigan economist Paul W. McCracken, "such actions merely change relative prices and thus interfere least with the operation of markets."[19]

How purist the President's commitment will be to liberal economics remains to be seen. Nevertheless, look for Washington to maintain an essential, but limited role, with business decision making made predominantly by private individuals acting within the limits set by competitive markets. The dynamics of a market-oriented economy, Reagan still believes, is the most effective and objective way of planning, of sorting out winners and losers. If a new product or technology makes its way on to the market and is accepted by consumers, it lives; if not, it dies. Treasury Secretary Donald Regan often is called upon to restate the White House's dictum: "We intend to create a climate in which business can flourish. But having created this climate, we then expect businesses to thrive or not on their own."[20]

"Planning, yes; national economic planning, no!" is the verdict of the Reagan administration, the business community, and many other sectors of American society. On the one hand, our government finds it quite impossible to respond to special-interest groups and still function in the interests of the majority. This national blemish makes the immediate prospects for a national industrial policy rather remote. On the other hand, the competitive realities of the global marketplace penalize heavily any nation that is ad hocing it along.

This double bind which the United States now finds itself in is best described by Mark Shepherd, Jr., chairman and chief executive officer of Texas Instruments, Inc. "The U.S. must develop a set of coherent and attainable national objectives that will stand for at least a decade, perhaps a generation," he says.[21] "The dilemma is how to accomplish this without falling into the trap of national planning."[22] Or, as the *New York Times* puts it: "The American economy is uneasily poised between 19th-century no-holds-barred capitalism and real central planning. The trick would be to move a step closer to planning without losing the benefits of competition."[23]

This balancing act, as it were, will not be resolved in the short term. But for how long is another question. To find the answer, Professor John E. Fleming and his colleagues at the University of Southern California's Center for Futures Research undertook a twenty-year forecast of government-corporate relations in the United States.[24] Relying heavily on the opinions of leading academics in the field of business and society, the U.S.C. team reached the following conclusions:

☐ The federal government will initiate some form of national planning for the economy in the early 1990s primarily because of the perceived need to synchronize more effectively our increasingly complex post-industrial society.

☐ The character of this planning process will be limited, participative, and largely indicative with regard to its impact on the private sector of the economy.

☐ Foreign planning models, such as Japan's, will not be useful predictors of what will happen in this country. "The U.S. social system will continue to be unique with little direct input from foreign models," Fleming believes.[25]

☐ Finally, the American economy will remain mixed and located near the center of the ideological continuum, with laissez-faire and totalitarian economics the two extremes.

If the U.S.C. predictions are correct, traditional national economic planning, an essential element in the consensual approach of Scenario II, could be a decade away for the United States.[26]

An Elite Bureaucracy

Any society, to paraphrase Abraham Lincoln, that plucks its most capable people from positions of importance and replaces them with those less capable is doomed. Unfortunately, this gloomy stratagem portrays the staffing profile of the public sector—at least in the eyes of most Americans. "In the end, it is not government that business fears; it is government incompetence."[27] So says former Undersecretary of Commerce Sidney Harman, an advocate of a national industry policy and an "America, Inc."

Frequently fingered as "incompetent" are the civil careerists assigned to keep the wheels of government turning. Contrary to the title of David Halberstam's best seller, the best and the brightest in this country have consistently opted out of positions of public responsibility. The emblem of this tragedy is the present plight of our civil institutions ranging from the Post Office to New York City. While democratic capitalism depends on a supply of able bureaucrats, the opposite, in fact, is taking place. What is more, those in the federal government are their own toughest critics. Of all the groups that I surveyed, civil servants were the most mindful of their limitations, besides being genuinely unwilling to assume a more direct role in managing the national economy.[27]

Notwithstanding the low self-esteem of the bureaucracy itself, outsiders are delighted to heap additional criticism on those in the public employ. To many, our Washingtonians are overpaid. Inflated titles, juicy fringe benefits, far-too-frequent cost-of-living adjustments, and lucrative pension benefits contribute to this problem. To others, the major rub is that Washington's "enterprising bureaucrats" (in George Gilder's words) actually promote the expansion of the state against its mortal enemy, the capitalist class. Whatever the dimension studied, our public servants are not up to snuff, or so say their critics.

"The American bureaucracy as now constituted," Ezra F. Vogel claims, "is simply too large and unwieldy, and its talent too uneven, to provide a high degree of coordination and direction."[29] But it is a *non sequitur* to suggest, as Professor Vogel does, that the solution is to create a small core of permanent, high-level bureaucrats. With the possible exception of the U.S. Foreign Service, the notion of elitism in government service is repugnant to our values of egalitarianism, individualism, and competitiveness. In my discussions, I found little serious interest in such a proposition, although Americans openly concede the merits of an elitist approach for the Japanese, Germans, Swedes, and the French.

Besides, the feeder schools of America's administrative talent remain the graduate schools of business, with their "golden passport," the M.B.A. degree. While the mission statements of some of these institutions—most notably, Cornell, Yale, and Stanford—have expanded to include public administration, these combined experiences have been shaky at best. Moreover, I disagree with the prediction of Irving Shapiro, retired board chairman of Du Pont Co., and those who see new coalitions forming between business schools and schools of government because of their close natural interests.[30] A more realistic outlook is continued differentiation, not integration. This, at least, is the organizational choice that Harvard University purposely made when it formed the Kennedy School of Government separate and apart from the business school. Whether the twain shall meet is arguable. The business school, after all, is located on the "wrong side" of the Charles River; and in view of the precedent set with its neighbor, the economics department, one could anticipate a growing schism to emerge between Harvard-trained careerists in business and government.[31]

In lieu of our propensity for either bureaucratic elitism or an American version of the *grandes écoles*, the best we may expect is a more systematic interchange of capable administrators from the private and public sectors. "If we are to retain any command at all over our own future," says John Gardner, "the ablest people in every field must give thought to the largest problems of the nation. . . . They don't have to be in government to do so. But they have to come out of the trenches of their own specialties and look at the whole battlefield."[32]

To date, however, businessmen have been reluctant to leave their trenches in product management, corporate lending, or public accounting for even short-term stints in government. Nothing short of a national emergency will pull junior and mid-level managers off their fast-track rollercoasters; and it may be unreasonable to expect anything different in our highly competitive, individualistic society.

I was vested with the chore of overseeing the "executive-on-loan" program of one leading multinational corporation. Although the project had considerable support of top management, replicating this enthusiasm into the bowels of the company took more than imagination. Invariably, our assignees to the public sector were the "old Charlies," who were "available"—that is, indefinitely between jobs. In one instance, when the stock of volunteers was at an all-time low, we had to go to Rome to snatch away an Italian manager for an assignment to New York City. The implicit code of the organization was "hands off" when it came to tapping our high-potential people for brief tours of duty in Washington or elsewhere. If my experiences are typical (and I expect they are), an American alternative to bureaucratic elitism—piggybacking on the talents of the best and the brightest in business—has a long way to go before it becomes a reality. Given this void, the chances of our adopting an economic ideology that requires a first-rate civil service, either built or borrowed, seems unlikely in the near term.

A COLLECTIVE SPIRIT

Whether the consensual approach to economic affairs will come easily or not at all also depends on our replacing individualism and egoism with group-oriented values and institutions. But can the United States shift from a self-interest society to one where community spirit abounds? Stated otherwise, will Americans opt to move from the "me decade" to the "we decade" in the 1980s?

When George Cabot Lodge and William F. Martin polled corporate executives for the *Harvard Business Review* in 1975, they found them pessimistically expecting a "communitarian" future.[33] This sample was convinced that socialist, humanist, and environmentalist values would drive out the more traditional American values of liberty, private property, competition, economic growth, and efficiency. My own findings run in the opposite direction. United States businessmen and their peers in organized labor and government are not inclined to pursue communitarian ends, and I do not expect the next round of America's leaders to follow a different heading. The "me generation" is alive, well, and going to college. That is the conclusion of Dean Hodge, a sociology professor at Catholic University in Washington, D.C. Based on his own research plus his analysis of the annual survey of college freshmen by the American Council on Education, Hodge claims that today's students still want the same personal freedoms that their predecessors of the sixties and seventies picketed to win.[34]

Every American, irrespective of age, is influenced by a culture that rewards individual rights and discounts collectivism. "The capacity of individual selfishness should surprise no one," says H. Justin Davidson, dean of the Ohio State Business School. "The capacity for organized self-gratification is a product of our times."[35] Indeed, there is ample evidence that our integrative institutions and organizations are losing, not gaining, ground. The death of compulsory military service, shrinking church attendance (notwithstanding the Moral Majority), declining camp enrollments, and the rising divorce rate are but a few examples. America seems unable to sustain, let alone build, the cultural conduits needed to synthesize the diverse elements of a heterogeneous society.

Reasons abound for this societal deficiency. Our shaky common spirit is the by-product of a narcissistic society, argues Christopher Lasch.[36] In another radical critique of contemporary life, Columbia's Marvin Harris contends that "cultural materialism" is the enemy.[37] To sociologist Daniel Bell, it is the hedonism that extends yet withdraws promises of the good life that gives America headaches.[38] The answer lies in our "celebrity culture," Michael Novak suggests; it glorifies self-centered personalities and inspires privileged elitists to take advantage of the system.[39] Underlying each explanation is a common theme: Pervasive undercurrents in American society run against our attaining a meaningful level of national esprit de corps.

One wonders: Would "My country, 'tis of *me*," be more appropriate lyrics to the well-known song? Perhaps not. But it might dispel fuzzy thinking when our leaders contemplate the practical realities of writing new social contracts.

"We must be practical idealists," cautions Roger B. Smith, board chairman of General Motors Corp.[40] "We must recognize this ideal relationship between government and business can never be a partnership in its literal sense. A government official who is charged to regulate an industry cannot be faithful to his responsibilities if he sees himself—or if others see him—as a partner to that industry. And a corporation executive's primary obligation must always be to his stockholders—as well as to society. And the extent of his commitment to the pursuit of a particular public objective, however commendable, must be judged in this light."[41]

Fortune's David Seligman is even more critical of the partnership proponents: "[They] talk about the 'common interest' that all the smiling partners have in a thriving and competitive U.S. economic system, and you are asked to believe that the partners would therefore undertake to sacrifice their own selfish interest to the long-run health of the economy. It is implicit in all this heavy breathing about partnership that the economy is driven by something other than business profits."[42] Nothing could be further from the truth, Seligman suggests.

To the camp followers of seductive slogans that seek such partnerships between our economic stakeholders goes the message: Remember the case of the missing institutions. Without national economic planning, an elite bureaucracy, and a communitarian ethic, the United States will be hard pressed to adopt an "America, Inc.," in the eighties. Rather than romanticize about the Japanese, Germans, or others, we would be well advised to chart a different course, one consistent with the realities of the times and the economic ethos of the United States. Such a course means rendering our present economic system more effective—while at the same time *selectively* applying the culturally acceptable elements of a more collaborative ideology. The next chapter tells how we might cast a composite system.

10

The Re-United States of America

FOR the past fifty years, the United States has dominated the global economy. Yet the system that has performed so capably in times of economic growth, abundant natural resources, and essentially domestic markets has done rather poorly when the economy is stagnating, resources are shrinking, and markets are internationalizing. While our major industrial competitors are coping successfully with these changes, the United States has clung to the ideological nostalgia of former times. And the question introducing the first chapter of this book must be reasked: "Whither America?"

The answer, as my research suggests, is not to be found in any sharp turn from our present course. "When the engine breaks down, you don't call the principle of internal combustion into question," warns Francois de Combert, former economic adviser to the president of France. "You fix or replace the engine."[1]

The repair, as it were, means preserving the basic principles of our mixed economy, while securing greater support from government and labor. No question, the regulated free enterprise system will remain synonymous with "the American way"; but there is also an emerging interest in reshaping our current habits.

The Split-Level Approach

"Dress me slowly, I'm in a hurry!" Napoleon once remarked. This describes the double bind of America's ideological transition: the challenge of recapturing the benefits of democratic capitalism while holding down the costs of stakeholder disputes to acceptable limits. But how?

It may be a matter of perspective—of applying elements of Scenario I to operational or day-to-day decision making and features of Scenario II to broad policy or strategic isues. Former Secretary of Labor and Ambassador to Japan James D. Hodgson offers some guidelines: "At the operational level, the adversarial tests of wills (for example, in traditional collective bargaining) is okay. But at the policy level, we must agree; international competition makes this a mandate."[2] In the years ahead, we should seek to define more precisely this *split-level approach.*

For starters, however, this means openly acknowledging once and for all that the United States is a "free" enterprise society with its economic lifeline inextricably tied to the modern-day corporation. This will not change; and any prospects of an "Inc.," American style, must reflect these realities.

Therefore, the foundation or *lower* level of the split-level approach will remain our regulated or mixed economy, although in a somewhat modified form. We may anticipate more serious attempts to redefine the "regulated" aspects of the present system—the objective being an unbridling of the competitive market forces that made the United States an economic superpower. Look for new and continued efforts to (1) rationalize regulation; (2) replace restrictive legislation with that accommodating U.S. business interests; and (3) redirect government's interventions in the economy along more productive, yet unobtrusive lines. In so doing, U.S. enterprise will be better positioned to compete more effectively in national and world markets.

While preserving the essence of America's competitive underpinnings, we must also work to reduce the antagonism of arm's-length attitudes of our major stakeholders in business, government, and labor. The *upper* level of our new economic home will include selected segments of an America, Inc. Confrontation will give way slowly to greater cooperation, particularly in national and international policymaking. The by-product, one hopes: a Re-United States of America.

The kind of conceptual framework we are proposing might best be described by an example or two. One case in point: the recent instance of U.S. semiconductor companies' banding together to finance basic research projects on American campuses. The new Semiconductor Research Cooperative will initially attempt to raise $5 million to give to selected universities for long-term research in areas of concern to all the participants, such as techniques for producing integrated circuits. Members of the cooperative, which include IBM, Digital Equipment, Motorola, Control Data, and National Semiconductor, will be asked to contribute one-tenth of on percent of their sales or use of semiconductor devices.

The motive behind this first effort at forming a hi-tech coalition is to stave off stiff Japanese competition by maximizing America's R&D dollars. "Why shouldn't two or more semiconductor companies join together to do research or to do research and development?" asks John R. Finch, vice-president and general manager of National Semiconductor.[3] Duplication of effort and expense can be reduced by pooling resources, he says.

Although research outlays are to be pooled, there will be no attempt to blunt the forces of market competition. In truth, every member of the cooperative will be on its own to win the hearts of prospective consumers. Darwinian survival, the philosophical basis of free enterprise, will be the rule; so this undertaking should not be interpreted as some sort of competitive cocoon. Quite the contrary, this joint venture blends the values of free enterprise on the one hand with the necessity for industrial cooperation on the other.

Another example is the foresight shown by both the United Auto Workers and Ford Motor Co. in their historic 1982 accord. Rather than waging war for higher wages, the UAW pressed for increased job security. For its part, Ford agreed to share future profits, not to close any plants as a result of shifting work to outside suppliers for two years, and to guarantee an income until retirement for workers with over fifteen years' seniority who are laid off. In this instance, what is good for Ford—and the United Auto Workers— should be good for the country. The "equality of sacrifice" principle that underlies this thinking may be a harbinger of more enlightened collective bargaining. To the *Wall Street Journal*, the Ford agreement "is part of a recognition by management of the legitimacy of the labor movement and a recognition by unions of the common interests of the workers and the corporation. . . . It is the kind of adaptation that competition forces, a benefit competition yields."[4] Hopefully, the *Journal*'s predictions will come true; at the time of this writing, the bets are still out on whether this kind of positive action, which typifies the split-level approach, will actually take hold. One thing is clear: the move by Ford (and later General Motors) and the UAW toward self-help is long overdue.[5] The auto industry—management and unions both—got itself into its present predicament. But by avoiding the industry's conventional response to its problems— looking to Washington for import restrictions, looser regulations, and loan guarantees—Detroit is proving that labor and management can collaborate on much-needed policy reforms without impinging on their respective roles in the world of work.

These cases and several others that are now surfacing suggest that the task of implementing the split-level approach will not be easy. The sharp realities of constructing such a mosaic from what today seems to be a series of cultural contradictions will call on deep reserves of strength.[6] The difficulty of forging new directions as well as new and proper roles for industry, government, and labor will present a severe test to our national will and resolve. But do we have an alternative? I (and most Americans) think not.

Building a Re-United States of America will require new attitudes and actions from our economic power brokers. This, in turn, means bold leadership, an all-too-often missing ingredient from the present scene. If our mixed economy is to be preserved and extended, deeds—not words that blindly beg for "reindustrialization" or "revitalization"—will be the answer. What follows is some practical counsel for leaders in business, government, and labor.

New Roles for American Business

The great majority of Americans agrees that the private sector is *the* driving force behind our nation's past success and its future hopes. Hence, the business community must carry a disproportionately heavy load in rebuilding the economy. This is the overriding opinion of the influential persons included in my research. Similarly, in a May 1980 poll, the American Enterprise Institute found that our countrymen still have positive views about business and its value to the economy. Almost seven out of ten Americans believe that we "must make sacrifices to preserve the free enterprise system"; and another 27 percent partially believe the same thing. What is more, by well over a three-to-one margin, Americans feel that business (versus government) has more intelligent people.[7] So, any partnership that emerges will be an unequal one, with the captains of industry and their lieutenants asked to take the lead. Their new platform should embrace the elements that follow.

1. ENLIGHTENED ACTIVISM

If they are to assume the mantle of leadership, those in American industry must adopt a more statesmanlike profile. Most businessmen (particularly those in charge) perceive our political economy as a divisible quantum of power, or what Lester Thurow calls "the zero-sum society."[8] Losses by one sector represent gains for another, with Washington invariably portrayed as the villain. Take, for instance, the remarks of the former head of a major U.S. steel company: "If the American economy has lost its competitive vitality in the world marketplace, it is more the result of government than of any 'inevitable' process connected with a mature industrial economy."[9] Hopefully, his comments were made with tongue in cheek. This same firm leads the steel industry's annual assault on Capitol Hill for handouts ranging from trigger-point prices to stiffer quotas against foreign imports.

Such two-sided tantrums, H. Justin Davidson feels, demonstrate "the tendency of corporate management to move toward monopoly, mercantilism, protectionism, and, finally, feudalism."[10] When asked about this new feudalism and the rising rhetoric from the business community about the virtues of "free enterprise" coupled with its cries for public handouts, Irving S. Shapiro, Du Pont's former board chairman, concedes: "[Businessmen] are just like everybody else. They sometimes talk out of both sides of their mouths, depending on their self-interest."[11]

Economically speaking, the self-interests of many American companies are inextricably linked to the public sector. The economic interdependency of U.S. business and government has grown to record proportions. To illustrate: federal outlays to consultants in business (and nonprofit organizations) approach $2.5 billion a year; government procurement of goods and services from private enterprise exceeds $120 billion a year; and nearly two hundred federal programs funnel some $200 billion in loan guarantees and subsidies to American industry. No matter how it is calculated, Washington's tab on the private sector runs extremely high.

Nevertheless, the American business community still sees itself on the defensive struggling to maintain its position in society. This, at least, is the finding of a *Harvard Business Review* survey conducted by Steven N. Brenner.[12] With its back against the wall, Corporate America is unlikely to retreat voluntarily. But rather than digging in for the territorial wars, the corporate community would do well to "look in another direction—toward more effective shaping of policy processes that will determine the character of the governmental advance."[13]

In the split-level approach, business must take the offensive by pressing those in government to create the kind of environment in which the private sector can unleash its incredible force. Yet "neglect of their public role," according to Leonard Silk of the *New York Times*, poses the greatest threat to the future of the corporation.[14] Generally speaking, American executives are a distant second to their foreign counterparts in coming to grips with public issues. This is the conclusion of Professor Leslie E. Grayson of the University of Virginia, who compared the relative abilities of American and non-American CEOs in the petroleum industry.[15] How generalizable these findings are is open to question; the top dogs of American enterprise, however, do seem to be uncomfortable in dealing with matters of public policy. But the next wave of business leaders must become more politically active. In assessing the chief executive's job over the next ten years, Roy L. Ash, former head of Litton Industries and AM International, believes that "the biggest change—I hope it will become the biggest change—will be the CEO's involvement in the political system."[16] Peter Drucker agrees. He insists that tomorrow's business executive "can no longer depend on the political process to be the integrating force; he himself must be the integrator."[17]

2. DUAL HEADQUARTERS

A radical way to promote effective integration is through structural change. It may be hard to influence Washington from a centralized command post in Terre Haute, Indiana, or Shreveport, Louisiana. "Any business of any size has to have a second headquarters in Washington, a co-headquarters," Roy Ash insists.[18] If the location of their head office is a serious stumbling block to effective governmental affairs, CEOs should pursue the notion of a dual headquarters.

There are some important international precedents for this proposal.[19] When its European operations began to generate approximately two-thirds of total overseas sales, IBM dissolved its World Trade headquarters in New York and replaced it with two international headquarters—IBM Europe (based in Paris) and IBM Americas/Far East (based in New York). Both organizations report directly to a vice-chairman in corporate headquarters. And Unilever and the Royal Dutch/Shell Group both established dual corporate headquarters in London and Rotterdam. In the political climate of today and tomorrow, why not Chicago-Washington or Dallas-Washington?

3. DIRECT COMMUNICATIONS

There are other more direct and less radical changes that can alter significantly the level of public-sector sensitivity in a company. In each instance, they depend on greater mutual trust and respect by those in business and government. "But to achieve it," insists Harvard's Robert B. Reich, "business executives and regulatory officials must restructure the means by which they communicate."[20] For too long now Washington's intermediaries—the lawyers, consultants, staff members, and public relations experts—have been impeding full and frank discussions between those in public and private life. The influence of these professional middlemen must be moderated. Our recommendation: the Business Roundtable approach.

Founded almost a decade ago, this uniquely conceived lobbying group brings the chief executives of the nation's largest corporations into direct and continuing contact with congressmen, civil servants, and members of the administration. Beyond merely buttonholing an influential senator or two, the Business Roundtable is institutionalizing corporate thinking on public issues.[21] Whether it is antitrust or foreign trade, the Roundtable reigns supreme in presenting corporate views to the Washington establishment. Neither the U.S. Chamber of Commerce nor the National Association of Manufacturers can rival its accomplishments in galvanizing business' political interests. "No question," says Congressman Leon E. Panetta, "business [now] is generally more sophisticated in its ability to lobby on Capitol Hill."[22]

The Business Roundtable has its obvious limitations. For one thing, it is very much an organ of big business, with its membership drawn from the *"Fortune* 500" lists. But a 1981 creation, the Washington-based Business Council, concentrates on the concerns of the much-neglected small- and medium-sized business segment.

And one hopes that further efforts are made to synthesize the interests of America's mini-concerns. Another rap on the Roundtable is its negative or defensive orientation. In the words of one critic: "[It] hasn't initiated legislation; it has no agenda other than survival of business interests."[23] Rather than communicating what business stands *against*, this high-powered forum should express more vocally what it stands for.

Blemishes aside, the Business Roundtable has helped to create a new relationship with the federal government. Predictably, its offsprings are being cloned at the state and local levels. The Sacramento-based California Roundtable is patterned along almost identical lines; embryonic versions of the national organization may be seen in Massachusetts, Pennsylvania, and Delaware; and similar activity is underway in New York, New Jersey, Connecticut, Virginia, and Indiana. On the local level, the Minneapolis-St. Paul consortium (referred to as "the Minnesota Business Partnership") probably serves as the best example of responsible and effective corporate involvement in public affairs.[24] The mirror image of the Business Roundtable, the MBP puts administrators and elected officials in direct contact with CEOs of leading companies, such as General Mills, 3M, Honeywell, and Dayton-Hudson. Working together, they have been able to deal with a variety of economic and other matters of mutual concern. Baltimore, Louisville, Seattle, and Phoenix are among those attempting to emulate the Twin Cities' success.

4. STATE AND LOCAL SUPPORT

In many respects, the dividends of building constructive partnerships may be higher at the state and local levels than at the national level. For one thing, the competency gap between those in government and industry widens typically as one proceeds "downstream." State and local officials are particularly uncertain about how to deal with complex social problems: urban renewal, unemployment, energy conservation, and productivity. What is worse, they are often awestruck by their counterparts in the local business community who seem to have some of the answers. Being uncertain and awestruck, state and local governments are often inclined to go on the defensive, to heighten their hostilities with the private sector—when the exact opposite, in fact, is needed.

Business can and must take the initiative in reversing this tradition of tension and neglect. By making its best people, resources, and ideas available to government—first in its own backyard, later at higher echelons—the corporate community can help to close the competency gap. But, as we have discussed earlier, industry's high flyers are reluctant to leave their corporate nests even for short-term stints in government. Top management, by its own example, can change all this. If an understanding of the political environment is critical to the success of the modern corporation, it should be reflected in the career patterns of tomorrow's business leaders.

5. MANDATORY PUBLIC SERVICE

John de Butts, before his retirement from AT&T, said he had come to believe that every aspiring chief executive officer in business should be required to spend at least one year in Washington.[25] This, he added, would better enable a young business executive to distinguish between the shadow and the substance in business-government relations. One year, in my opinion, is not enough, and I would challenge U.S. enterprise to announce openly a policy requiring those aspiring to the corporate throne to spend a minimum of three years in public service as an elected or an appointed official. Making tours of duty in government a prerequisite for entry into top management would produce markedly different attitudes in our companies. After all, high-potential candidates have been known to transcend tall buildings if that is what it takes to enter the executive suite.

This proposal of "mandatory" public service is not as bizarre as it may appear at first blush. In earlier times, when ambitious managers discovered that actual experience in the global side of their company's businesses was vital to their career advancement, they volunteered in droves for overseas postings. Internationalism quickly became the fast track, and those on it never looked back. Public service is somewhat analogous to foreign service. Both provide the opportunity for greater insight into external areas essential to the enterprise; both place a premium on direct experience under fire; and both rely on similar personnel systems — selection procedures, preassignment orientation, special salary supplements, and re-entry mechanisms. By drawing on these similarities, American industry can and must reroute the careers of its future leaders through the halls of government *before* they move into the corporate boardroom.[26]

An industrywide mandate for public service assignments would also inject new life into the sorry state of business-government exchanges. Executive commitment can do wonders, and this under-gunned area is no different. Besides overhauling their own company's approach to billeting midmanagers in government, business executives should participate in national efforts with the same end. Perhaps the best is the Conference Board's Congressional Assistance Program, which enables a dozen or so mid-career businessmen to spend a year in Washington working on the staff of a congressional committee, preceded by an intensive series of orientation, education, and briefing sessions. "They learn the meaning of coalition, compromise, and consensus," boasts Elmer B. Staats, one of the program's founding fathers.[27]

By definition, personnel exchanges must be a two-way street. As valuable as firsthand experience in the public sector is to those in industry, the reverse is also true. It would be most helpful if more businesses could also plan to provide a period of time, such as two to four years, for selected public administrators to work in industry as a normal part of their development.

6. INTEGRATED LEARNING

Alternatively, some of the best learning and understanding takes place in executive development programs conducted across this country. Yet, barriers to entry (steep tuition, in particular) exclude our government's blue chippers from attending these sessions. Unlike Brazil, Sweden, and several other countries where mixed participation of bureaucrats and businessmen is "encouraged," U.S. enrollments in advanced training sessions are almost totally skewed toward private enterprise. American corporations should either open the doors of their own in-house seminars to selected civil servants or offer scholarship help to those in government who are eager to study in similar sessions on university campuses. By promoting a higher level of human contact between those in the private and public sectors, Corporate America can more closely ally its interests with those of government.

Taken together, these proposals should enhance industry's ability to become more politically astute and more in touch with big government. Our intention, though, is not to establish a cadre of corporate lobbyists and the supra-institutions to support them. Rather, we would hope that these measures might enable big business to move away from its traditional preoccupation with matters of narrow special interest to those of greater societal consequence.

"Business needs better managers more urgently than it needs more effective lobbyists," argues Berkeley's David Vogel. "Unless managers can improve employee productivity, upgrade the quality of products and become more entrepreneurally minded,"[28] transforming business-government relations will not by itself cure America's economic malaise. Nevertheless, by encouraging greater patterns of convergence with Washington, we stand a far better chance of preserving—indeed, extending—the primacy of private enterprise and, with it, America's rightful place in the global industrial system.

A New Role for Government

Another key element in the split-level approach is a reexamination of government's role in the economy. "Call it what you will—'quasi-public,' 'half-free enterprise,' 'the mixed economy.' By any name," says Irving S. Shapiro, "it is a system in which heavy government involvement will remain a fact of life for business."[29] An activist public sector is here to stay, whether we like it or not. With Japan as his idealized model, Ezra F. Vogel puts it more forcefully:

"Government and only government can make the strategic decisions, but to make those decisions wisely requires drawing on the competence which only businessmen and labor bring."[30] The lesson of Japan, West Germany, and other nations on the rise is that government *can* make positive contributions to the promotion and encouragement of industry. But for the lesson to "take," our political leaders must replace rhetoric with results. Some suggested actions follow.

1. NEED FOR NEW ATTITUDES

"We've spent the last few decades worrying about the distribution of the golden eggs," Senator Paul E. Tsongas concedes. "The time has come to worry about the health of the goose."[31] If a prominent member of the liberal Democrats can make such an admission, one might expect others to follow. Indeed, a broad base of popular support for American industry is taking root today, and the Congress is picking up on these sentiments. Increasingly, those on Capitol Hill, irrespective of their party ties, are voicing an aye for business.

Since 1981, a progressive shift in government's attitudes has been taking place. Take the area of regulatory reform, where restrictive legislation and thinking are slowly giving way to those accommodating U.S. business interests. Consider, for instance:

☐ The appointment of Vice-President George Bush to head a cabinet-level task force to identify and revise regulations deemed unnecessary.

☐ The removal of price controls on domestic crude oil.

☐ The push to deregulate airlines, trucking, and communications, with similar moves likely for banking and other key industries.

☐ The administration's intentions to hold constant the growth in the budgets of regulatory agencies for fiscal year 1981, with a 4 percent reduction projected for the following year.

☐ The self-initiated efforts of the Occupational Health and Safety Administration to drop over a thousand pages of regulations and design standards from its books.

☐ The pending legislation to provide better criteria for determining whether and when the benefits of regulation exceed its costs. Plus the calls for stricter impact analysis of regulations, as well as for tougher congressional oversight.

How profound Washington's mood change will be remains to be seen. But by melting its once-frosty position with industry, government is taking an important first step in demonstrating the viability of a modified adversarial approach. What is more, the captains of commerce are impressed.

"Across the country," writes Winston Williams of the *New York Times*, "business leaders are applauding the Administration's plans to simplify the confusing image of federal regulations that, they say, discourages investment, aggravates inflation, and suffocates productivity."[32] Yet much more can be done—particularly in the area of international business.

2. SPECIAL HELP FOR MULTINATIONALS

Once maligned in congressional circles, the global corporation takes on a public or quasi-public character in most other industrialized countries. Our government must express greater sensitivity to the special role of American multinational enterprises if we are to compete effectively in world markets. Senator Lowell Weicker is one of many elected officials who believes that the traditional ideology is ill-suited to meet our global needs. "I want to usher in America Inc.," he says. "I want to see our industries able to act in concert abroad with the federal government as their foreign business partner."[33] There is no better starting place to foster such a partnership, albeit an unequal one, than by removing the plethora of unnecessary restrictions that handicap U.S. multinationals.

Our political leaders seem inclined to meet this challenge, if the recently approved federal tax package is an accurate barometer of their feelings. Besides the widely endorsed sweeteners—accelerated

depreciation, investment tax credits, and lower corporate tax rates—
global companies were delighted to learn that U.S. citizens working
abroad would be tax-exempt on the first $75,000 of income in 1982,
with further $5,000 increments in subsequent years up to a maximum
of $95,000. Opportunities abound for Washington to create a more
favorable environment in which U.S. MNCs can operate, whether it
is clarifying the Foreign Corrupt Practices Act or revamping the
Export-Import Bank. To these vital areas should be added legislative
proposals that (1) strengthen Domestic International Sales Corporations (or "DISCs") by permitting the deferral of 100 percent of
qualified export income; (2) retain the foreign tax credit system as
well as the present procedures of not taxing accumulated overseas
earnings prior to their remittance as dividends; (3) permit setting up
trading companies to act as agents for smaller firms; (4) tighten the
enforcement of antidumping statutes; and (5) beef up federal agencies
responsible for developing long-term foreign trade policies.

3. ANTITRUST REFORM

These remedies will not spell relief for U.S. multinationals,
though. Without fundamental changes in our antitrust laws and
enforcement procedures, they will remain at a competitive disadvantage. Key members of the Reagan team are sensitive to the
problem as well as to the upswing in foreign conglomeration. David
Stockman, director of the Office of Management and Budget,
describes our restrictive antitrust approach as "misguided,"[34] while
James Miller, head of the Federal Trade Commission, pledges a
"thoroughgoing" review of his agency's past practices.[35] "Bigness
doesn't necessarily mean badness," declares Attorney General William
French Smith, who adds that our antitrust laws have been "misguided and mistaken."[36] Even the chief of the Justice Department's
antitrust division, William Baxter, chimes in with his claim that big
businesses are "very valuable things" because they tend to be most
efficient.[37]

Is all this simply the huff-and-puff of any energetic administration? The results to date suggest not. First, there are the Justice
Departments decisions to drop its twelve-year antitrust suit against

IBM and to settle out of court its eight-year suit against AT&T. Then there is the White House's decidedly novel approach to antitrust, spurring on an unprecedented urge to merge. By October, merger bids for 1981 surpassed the full-year record of $44.3 billion set in 1980. No single tender attracted more attention than the $7.3 billion takeover by E. I. du Pont de Nemours & Co., the largest U.S. chemical company, of Conoco, the ninth largest oil company. It represented the biggest corporate merger in history — paving the way for the second largest takeover, U.S. Steel's $6.3 billion bid for Marathon Oil.

Consistently, the administration has rejected the relevancy of an eighty-three-year-old antitrust act to present-day mergers. In its place, it is offering simple, but revolutionary criteria to evaluate corporate coalitions: the performance effects on domestic *and* international competition as well as the implications for national security. By removing the traditional taboos against bigness per se, government stands a good chance of extricating U.S. industry from the legalistic morass of the past. If successful, the United States should next address the elusive task of shaping an effective economic strategy.

4. AN INDUSTRIAL GAME PLAN

Industrial policymaking, American style, need not mean economic forecasting, national planning, or sectoral targeting in the usual sense. These features, as we have seen, are ideologically alien to most of us, and if they appear on the U.S. scene, it will not be in the immediate future. Nevertheless, Americans from all walks of life are prepared to replace the current practice of muddling through with some elements of a more rational and cohesive industrial strategy.

"What is needed," says Ruben F. Mettler, chief executive officer of TRW, Inc., "is *not* an extensive blueprint or a plan for intrusion in the market economy, nor a planning approach appropriate to command organizations."[38] He advocates an "incentive system" with government inducement aimed at (1) stimulating investment for more productive plants and equipment, (2) ensuring higher quality, safer products, and (3) increasing private training programs to upgrade white- and blue-collar skills.

Mark Shepherd, Jr., CEO of Texas Instruments, takes a slightly different tack—proposing instead a "board of national objectives" with a status similar to that of the Federal Reserve Board, but with no independent powers of implementation.[39] The members of the board, whose tenure would extend beyond normal political terms, would include former presidents, congressmen, and cabinet members along with representatives from business, labor, and the general public. Its mission: to formulate a set of national objectives for consideration of the President, Congress, and the public by initiating public debate and by generating a national consensus. Shepherd's proposal closely parallels that of his business rival at TRW, especially its "emphasis . . . on technical and vocational skills and retraining for those whose capabilities are being overtaken by rapid technological change."[40]

5. HIGH PRIORITY FOR HIGH TECHNOLOGY

That these highly respected leaders of two of America's most successful enterprises in a vanguard industry are taking the initiative in speaking out for selected pieces of a national industrial policy could not come at a better time. According to German economist Gerhard Mensch, the world is on the threshold of an innovative revolution in several areas: microprocessing, ocean farming, genetic engineering, and space exploration.[41] He believes these emerging technologies will trigger a period of "hyperindustrialization" that can only be exploited by giant partnerships of private companies and their governments. Whether the United States will lag or lead this industrial renaissance depends largely on the combined abilities of Washington and Corporate America to stimulate R&D and productivity.[42]

Government, for its part, must foster the institutional and attitudinal framework within which an economic policy based on future technology can be shaped.[43] This means continuing its efforts to rationalize regulation; to create tax incentives through accelerated depreciation and direct credits; to improve federal patent policies, while pressing for international patent protection; and to support basic research. That leaves it up to industry to develop a stream of new ideas and concepts, and to apply them to America's goods and services.

On the R&D side, most observers are bullish on the prospects for the United States in the eighties and nineties. While several nations are closing the innovation gap and in some cases even surpassing us, there is no need for America's spirits to sag. "Yankee ingenuity is as present in America now as before," contends Simon Ramo, co-founder and the "R" of TRW.[44] In almost every high-technology segment, our companies and products are well positioned to participate in an innovative rebirth. We are ahead in solid-state technology, large-scale integrated circuits, digital computers, and communications equipment, and virtually every other aspect of information technology. "I'm absolutely convinced," waxes Friedrich Schroeder, a native German who heads corporate development at Hewlett-Packard Co., "that the U.S. will be the leading technological country to the end of this century."[45] For this rosy scenario to become a reality, though, greater capital formation (and recovery) as well as substantially better industrial productivity will be required.

The decrepit state of America's industrial base has been the subject of much attention. The United States reinvests only 15 percent of its GNP, or far below West Germany (22 percent) and Japan (29 percent). To generate a rate of capital formation compatible with our basic growth needs and socially mandated expenditures means a major infusion of investment spending. If the United States is to exploit the technological opportunities of the future, we must add new plant and equipment at a dramatic rate. The tax tonic of the Reaganites, oriented toward the supply side of the economy, should provide some inducement for the sort of savings and investment needed to yield a more modern and efficient American economy.

6. IMPROVING PRODUCTIVITY

Even if we are able to restore our industrial machine, and patentable ideas flow, there remains the difficult task of restoring American productivity. As a nation, we had become accustomed to respectable productivity increases of 3 percent a year during the fifties and sixties. The downturn came in the seventies and only recently perked up. In 1981, U.S. productivity rose a modest 0.9 percent, after declining three years in a row: 0.3 percent in 1980, 0.7 percent in 1979, and 0.2 percent in 1978. To the surprise of no one, the Joint Economic Committee recently called our sluggish productivity growth "the most important factor contributing to our present economic malaise."[46] Yet the cause of the decline remains a puzzle to all of us, including leading experts in the field. "It could be," hypothesizes Nobel laureate Lawrence R. Klein, "demographic change, economic regulations, poor capital formation, changed social values, poor economic management, or any number of factors."[47]

Even without a clear perception of the causes, there is widespread agreement that the downturn in U.S. productivity will not be solved by a separatist, piecemeal approach to the problem. To Elmer B. Staats, former comptroller general of the United States, one thing is clear: "improvements will require the cooperative efforts of all sections of our economy — government, industry, and labor."[48] When, for instance, a General Accounting Office forum of leaders from business, government, labor, and academia met in 1979 to consider a collective response to the problem, the participants agreed that the "government and the private sector have to work together to remove disincentives and create new incentives for productivity improvement."[49]

Actually, the federal government has been spearheading a number of important efforts in this vital area. In February 1980, the secretary of commerce announced the establishment of an Office of Productivity, Technology, and Innovation to "work with the private sector to identify targets of opportunity for advancing industry's development and its competitive position in world markets." This new unit is under strict orders to work closely with private industry and organized labor. At about the same time, Senator Lloyd Bentsen and Congressman Stanley Laudine introduced legislation, based largely on the recommendations of the General Accounting Office, that would give the federal government an even stronger hand in enhancing private-sector productivity. They proposed a productivity council that would have an advisory board of private executives and would be the central focus for Washington's efforts to modify regulatory and tax policies designed to promote industrial output.[50]

7. TAX RELIEF

As encouraging as these developments are, the federal government can do much more to create a more favorable environment for technological gain and improved productivity. For one thing, Washington's support of industrial research and development has fallen sharply in recent years; only by providing special tax credits for private R&D can this trend be reversed. Government should also look to the halls of ivy and offer a full range of direct subsidies for *basic* research conducted on university campuses. William F. Miller, president of SRI, is one of several authorities on industrial innovation who believe that the present tax system works to the added disadvantage of high-technology industries. He would like to see government (1) encourage a shift of shareholder equity from mature industries to innovative ones without the usual capital gains tax on such a transfer, and (2) stimulate banks, through special tax incentives, to offer easier, more accessible financing to our industrial high flyers.[51]

By taking the shackles off business and by injecting positive incentives into the economy, Washington *can* continue to strengthen the modern market system. The challenge of the split-level approach is how to take full advantage of an increasingly favorable political environment without compromising the spirit of our arm's-length safeguards. Striking such a balance depends on heightened human contact and shared experience. Only by bringing together the talents of all Americans can we achieve the pragmatic harmonization needed to renew our economy.

8. COMPULSORY NATIONAL SERVICE

Government can begin the process by drawing on the immense untapped reservoir of energy, enthusiasm, and ability of America's youth. More specifically, the United States should introduce a system of compulsory national service with the following features: (1) an age band of eighteen to twenty-three years for entry into the system; (2) a minimum two-year period of active duty, including six months of rigorous basic training; (3) a four-year reserve requirement; and (4) a wide range of assignments in military or nonmilitary branches of government. Above all, such a scheme must be applied uniformly and equitably in all areas: registration, selection, and assignment policies. "The past has shown," warns Bernard Rostker, former director of the Selective Service System, "that the American people will not accept conscription unless it is perceived as fair."[52] Hence, we must press for equal, but enforced, opportunity for every American.

The mood is right for inciting national esprit. On the much more sensitive subject of compulsory military draft, the latest poll showed that, by a margin of 59 to 33 percent, the American people favor a return to the draft. A more comprehensive plan, including nondefense assignments, could help to replace the current ethic of divisive self-interest with one of the national service. At the very least, a program of effective conscription might foster a new, contemporary meaning of "duty, honor, and country"—and, with it, the communitarian values and institutions needed to survive future decades.

New Clothes for Labor

Industry and government alone cannot effect a fundamental ideological transition. "Without labor," insists Senator Bill Bradley, "developing a national consensus is not possible."[53] Union leaders, as we have seen, boast that they are primed for change. Of all the groups I surveyed, organized labor claims to be the most committed to a Re-United States. And for good reasons.

1. GEARED FOR CHANGE

First, unions like any other social institution, are image conscious; they should be. According to The Garth Group, Inc., more than two-thirds of our people think unions have acted irresponsibly in taking more than they deserve; and 62 percent of union members agree with that statement.[54] Perhaps more serious, a majority of the American public would like to vote for a political candidate who favors reducing the power of organized labor. And certainly the 1981 air traffic controllers' strike did little to rekindle popular support for the House of Labor.

Second, union membership is down—and falling. By 1980, organized labor's share of private-sector employment declined to less than 20 percent from its all-time high of about one-third in 1945.[55] What is more, potential growth segments, the service industry, small businesses, and professional and managerial occupations, have always been especially difficult for labor to organize.

Third, Big Labor's favorite ally, the Democratic party, can no longer be counted on for support. Unions' special relationship with Washington ended when the allegedly apathetic (to labor, at least) Republican party captured the White House and Senate. "We'd grown so accustomed to getting things from the Federal Government that we forgot how to get things on our own," asserts an official with one of the AFL-CIO's major departments.[56]

Fourth, the poor state of the economy is also making union leaders look elsewhere for support. Budgetary cutbacks plus unemployment levels in excess of 9 percent are forcing unions to reconsider the partnership approach. Under these present conditions, says John Laslett, a labor historian at UCLA, "the pressure to collaborate is enormous."[57]

Fifth, a distinctly different work force has sapped labor of its strength and left it groping for new directions; or so says William

Serrin of the *New York Times*.[58] Nowadays, blue-collar types are less swayed by the tough, anticorporate positions of the past. The advantage of their youth removes them from the bitter ideological clashes of earlier generations of unionists and managers.

The rank-and-file of the eighties are voicing two new sets of interests. They are pressing for greater participation in areas that have been the exclusive province of management: redesign of jobs and work processes, quality control, shop floor decision making, and quality-of-work-life programs. In addition, today's enlightened employees want positive social legislation to help all workers, but not if it means costly, self-defeating regulation of the workplace in areas such as pension reform, health and safety, and minimum wages. Union leaders are under the gun to deliver on both fronts. This will mean more, not less, collaboration with business and government.

2. A NEW MIND-SET

Organized labor's current problems may be averted by converting a combative relationship into a partly constructive one. True, the adversary principle is endemic to American society, and collective bargaining in its traditional form could not function without it. Still, "the founding fathers of the modern industrial revolution thought that once we overcame the historic class struggle, the adversarial relationship would develop into a collaborative relationship," says Jack Barbash, a labor economist at the University of Wisconsin.[59]

Until very recently, union leaders clung religiously to their headbutting gospel. Times may be changing, though. The evidence is mounting that the shortsighted animosity of collective bargaining, American style, may be giving way to greater collaboration. "We've been teaching our local leaders and members all these years to be aggressive and militant toward the companies," admits a high official in the United Auto Workers. "Now we have to turn around and undo all that."[60] No doubt, the distressed state of the U.S. auto industry is inducing all sides to modify the old ways. Even Lee A. Iaococca, chairman of Chrysler Corporation, concedes that "we have to develop a new relationship based on cooperation."[61]

This abrupt change in the way business and labor in the automobile industry view each other philosophically is producing marked changes. Now the United Auto Workers is trying to carve itself a role in management. Borrowing ideas from German and Japanese labor, the union has charted a course intended to involve workers in decision making, a clear break with American labor traditions. In doing so, they are imitating the Japanese, who credit much of their individual success to labor-management cooperation. One payoff? In every plant where the UAW is collaborating with management to set up a successful work innovation program, the local labor leaders who pushed it have been reelected.[62]

To some, U.S. Steel's turnaround from a net loss of $293 million in 1979 to a profit of $504.5 million in 1980 is also due, at least in part, to its adopting a more consensual approach. One element of this strategy is the so-called labor-management participation teams, jointly sponsored by the company (and all other major steel employees) and the U.S. steelworkers' union. "The concept," writes *Business Week*, "is an old one. It begins with the assumption that experienced steelworkers know a great deal about the production processes of the mills in which they work. If this knowledge is tapped through collaborative programs, it can help management run existing programs more efficiently. The participation team approach, carried on outside the usual adversarial relationship typified by the grievance procedure, enables labor and management to work jointly on production problems."[63]

The togetherness trend of employers and employees in autos, steel, and other industries will not invoke a return to industrial paternalism. But the success of these experiments (in what Robert E. Cole of the University of Michigan calls "career enlargement") does represent at least one vector on which the United States can learn from Japan and Germany.[64] "I'm absolutely convinced that the future of collective bargaining is in [these] quality-of-work-life programs," insists Irving Bluestone, a retired UAW vice-president.[65]

Nevertheless, labor's recent tilt toward greater collaboration must be viewed in the context of the split-level approach. As Bluestone himself admits: "We can be cooperative on the plant floor and adversarial at the bargaining table."[66]

3. TRIPARTITE PROSPECTS

As successful as these joint industry-labor efforts have been in getting America back on track, some experts sense that they do not go far enough. Without government's participation, the payoffs may be limited. Glenn Watts, president of the Communications Workers of America, is among those who believe that the United States should follow the West German program of tripartite "concerted action," where business, labor, *and government* agree on the worker-related methods needed to achieve national economic objectives.[67] To some extent, Watts's prescription is taking.

Automobiles, coal, construction, and steel are just four examples of troubled industries that have shifted to *tripartite* negotiations. An optimistic former Assistant Secretary of Labor William P. Hobgood believes that "for the first time in many years, there is a coherent pattern developing of bringing labor, management and government together to solve serious industry problems."[68] By combining knowledgeable experts from all three sectors, the potential is greatly enhanced to take on the tough tasks of revitalization: industrial relocation, job preservation, capital formation, technological innovation, and government incentives.

4. BEFRIENDING BUSINESS

Again, business will have to play a disproportionately greater role in this uneven partnership if a more sensible approach to managing America's human resources is to be realized. As organized labor moves into a mode of reduced radicalism and militancy, industry must respond in kind. Far too often, Corporate America has preferred to sidestep its common interests with the rank-and-file. Our industrialists seem to forget Harry S. Truman's important advice that "labor has become a full partner in our economy."

Whether it is hiring additional consultants to blunt off unions or supporting federal legislation to lessen the power of organized labor, big business views itself in a fight for survival with the House of Labor.

"Management must recognize that organized labor has a role to play in American society," insists AFL-CIO executive assistant Kenneth Young. "We still find it is a gut issue that management is trying to knock us out of the box at every opportunity."[69] On more than one occasion, I found Mr. Young's perceptions to ring true. With union membership at its nadir, several CEOs confided to me that the timing is now right to deliver the death knell to big labor. Such a strategy, in my opinion, could countermand the very essence of our society. If a Re-United States of America is to be forged, it will require a markedly higher level of vision by our captains of industry. The natural starting place is a greater corporate commitment to career development, quality-of-work-life programs, manpower development, and supervisory workshops. These efforts are already in motion, but they need to be improved, intensified, and extended to include every element of our economy, including the public sector.

5. BETTER JOB SECURITY

Worker participation in matters ranging from productivity to career pathing cannot by itself restore the American dream. Job security, as we know, is commonly rated among the most important benefits available to the American workers. Yet we persist in adjusting our labor force up and down with the vagaries of the business cycle. In reuniting this country, the greatest candidate for oblivion is cyclical unemployment.

United States industry must embark on a full-scale attempt to restore systematic job security to the workplace—if only on a modified basis. Any progress in molding labor-management teams will be short-lived if workers feel that their help leads to layoffs. So, Michigan's Robert Cole contends: "It may be time for America to reflect more on whether the welfare society can have any real meaning if we persist with the anachronistic practice of making selected workers arbitrarily vulnerable to protracted periods of unemployment."[70] Lacking a system of permanent or semipermanent employment, the United States is unable to leverage its human capital against Japan, West Germany, and other nations on the rise. Precisely because unionism is presently on its knees, the business community should move with full dispatch to correct this national deficiency.[71]

6. ENLIGHTENED LEADERSHIP

Organized labor, for its part, must continue to promote "the new industrial relations." Union leaders can represent their constituents more effectively by dropping their antiprofit rhetoric of the past. They should also be aware that workers in American industries losing out to international competition (autos, for instance) earn half again as much as the average industrial worker — and far more than their Japanese counterparts. Accordingly, the top echelon of the labor movement should divert its attention from ill-conceived notions of across-the-board pay increases, codetermination, and comprehensive welfare reform. Rather, labor should press for increased job security, worker participation, educational and training benefits, and productivity-based wage hikes. Clearly, the UAW's talks with Ford and General Motors represent a positive first step. In addition, labor leaders should develop better techniques for impasse resolution, increase the use of final-offer arbitration and national accords, penalize unexcused absenteeism, and seek a wider application of the kind of local labor-management committee approach (coupled with a no-strike agreement) that has worked effectively in the steel industry. By pursuing these new directions, our unions will be more able to survive their present life crises, while contributing to national reunification.

Progress may be within reach in the not-too-distant future. Already, laborites and businessmen appear interested in shifting away from the siege mentality of former times. In 1982, for instance, several prominent business leaders joined with labor leaders to form the Labor-Management Group, with Professor John T. Dunlop of

Harvard, former secretary of labor in the Ford cabinet, as coordinator.[72] The group, which pits the AFL-CIO's Lane Kirkland with the likes of Roger B. Smith of General Motors, Ruben F. Mettler of TRW, and Clifton C. Garvin, Jr., of Exxon, has agreed on a mission statement. They will search for voluntary solutions to a wide range of issues, such as how to create new and expanded job opportunities, higher living standards, increased competitiveness in world markets, and the capacity to meet social commitments. "The national interest," the group declared, "requires a new spirit of mutual trust and cooperation, even though management and organized labor are, and will remain, adversaries on many issues."[73] While their pronouncements do not necessarily signal greater cupidity between big business and big labor, they do embody the spirit of the cultural cocktail which we have termed "the split-level approach"—an admixture that, in our opinion, offers the best hope for economic renewal.

A Final Plea

For the balance of this century, America's charge is to shape the type of social, economic, and political system in which its children and their children will prosper. For this to happen, U.S. business, government, and labor must replace the ethic of head-to-head competition with the ethic of collaboration. Only by letting their talents work in tandem will the principals in our economic society weed out old myths and allow new dreams to be realized. Or, as Henry Ford once put it: "Coming together is a beginning; keeping together is progress; working together is success."

The principle of indivisibility—of coming together, keeping together, and working together—is deeply ingrained in the American character. We should follow our origins to pursue the modern-day meaning of "one nation indivisible." That meaning, we predict, will reside in a Re-United States of America, where an accommodation, if not an alliance, gradually begins to emerge among industry, government, and labor.

"The history of man," wrote psychologist and thinker Erich Fromm, "is a graveyard of great cultures that came to catastrophic ends because of their incompatibility for planned, rational and voluntary reaction to challenge." Nothing short of meeting this challenge will brake America's economic slippage and revitalize its self-esteem.

Appendix One

Research Methodology

The data upon which this study is based were derived from a survey begun in 1979 and completed in late 1981.* Influential men and women from American business, government, and labor were asked to evaluate the three scenarios in Exhibit 8.1 from the following perspectives:

1 Which scenario do they *prefer?*

2 Which scenario do they think would *dominate* the United States in the 1980s?

3 Which scenario would be *most effective* in solving America's problems in the 1980s?

4 What is their rationale in answering question 3?

---

* This approach closely parallels that used by William F. Martin and George Cabot Lodge in "Our Society in 1985—Business May Not Like It," *Harvard Business Review,* November-December 1975. For a more detailed description of my survey design, sampling technique, confidence intervals, and tests for significance differences, see my "Ideology Revisited: America Looks Ahead," *Sloan Management Review,* Winter 1982.

APPENDIX ONE

Participants in the poll included:	Sample	*Response* *Rate*
CEOs—chairmen of the board or those in the president's office. Names were obtained from the *Forbes* "750" listing of American companies.	302	40.2%
Midmanagers—individuals in a variety of line and staff positions, who were sampled while attending advanced management programs at major American universities.	320	37.2%
U.S. senators and congressmen—elected national officials in the Ninety-sixth and Ninety-seventh Congresses.	215	34.1%
State legislators—elected state officials chosen from New York, California, Texas, Ohio, and Hawaii.	201	35.8%
U.S. bureaucrats—federal administrators and civil servants representing several major departments and agencies.	246	31.1%
Union leaders—senior officials in the U.S. labor movement.	181	21.4%

We used various statistical techniques, ranging from standard Chi-square analysis to multidimensional mapping, to give added meaning to the questionnaire results. Finally, follow-up interviews were conducted with over fifty respected leaders on the central problem of improving the relationship between business, government, and labor in the United States.

Appendix Two

Scenario Preferences Uncovered

Respondents' Reasons for Preferring Scenario I

☐ "Government did not make America great—the people did. A return of government to the people is needed to move ahead." (State senator)

☐ "Big government has generally proved ineffective and a disaster with the possible exception of Japan and Singapore, where free market economies are understood and political expediency does not control." (CEO)

☐ "Central planning produces DOE-type screwups on a fantastic scale engineered oftentimes by people who couldn't hold a job in a competitive environment." (Labor leader)

☐ "Within the U.S. economy, free enterprise competition provides the most effective approach for resource allocation and problem solution." (Bureaucrat)

☐ "The Japanese system is more efficient, more rational, and ought to serve as a model for *limited* efforts on critical issues where a true mutuality of interests is apparent. It cannot become the dominant mode in the United States in a mere decade." (CEO)

☐ "Government has consistently proven its ineptitude in planning and operating business enterprise." (Midmanager)

☐ "The free enterprise marketplace built this country and is more capable of pulling it out of its present troubles." (CEO)

☐ "I think that the public will assign increasingly higher value to private sector productivity as they begin to realize the fact that there is a direct trade-off between government-provided services and private sector growth." (U.S. senator)

☐ "What we need is a rebirth in our confidence in the market system in all aspects of business and labor—freedom to succeed, freedom to fail, and freedom to compete." (CEO)

☐ "Government bureaucrats are concerned mainly with police action rather than promotion, and it will take years to weed out this mentality." (State senator)

Respondents' Reasons for Preferring Scenario II

☐ "Government should play a role in bringing business and labor together—as a partner, not as a regulator or 'dictator.' We need cooperation rather than confrontation, with as little government regulation as possible." (State senator)

☐ "With the increased trends in international business, U.S. corporations will need clout of U.S. government in order to effectively continue business worldwide." (Midmanager)

☐ "Monumental problems facing the United States in the 1980s need to be solved *more quickly* than is possible in Scenario I." (CEO)

☐ "Only by adopting methods followed by other countries, but shaped by our own values, can we hope to reassert our legitimate authority." (U.S. senator)

☐ "The enormity and complexity of the problems and relationships, domestic and international, are simply too difficult for the separate, competing players to handle successfully. Some added degree of forced coordination and planning is essential." (Bureaucrat)

☐ "Scenario I is not working, and the bureaucracy and opportunity for fraud in Scenario III are tremendous." (Labor leader)

☐ "The current adversarial relationship between the government regulators and business has led to our current difficulties." (Labor leader)

☐ "A kind of neo-corporatism (that is, a partnership between labor, business, and government) seems to be the wave of the future." (Bureaucrat)

☐ "Business cannot do it alone, nor can labor. Government will have to take the lead. The free enterprise ethic is a 'drag' factor, but the fear of bureaucracy, red tape, and increased taxes is justifiable." (State senator)

☐ "We need to become more effective in reconciling some, if not all, of the objectives of our myriad interest groups in order to increase our ability as a nation to react more quickly and more positively to crises." (CEO)

☐ "I for one can't take much more of the free enterprise, full competition system." (Bureaucrat)

☐ "In today's increasingly complex society, the free market system even when regulated cannot cope." (U.S. senator)

☐ "The U.S. market-oriented, adversary system cannot cope with the international economic situation, which increasingly is being dominated and influenced by rigid, self-serving, nonmarket-oriented policies of foreign governments." (Bureaucrat)

Respondents' Reasons for Preferring Scenario III

☐ "As our institutions grow beyond limits, we leave no other choice. Our economy has no way to go. We can't control it without this kind of planning." (State senator)

☐ "Advanced capitalist societies necessarily are becoming increasingly collectivized. Only a democratic social market system offers a chance of achieving both a democratic and an economically successful society." (Bureaucrat)

☐ "We need a responsibly directed economy structured so as to control the expansionist, exploitive tendencies of big business. This, I feel, can only be orchestrated by a centrally planned economy." (U.S. senator)

☐ "We must give more power to our government, not to those untouchable individuals currently guiding America's industry." (Labor leader)

☐ "Those in control of private enterprise lack everything (values, morals, ethics, incentives, altruism, unselfish interests) required to make decisions protective of and nurturing to an open society capable of accommodating a plurality of group (and individual) interests." (State senator)

☐ "The American 'free enterprise' system has been so abused by monopolistic practices and deception that, unfortunately, it will have to be completely wiped out to allow a new start." (Labor leader)

☐ "Government planners are, at least to some extent, accountable to the electorate. Corporate planners, for all practical purposes, are accountable to no one at all." (State senator)

☐ "The free enterprise system, particularly since the end of World War II, has been neither free nor enterprising. In the last twenty-five years, a society has evolved which can best be described as socialism for the rich and free enterprise for the poor." (Labor leader)

☐ "Corporate criminals . . . are destroying the quality of life for all but themselves." (State senator)

☐ "In today's international trade, business without government support is just like an individual acting against a syndicate." (Midmanager)

☐ "Only Scenario III preserves economic viability, absent war." (Labor leader)

☐ "We do not have enough private capital and incentives to effectively compete against other nations." (Midmanager)

Appendix Three

Significance Difference Testing

Pairwise Chi-square tests of identical distribution of scenarios. (Exhibit values are levels at which a null hypothesis of identical distributions can be rejected. Not significant [*ns*] is measured at p = 0.05 level.)

Exhibit A.1 Tests for *preferred* scenario.

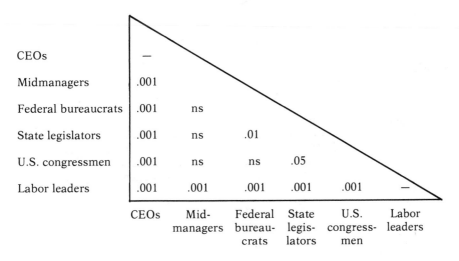

	CEOs	Mid-managers	Federal bureau-crats	State legis-lators	U.S. congress-men	Labor leaders
CEOs	—					
Midmanagers	.001					
Federal bureaucrats	.001	ns				
State legislators	.001	ns	.01			
U.S. congressmen	.001	ns	ns	.05		
Labor leaders	.001	.001	.001	.001	.001	—

Exhibit A.2   Tests for *dominant* scenario.

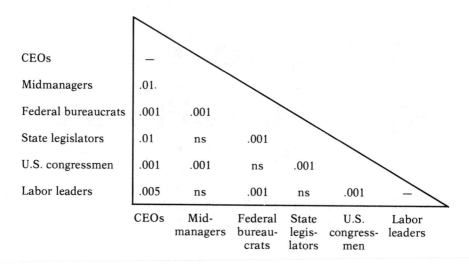

	CEOs	Mid-managers	Federal bureaucrats	State legislators	U.S. congressmen	Labor leaders
CEOs	—					
Midmanagers	.01.					
Federal bureaucrats	.001	.001				
State legislators	.01	ns	.001			
U.S. congressmen	.001	.001	ns	.001		
Labor leaders	.005	ns	.001	ns	.001	—

Exhibit A.3   Tests for *most effective* scenario.

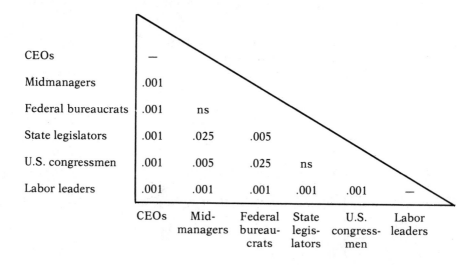

	CEOs	Mid-managers	Federal bureaucrats	State legislators	U.S. congressmen	Labor leaders
CEOs	—					
Midmanagers	.001					
Federal bureaucrats	.001	ns				
State legislators	.001	.025	.005			
U.S. congressmen	.001	.005	.025	ns		
Labor leaders	.001	.001	.001	.001	.001	—

Notes

PREFACE

1. Charles E. Lindblom, *Politics and Markets: The World's Political-Economic Systems* (New York: Basic Books, 1977), p. ix.
2. Father Hesburgh as quoted in George M. Taber, "Capitalism: Is It Working . . . ?" *Time,* April 21, 1980, p. 54.
3. See David A. Heenan and Warren J. Keegan, "The Rise of Third World Multinationals," *Harvard Business Review,* January-February 1979. See also David A. Heenan, "Moscow Goes International," *Harvard Business Review,* May-June 1981, and "Ideology Revisited: America Looks Ahead," *Sloan Management Review,* Winter 1982.

CHAPTER ONE

1. See *America's Competitive Challenge: The Public's Response,* edited by Philip J. Friedman (New York: The Garth Group, Inc., 1980). This document is popularly referred to as "The Garth Report."
2. For a discussion of the evolution of corporate multinationalism, see David A. Heenan and Howard V. Perlmutter, *Multinational Organization Development: A Social Architectural Approach* (Reading, Mass.: Addison-Wesley, 1979), chapter 1.
3. *Ibid.,* pp. 15-16.
4. Jean-Jacques Servan-Schreiber, *The American Challenge* (New York:

Avon Books, 1969), or in its first form, *Le défi américain* (Paris: Editions Denoel, 1967).

5. "An Economic Dream in Peril," *Newsweek*, September 8, 1980, p. 50.
6. For an excellent survey of this phenomenon, see Lawrence G. Franko, "Multinationals: The End of U.S. Dominance," *Harvard Business Review*, November-December 1978, p. 93. See also Raymond Vernon, "Gone Are the Cash Cows of Yesteryear," *Harvard Business Review*, November-December 1980, p. 150.
7. Mark N. Dodosh, "U.S. Firms Dissatisfied with Earnings Abroad as Economics Sputter," *Wall Street Journal*, September 23, 1977, p. 1.
8. "American Investments Abroad: Less Next Year," *Economist*, December 27, 1980, p. 54.
9. Doctoral research by Brent Wilson at the Harvard Business School as quoted in Sanford Rose, "Why the Multinational Tide Is Ebbing," *Fortune*, August 1977, pp. 111-112.
10. Business International (J. J. Boddewyn, main reporter), *International Divestment: A Survey of Corporate Experience* (Geneva and New York, 1976).
11. Jean J. Boddewyn, "Foreign Divestments: Magnitude and Factors," *Journal of International Business Studies*, Spring-Summer 1979, p. 21.
12. Mark N. Dodosh, "Foreign Earnings of U.S. Multinationals Are Down and Should Stay There Awhile," *Wall Street Journal*, February 13, 1981, p. 38.
13. *Ibid.*
14. *Ibid.*
15. James Cook, "A Game Any Number Can Play," *Forbes*, June 25, 1979, p. 51.
16. Boddewyn, p. 26.
17. Vernon, p. 150.
18. Heenan and Perlmutter, pp. 6-7. Similarly, see: "A Need for Choosiness Overseas," *Business Week*, December 31, 1979, p. 134; Ralph E. Winter, "Many Companies See Chancy Times Ahead and Act to Cut Danger," *Wall Street Journal*, March 23, 1981, p. 11; "The Chilling Climate for U.S. Investment," *Business Week*, December 7, 1981, p. 77; "Foreign Markets Turn More Hazardous," *Business Week*, December 28, 1981, p. 129.
19. Study cited in "U.S. Business Is Staying at Home," *World Business Weekly*, June 9, 1980, p. 48.
20. "Heinz Comes Home and Discovers Advertising," *Business Week*, November 14, 1977, p. 224.
21. "ITT Looks to the U.S. Again," *Business Week*, September 27, 1976, p. 104. See also "A Frustrated ITT Quits a Hot Market," *Business Week*, November 2, 1981, p. 67.

22. For other examples of this trend, see: "Boise Cascade: Expansion That Now Sticks Close to Home," *Business Week*, February 19, 1979, p. 54; "Back Home for Farm Equipment," *Business Week*, May 7, 1979, p. 74; Pamela G. Hollie, "Global Builder Coming Home," *New York Times*, November 21, 1979, p. D1; "F. W. Woolworth: A Worldly Retailer Looks Homeward," *World Business Weekly*, June 8, 1981, p. 20; "The Frustrations behind Penney's Cutbacks," *Business Week*, November 16, 1981, p. 60.

23. For more on foreign interest in the U.S. market, see: Malcolm Burn, "The Transatlantic Take-over Spree," *International Management*, May 1979, p. 55; Hugh G. Menzies, "It Pays to Brave the New World," *Fortune*, July 30, 1979, p. 86; "Look Who's Investing in America's Future," *Economist*, October 25, 1980; Arlene Wilson, "Foreign Investment in U.S. Industry," Issue Brief No. IB78091 (Washington, D.C.: The Library of Congress, Congressional Research Service, updated November 18, 1980); Robert Ball, "Europe's U.S. Shopping Spree," *Fortune*, December 1, 1980, p. 82; and Linda Bernier, "Wide Range of Investments Lures Foreigners," *International Herald Tribune*, May 1981, p. 145.

24. "Drang Nach U.S.A.," *Forbes*, July 7, 1980, p. 83. See also "Hoechst's Patient Pursuit of the American Market," *World Business Weekly*, June 22, 1981, p. 22.

25. "The Buying of America," *Newsweek*, November 27, 1978, p. 78. See also "Michelin Goes American," *Business Week*, July 26, 1976, p. 56.

26. Ann Crittenden, "Fast Growth for Foreign Banks," *New York Times*, July 29, 1980, p. D1. See also: "Here Come Foreign Banks Again," *Business Week*, June 26, 1978, p. 78; "The Foreign Grab for America's Banks," *Economist*, August 30, 1980, p. 72; and "Foreign Banks Bid for U.S. Capital," *Business Week*, April 27, 1981, p. 113.

27. "Here Come Foreign Banks Again," *Business Week*, June 26, 1978, p. 78.

28. *Ibid.*, p. 79.

29. Quoted in David Rockefeller, "America's Future: A Question of Strength and Will," *Atlantic Community Quarterly*, vol. 17, no. 1 (Spring, 1979), pp. 14-19.

30. Vernon, p. 151.

31. *Ibid.*

32. Quoted in Joseph C. Harsch, "The Decline of the Superpowers," *Christian Science Monitor*, April 30, 1981, p. 23.

33. "Embattled America: The Struggle for Global Markets," *Saturday Review*, July 7, 1979, p. 18.

34. George Chaplin, "Challenge to U.S.: Catch Up with Japan," *Honolulu Advertiser*, December 17-23, 1981, editorial section.

35. "Revitalizing the U.S. Economy," *Business Week*, June 30, 1980, p. 57.

36. Jesse W. Markham, "The Changing Nature of the Marketplace," in *Business Problems of the Eighties*, edited by Jules Blackman (Indianapolis: Bobbs-Merrill Educational Publishing Co., 1980), p. 104.

37. "The Emerging Consensus: Public Attitudes on America's Ability to Compete in the World," a survey conducted by Cambridge Reports, Inc., for Union Carbide Corp., New York, 1981, pp. 47-49.

38. Ronald Reagan, "Government and Business in the 80's," *Wall Street Journal*, January 9, 1981, p. 18.

39. *Ibid.*

40. Leonard Silk, "A 'Dissensus' on U.S. Policy," *New York Times*, March 25, 1981, p. D2.

41. See Robert C. Merry, "Bill Bradley on the Democrats and the Economy," *Wall Street Journal*, December 10, 1981, p. 22.

42. "Reagan's Policy Gamble Sets the Investment Climate," *Business Week*, December 28, 1981, p. 76.

43. Throughout this book, I will be using the United Nations' definition that "the term 'multinational corporation' . . . in the broad sense [covers] all enterprises which control assets — factories, mines, sales offices and the like — in two or more countries." See *Multinational Corporations in World Development* (New York: United Nations Department of Economic and Social Affairs, U.N. publication no. E.73 II. A. II, 1973), p. 5.

44. "Kearns Speaks at Distinguished Lecture Series," *Hermes*, Fall 1981, p. 75.

45. *Ibid.*

CHAPTER TWO

1. For an explanation of Japan's rapid economic rise, see: Kazushi Ohkawa and Henry Rosovsky, *Japanese Economic Growth* (Palo Alto, Calif.: Stanford University Press, 1973); Hugh Patrick and Henry Rosovsky (eds.), *Asia's New Giant* (Washington, D.C.: Brookings Institution, 1976); Edward F. Denison and W. Chung, *How Japan's Economy Grew So Fast* (Washington, D.C.: Brookings Institution, 1977); Kiyoshi Kojima, *Japan and a New World Economic Order* (Tokyo: Tuttle Press, 1977); Herman Kahn and Thomas Pepper, *The Japanese Challenge: The Success and Failure of Economic Success* (New York: Thomas Y. Crowell, 1980). For a recent contrary viewpoint, see Daniel Yergin, "The Last Locomotive?" *New Republic*, January 20, 1982, p. 22.

2. Ezra F. Vogel, "The Challenge from Japan," an address delivered at the Conference on U.S. Competitiveness, Harvard University, Cambridge, Mass., April 25, 1980, p. 2.

3. Terutomo Ozawa, *Multinationalism, Japanese Style* (Princeton, N.J.: Princeton University Press, 1979), p. 3. See also Yoshi Tsurumi, *The Japanese Are Coming: A Multinational Interaction of Firms and Politics*

(Cambridge, Mass.: Ballinger, 1976), especially chapters 1 and 11; Michael Y. Yoshino, *Japan's Multinational Enterprises* (Cambridge, Mass.: Harvard University Press, 1976); and "Japan's Strategy for the '80s," *Business Week*, December 14, 1981, pp. 39-120.

4. See Mike Tharp, "Computers: Here Comes Fujitsu," *New York Times*, November 16, 1980, p. D1; "Computers: Japan's Bid to Out-design the U.S.," *Business Week*, April 13, 1981, p. 123; "Computers: The Coming Challenge from Japan," *World Business Weekly*, April 20, 1981, p. 32; Steve Lohr, "Japan's Computer Plans Worry U.S. Experts," *New York Times*, September 5, 1981, p. 1; "Japan: The Information Era Beckons," *World Business Weekly*, September 14, 1981, pp. 27-41; and Andrew Pollack, "Japan's Big Lead in Memory Chips," *New York Times*, February 28, 1982, p. 1F.

5. See Urban C. Lehner, "Japan Starting 10-Year Effort to Create Exotic Computer," *Wall Street Journal*, September 25, 1981, p. 29.

6. See Robert B. Reich, "Hi-Tech Rivalry," *New York Times*, November 20, 1981, p. 27. See also: "Japan Plans to Spend $466 Million to Spur Advanced Technologies," *Asian Wall Street Journal*, July 13, 1981, p. 14; "MITI Plans Policy to Govern Japan's Biotechnology Firms," *Asian Wall Street Journal*, July 13, 1981, p. 15; "MITI Has Designs on Robots Tailored to Clothing Firms," *Asian Wall Street Journal*, August 10, 1981, p. 17; Masayoshi Kanabayashi and Hal Lancaster, "Japan's Aggressive Move in Biotechnology Worries U.S. Firms Fearful of Losing Lead," *Wall Street Journal*, October 9, 1981, p. 29; "Japan, Inc., Goes International with High Technology," *Business Week*, December 14, 1981, p. 40; Gene Gregory, Mike Tharp, and James Bartholomew, "Japan's 'Third Revolution,'" *World Press Review*, March 1982, p. 23; and many other articles on this theme.

7. "Japan's Bid to Out-design the U.S.," p. 124.

8. See Gary R. Saxonhouse, "Industrial Restructuring in Japan," *Journal of Japanese Studies*, Summer 1979, pp. 273-320. See also Robert C. Wood, "How Japan Rescues Companies," *New York Times*, September 19, 1979, p. A25.

9. Ozawa, p. 7.

10. See Ozawa, chapter 3. See also Toyomitsu Tamao, "Asia Remains Prime Target," *Asian Finance*, February 15, 1981, p. 71.

11. Ozawa, chapter 3.

12. John Marcom, "Small Firms in Japan Are Stepping Up Investments Abroad," *Wall Street Journal*, October 22, 1980, p. 37.

13. "Japanese Multinationals: Covering the World with Investment," *Business Week*, June 16, 1980, p. 99.

14. *Ibid.*, p. 92.

15. *Ibid.*

16. "The 500 by Country," *Fortune*, August 10, 1981, p. 218.

17. These results were published by the Washington-based Japan Economic Institute. See "Japanese Companies Control 225 U.S. Concerns, Study Says," *New York Times*, May 13, 1981, p. D4.
18. See Peter F. Drucker, "Japan Gets Ready for Tougher Times," *Fortune*, November 3, 1980, pp. 108-111.
19. For an excellent overview of Japanese trading companies, see *The Role of Trading Companies in International Commerce* (Tokyo: Japan External Trade Organization, 1977). See also Yoshi Tsurumi (with Rebecca R. Tsurumi), *Sogoshosa: Engines of Export-Based Growth* (Montreal: Institute for Research on Public Policy, 1980), and Masayoshi Kanabayashi, "Japan's Trading Companies Are Serving as Middlemen between Other Nations," *Asian Wall Street Journal Weekly*, December 22, 1980, p. 4.
20. See Vogel, "The Challenge from Japan," p. 3. See also Steve Lohr, "U.S. Tides Growing for Japan's Traders," *New York Times*, August 10, 1981, p. D4.
21. Thomas B. Lifson, "Japanese Business Strategies for the 1980s," *Japan Report*, May 1, 1980, p. 5.
22. "How Japan Competes," *Dun's Review*, July 1979, p. 69.
23. Urban C. Lehner, "Leader of Japanese Car Unions Supports Building U.S. Plants," *Wall Street Journal*, October 10, 1980, p. 29.
24. Quoted in Masayoshi Kanabayashi, "Getting to the Top Means a Union Stint in Japan's Industry," *Wall Street Journal*, October 14, 1981, p. 33. See also Masayoshi Kanabayashi, "Japan's Unions Try a New Approach," *Wall Street Journal*, February 18, 1982, p. 27.
25. Kanabayashi, "Getting to the Top."
26. James Cook, "A Tiger by the Tail," *Forbes*, April 13, 1981, p. 128.
27. Quoted in John T. Gillespie, "Loyalty to Their Companies Produces Better Workmanship by the Japanese," *Philadelphia Bulletin*, April 12, 1981, p. 1.
28. *Ibid.*
29. Cook, p. 124. See also Steve Lohr, "Japanese Earned Labor Harmony," *New York Times*, February 13, 1982, p. 21.
30. Among the many references on the Japanese worker, see: Michael Y. Yoshino, *Japan's Managerial System: Tradition and Innovation* (Cambridge, Mass.: M.I.T. Press, 1968); Chie Nakane, *Japanese Society* (Berkeley and Los Angeles: University of California Press, 1970); Robert E. Cole, *Japanese Blue Collar: The Changing Tradition* (Berkeley and Los Angeles: University of California Press, 1971); James C. Abegglen, *Management and Worker: The Japanese Solution* (Tokyo: Kodansha International, 1973); Kazuo Okochi, Bernard Karsh, and Solomon B. Levine, *Workers and Employees in Japan* (Princeton, N.J.: Princeton University Press, 1974); Edwin O. Reischauer, *The Japanese* (Cambridge, Mass.: Harvard University Press, 1977); and James D. Hodgson, *The Wondrous Working World of Japan* (Washington, D.C.: American

Enterprise Institute, 1978). See also: Peter F. Drucker, "What We Can Learn from Japanese Management," *Harvard Business Review*, March-April 1971; Robert C. Christopher, "The Psychic Rewards of the Japanese Company," *Asia*, September-October 1978; Terutomo Ozawa, "Japanese World of Work: An Interpretive Survey," *MSU Business Topics*, Spring 1980; Nina Hatvany and Vladimur Pucik, "Japanese Practices and Productivity," *Organizational Dynamics*, Spring 1981; Robert H. Hayes, "Why Japanese Factories Work," *Harvard Business Review*, July-August 1981; and Steve Lohr, "Japan's Enviable Jobless Rate," *New York Times*, December 21, 1981, p. D1.

31. William Ouchi, *Theory Z: How American Business Can Meet the Japanese Challenge* (Reading, Mass.: Addison-Wesley, 1981).

32. Hobart Rowen, "Management in Japan and the U.S.," *Honolulu Advertiser*, April 16, 1981, p. A20.

33. Richard Tanner Pascale and Anthony G. Athos, *The Art of Japanese Management* (New York: Simon and Schuster, 1981).

34. Ozawa, p. 235. Similarly, see Robert Stewart Emerson, "The Rationale of Multinationals," *Asian Finance*, July 15, 1980, p. 60.

35. See Terutomo Ozawa, "Japan's New Resource Diplomacy: Government-Backed Group Investment," *Journal of World Trade Law*, January-February 1980. Note particularly the excellent description of the Asahan project. See also Susumu Awanohara, "Indonesia Turns Its Asahan Ambition into Reality," *Far Eastern Economic Review*, February 5, 1982, p. 87.

36. Douglas R. Sease and Urban C. Lehner, "MITI Guides Japanese Steel Makers, But Not as Much as Americans Think," *Asian Wall Street Journal Weekly*, April 13, 1981, p. 4.

37. "Sony's Akio Morita Opens Distinguished Entrepreneur Lecture Series," *Pacific Basin Quarterly*, Spring-Summer 1980, p. 4.

38. Kenichi Ohmae, "Japan vs. Japan: Only the Strong Survive," *Wall Street Journal*, January 26, 1981, p. 20.

39. *Ibid.*

40. Steve Lohr, "Japan's Challenge to U.S. Is Policies, Not Products," *New York Times*, January 3, 1982, p. E3. See also Robert C. Wood, "Japan's Industrial Vision," *Asia*, January-February 1982, p. 8.

41. Cook, p. 128. For an excellent criticism of Japan's financial markets and risk management system, see Lewis P. Freitas, "Comparative Management Practices: Japan-U.S.," an address to the 5th Tsukuba International Symposium, Tsukuba University, Japan, September 29, 1979.

42. Quoted in James Flanigan, "The Wrong Bottom Line," *Forbes*, May 25, 1981, p. 46.

43. "How Japan Will Finance Its Technology Strategy," *Business Week*, December 14, 1981, p. 50.

44. *Ibid.*, p. 49.

45. *Ibid.*
46. Kent E. Calder, "Japan's 'Minimarket' Government," *Wall Street Journal,* February 13, 1981, p. 16.
47. Sease and Lehner, p. 4.
48. Drucker, "Japan Gets Ready for Tougher Times," p. 114. See also Kenichi Ohmae, "The Long and Short of Japanese Planning," *Wall Street Journal,* January 18, 1982, p. 18.
49. Calder, p. 16.
50. See Jean Ross-Skinner (with Susan Antilla), "Germany: Why It Thrives," *Dun's Review,* December 1979, pp. 106-110. See also Edwin Hartrich, *The Fourth and Richest Reich* (New York: Macmillan, 1980).
51. Guido Goldman, "German Competitiveness," *The Proceedings of the Conference on U.S. Competitiveness; Harvard University, April 25, 1980* (Washington, D.C.: U.S. Government Printing Office, August 1980), p. 21. For an excellent comparative analysis of the economies and business systems of Germany, Japan, and the United States, see Arlene Wilson, "Major Structural Differences between the Economies of the United States, Germany, and Japan: An Overview" (Washington, D.C.: Congressional Research Service, Library of Congress, October 31, 1979).
52. See Alice L. Ahmuty, "Worker Participation in Management Decision-Making in Western Europe: Implications for the United States" (Washington, D.C.: Congressional Research Service Report No. 79-136, April 23, 1979), especially pp. 21-31. See also Wilson, pp. 58-59.
53. See James C. Furlong, *Labor in the Boardroom: The Peaceful Revolution* (Princeton, N.J.: Dow Jones Books, 1972), pp. 37-51.
54. Ross-Skinner, p. 108.
55. John M. Geddes, "Germany Profits by Apprentice System," *Wall Street Journal,* September 15, 1981, p. 27.
56. *Ibid.*
57. Paul Gibson, p. 161.
58. "Germany's Volkswagen Switches to Worker Groups," *Business Europe,* March 13, 1981, p. 84.
59. *Ibid.*
60. Ross-Skinner, p. 108.
61. *Ibid.*
62. John Tagliabue, "German Aircraft Merger Nears," *New York Times,* October 13, 1980, p. D1.
63. Goldman, p. 27. See also Wilson, pp. 10-28.
64. See "West Germany: Competition's Weaker," *World Business Weekly,* July 19, 1980, p. 75, and "Bonn's Antitrust Agency Fights Bigness, But Actual Breakup of Firms Is Doubted," *Wall Street Journal,* August 21, 1979, p. 46.
65. See Wilson, pp. 39-43. See also Philip Thorn and Jean M. Lack (eds.),

Banking and Sources of Finance in the European Community (London: Financial Times, Ltd., Banker Research Unit, 1977).
66. Goldman, p. 27.
67. "West German Banks Defend Their Industrial Shareholdings," *World Business Weekly,* November 3, 1980, p. 49.
68. *Ibid.,* p. 48.
69. John B. Geddes, "West Germany's Economic Slump Seen at an End," *Wall Street Journal,* June 22, 1981, p. 25. See also "Bonn Gives the West German Economy a Miniboost," *World Business Weekly,* April 27, 1981, p. 22; "Encouraging Signs Brighten the Gloom," *World Business Weekly,* June 22, 1981, p. 7; and "An Insider's and an Outsider's Look at West Germany," *World Business Weekly,* July 20, 1981, p. 6.
70. See "West Germany: Still King of the Mountain?" *World Business Weekly,* November 10, 1980; John M. Geddes, "Trouble in Bonn: Ailing Economy and Missiles Peril Stability," *Wall Street Journal,* October 30, 1981, p. 1: and David B. Tinnin, "The Miracle Economy Hits the Skids," *Fortune,* April 20, 1981.
71. See John Vinocur, "Now the 'Swedish Disease' Has Struck West Germany," *New York Times,* November 16, 1980, p. E3.
72. See "Germany: Will Workers Accept a Cut in Real Wages?" *Business Week,* February 9, 1981, p. 34; "German Unions Regional Accord May End Strike," *Wall Street Journal,* April 30, 1981, p. 30; and "German Union Accepts 4.2% Rise in Wages for 1982," *Wall Street Journal,* March 8, 1982, p. 32.
73. "The Sticking-Place: A Survey of the West German Economy," *Economist,* November 8, 1980, p. 5.
74. "Interview with Otto Graf Lambsdorff, *Business Week,* November 24, 1980, p. 27.
75. "Growing German Economic Strains Threaten the West," *Business Week,* November 24, 1980, p. 65.
76. *Ibid.*
77. "Interview with Otto Graf Lambsdorff," p. 72.
78. *Ibid.*
79. *Ibid.*
80. "Growing German Economic Strains Threaten the West," p. 69. See also "A Structural Problem?" *World Business Weekly,* May 11, 1981, p. 31, and "Germany Plagued by High Costs and Technology Gap," *New York Times,* April 13, 1981, p. D1.
81. Goldman, p. 23.
82. *Ibid.,* p. 24. See also: "Away from Oil," *Economist,* November 8, 1980, p. 31; "Germany's Turning Point for Nuclear Energy?" *Business Week,* February 23, 1981, p. 52; and "German Technology Teams Up with Soviet Coal," *Business Week,* November 30, 1981, p. 29.

83. Paul Gibson, "How the Germans Dominate the World Chemical Industry," *Forbes,* October 13, 1980, p. 156.
84. *Ibid.*

CHAPTER THREE

1. James C. Abegglen, "The Impact of the Newly Industrializing Countries on U.S.-Japanese Economic Relations," condensation of opening remarks at the second meeting of the Columbia University East-Asian Institute Toyota Seminar, November 19, 1979. See also Saburo Okita, *The Developing Economies and Japan: Lessons in Growth* (Tokyo: University of Tokyo Press, 1980).
2. Geoffrey Barraclough and Takeo Kuwabara, "The Limits of Westernization," *World Press Review,* March 1981, pp. 24-26.
3. "Doing Business with a Blacker Africa," *Business Week,* February 14, 1977, p. 75.
4. Quoted in Roy Rowan, "There's Also Some Good News about South Korea," *Fortune,* September 1977, p. 174.
5. Nam Duck Woo, "The Development Model of Korea," an address to the Pacific Forum, Seoul, Korea, September 9, 1979.
6. See Jane Seaberry, "U.S. Firms May Face Competition from the World's Budding 'Japans,'" *Honolulu Advertiser,* December 15, 1981, p. E12. See also Louis Kraar, "Make Way for the New Japans," *Fortune,* August 10, 1981, pp. 176-183.
7. Willard D. Sharpe, "The Outlook for Asia's Star Performers," *Asian Wall Street Journal,* February 14, 1980.
8. Jean-Jacques Servan-Schreiber, *The World Challenge: OPEC and the New World Order* (New York: Simon and Schuster, 1981).
9. Quoted in Felix Kessler, "Servan-Schreiber's New Challenge," *Wall Street Journal,* December 26, 1980.
10. Abegglen, p. 1.
11. See Henry Scott Stokes, "Japan Goes Courting in Southeast Asia," *New York Times,* January 11, 1981, p. E5.
12. Derek Davies, "What Asia Wants from America," the Fourth Annual Boyd MacNaughton Memorial Lecture, College of Business Administration, University of Hawaii, Honolulu, November 15, 1979, p. 10.
13. *Ibid.*
14. Robert A. Scalapino, "Emerging Trends in the Pacific-Asian Region," in *ASEAN and a Positive Strategy for Foreign Investment,* edited by Lloyd R. Vasey (Honolulu: University Press of Hawaii, 1978), p. 28.
15. Nam Duck Woo, "Development Model of Korea."
16. *Ibid.*
17. Choong Hoon Park, "Political Change and Economic Future of East Asia," an address to the Pacific Forum, Seoul, Korea, September 8, 1979.

18. Milton Friedman and Rose D. Friedman, *Free to Choose: A Personal Statement* (New York: Harcourt Brace Jovanovich, 1980), p. 34.
19. See "Hong Kong Has Second Thoughts about Laissez-Faire," *World Business Weekly*, October 20, 1980, pp. 49-50; "What Would Milton Friedman Say?" *World Business Weekly*, April 6, 1981, pp. 22-23; and "The Cost of Laissez-Faire in Hong Kong," *Business Week*, January 26, 1981, pp. 48-50.
20. Another indicator is the growing exchange between the colony and its colossal neighbor, the People's Republic of China. Hong Kong obtains nearly half its food, 60 percent of its water, and 30 percent of its fuel from the mainland. These relationships plus a sixfold growth in China trade over the past three years have been aided particularly by the public sector. See Stephen K. Beckner, "Hong Kong's Success," *New York Times*, August 2, 1981, p. 23.
21. "A Shabby Affair," *Asian Wall Street Journal*, July 1, 1980, p. 4 (an editorial).
22. "Hong Kong Has Second Thoughts about Laissez-Faire," p. 48.
23. Other critics are pressing for an abandonment of flexible exchange rates and Hong Kong's adoption of either fixed exchange rates or a bank reserve system. See Yeung Wai-Hong, "Colony's Adjustment Mechanism Needs an Overhaul," *Asian Wall Street Journal*, September 7, 1981, p. 12.
24. See "The Cost of Laissez-Faire in Hong Kong," p. 50.
25. "What Would Milton Friedman Say?" p. 23.
26. "Kahn's Asia," *Insights*, April 1979, p. 7.
27. Quoted in *ASEAN Briefing*, no. 26, September 1980, p. 2. See also Andy McCue, "Singapore Looks to Japan Model to Push Exports," *Asian Wall Street Journal*, February 12, 1980, p. 1, and "Singapore's Success Story," *Time*, January 25, 1982, p. 4.
28. Davies, p. 21. Many, however, do not think that the Confucian ethic theory holds water. Saburo Okita, an economist and former foreign minister of Japan, cites China to prove this point. "If it were all Confucius, China would be the most powerful country in the world," he says. Okita believes that a particular, but not necessarily Confucian, social discipline does lie at the roots of success. Brazil and Mexico are moving up fast economically, he points out, and other Asian countries not much touched by Confucianism—the Philippines, Thailand, and Indonesia—have achieved respectable growth rates. See Will Chapman, "Confucius and Successful Asians," *Honolulu Advertiser*, September 4, 1981, p. A21.
29. Henry Kamm, "Singapore Worries about Its Values as It Seeks Even Greater Prosperity," *New York Times*, September 24, 1980, p. A8.
30. See "A 'Second Industrial Revolution,'" *World Business Weekly*, December 22, 1980, pp. 29-40. See also "Singapore: Cheap Labor Is on the Way Out," *Business Week*, July 16, 1979, p. 48, and "Trying for a

'Second Industrial Revolution,'" *Business Week,* May 25, 1981, p. 75.

31. At the Institute for Information Industries, Taiwan is also undertaking its own industrial restructuring. Four major areas have been singled out for development over the next decade: energy science, material science, information science, and automation. See Robert King, "Taiwan's K.T. Li on Industrial Restructuring," *Asian Wall Street Journal,* October 6, 1981, p. 2.

32. Quoted in Barry Newman, "Can Singapore Become Japanese?" *Wall Street Journal,* January 1, 1981, p. 23. Much the same plea is being made in neighboring Malaysia. See "Malaysia Urges Citizens to Learn Japanese Work Ethics," *Business Standard,* February 23, 1982, p. 3.

33. Kamm, p. A8, and Andy McCue, "Souring of the 'Sweetness' of the Singapore Model," *Asian Wall Street Journal,* January 4, 1980, p. 4.

34. Kamm, p. A8.

35. See Andy McCue, "Asian Nations Are Attracted to Singapore as Industrial Model and Capital Exporter," *Asian Wall Street Journal,* p. 1; "Sri Lanka Copies Singapore," *Insight,* December 1979, pp. 14-15; Michael T. Kaufman, "Sri Lanka Lures Business, Singapore-Style," *New York Times,* November 12, 1980, p. D18; and Marcel Barang, "Singapore and Sri Lanka Begin to Talk Shop," *South,* January 1982, p. 22.

36. McCue, "Asian Nations Are Attracted to Singapore as Industrial Model and Capital Exporter."

37. Alvin Rabushka, "Sri Lanka's Experiment in Economic Liberalism," *Wall Street Journal,* May 18, 1981, p. 27.

38. See Ho Kwon Ping, "Thailand Inc.: An Open Door for the World's Multinationals," *Far Eastern Economic Review,* May 23, 1980, p. 40.

39. *Ibid.,* p. 42.

40. *Ibid.*

41. "Picking Winners with a Japanese Formula," *World Business Weekly,* February 23, 1981, p. 7. This analysis was based on an earlier article written for the *Financial Times* by Paul Krauss, managing director of the Paris office of McKinsey & Co. See also Ann Corbett, "Research Spending Up 14 Percent in France, Science Seen as Key to Economic Growth," *Chronicle of Higher Education,* January 27, 1982, p. 15.

42. "Picking Winners," p. 8.

43. Joseph Kraft, "European View of U.S. Decline," *Honolulu Advertiser,* December 16, 1980, p. A10. See also Michael Crozier, *Le mal américain* (Paris: Librairie Arthème Fayard, 1980 [in French]).

44. Crozier, *Le mal américain.*

45. Alfred Grosser, "Western Europe," *The United States in the 1980s,* edited by Peter Duignan and Alvin Rabushka (Palo Alto, Calif.: Hoover Institute, 1980).

46. *Ibid.*

47. *Ibid.,* p. 731.

CHAPTER FOUR

1. This term was coined by Clyde H. Farnsworth in his "The New Multi-nationals," *New York Times*, March 4, 1979.
2. James Cook, "A Game Any Number Can Play," *Forbes*, June 25, 1979, p. 49.
3. Many of these thoughts were contained in my earlier article co-authored with Professor Warren J. Keegan of New York University. See Heenan and Keegan, "The Rise of Third World Multinationals," *Harvard Business Review*, January-February 1979, pp. 101-109. For further background on the subject of Third-World multinationals, see: *Multinationals from Developing Countries*, edited by Krishna Kumar and Maxwell G. McLeod (Lexington, Mass.: Lexington Books, 1981); K. Balakrishnan, "Indian Joint Ventures Abroad: Geographic and Industry Patterns," *Economic and Political Weekly*, May 29, 1976, pp. M35-48; Donald Lecraw, "Direct Investment by Firms from Less Developed Countries," *Oxford Economic Papers*, vol. 29, no. 3, pp. 442-457; Louis T. Wells, Jr., "Foreign Investment from the Third World: The Experience of Chinese Firms from Hong Kong," *Columbia Journal of World Business*, Spring 1978; Carlos Diaz-Alejandro, "Foreign Investment by Latin Americans," and Louis T. Wells, Jr., "The Internationalization of Firms from the Developing Countries," in *Multinationals from Small Countries*, edited by T. Agmon and C. P. Kindleberger (Cambridge, Mass.: M.I.T. Press, 1977).
4. "The Foreign 500," *Fortune*, August 10, 1981, p. 218.
5. Ray S. Cline, *World Power Assessment 1977: A Calculus of Strategic Drift* (Boulder, Colo.: Westview Press, 1977). His power equation includes such items as geography, population size, economic strength, military capability, and the critical but elusive factors of strategic purpose and national will.
6. "Arab Banks Grow: A Tool to Control World Capital," *Business Week*, October 6, 1980, pp. 69-84.
7. "How Kuwait Finds a Home for a $70 Billion Surplus," *World Business Weekly*, April 6, 1981, p. 32. See also "Kuwait's Drive to Be Oil's 'Eighth Sister,'" *Business Week*, January 11, 1982, p. 36, and Yousse F. M. Ibrahim and R. Mohan, "Kuwait Petroleum May Be Seeking to Buy Gulf Oil's Refining Facilities in Europe," *Wall Street Journal* January 28, 1982, p. 4.
8. Debra Whitefield, "Kuwait, U.S. Firm in Oil Deal," *Los Angeles Times*, April 23, 1981, p. 12.
9. Stephen J. Sansweet, "Santa Fe International Agrees to Takeover by Kuwait for $2.5 Billion, a Record for Mideast Oil Investment," *Wall Street Journal*, October 6, 1981, p. 3.
10. "Korean Contractors Invade the Mideast," *Business Week*, May 29,

1978, p. 34. See also Eduardo Lachica, "U.S. Faces Stiff Competition for Asian Engineering Work," *Asian Wall Street Journal*, January 21, 1982, p. 1.

11. Urban C. Lehner, "South Korea Faces Fight to Retain Place as a Leader in International Construction," *Wall Street Journal*, September 17, 1981, p. 48.

12. "Why Korea Plans U.S. Plant," *New York Times*, May 12, 1981, p. D2.

13. This process of international evolution through initial successes at home underlies the produce life cycle theory of international trade and investment; see Raymond Vernon, "International Investment and International Trade in the Product Life Cycle," *Quarterly Journal of Economics*, May 1966.

14. Louis T. Wells, Jr., "The Internationalization of Firms from Developing Countries," in *Multinationals from Small Countries*, edited by Tamir Agmon and Charles B. Kindleberger (Cambridge, Mass.: M.I.T. Press, 1977), p. 133. See, for instance, David Zielenziger, "Malaysia Woos Korean Investment to Promote Its Industrial Growth," *Asian Wall Street Journal Weekly*, May 11, 1981, p. 3; "Bangkok Bank Expands in Hong Kong," *Asian Finance*, October 15, 1981, p. 30; Andy McCue, "Sime Darby to Use Goodrich Subsidiary as Foothold for Philippine Expansion," *Asian Wall Street Weekly*, August 17, 1981, p. 19; Rafael Pura, "Joint Projects in Thailand, Philippines Get Go-Ahead from ASEAN Minister," *Asian Wall Street Journal*, January 25, 1982, p. 16; and Pura, "Since Darby Plans to Join Philippine Rubber Venture," *Asian Wall Street Journal*, January 25, 1982, p. 22.

15. "Preference for Investors from Small Countries," *Hong Kong Standard*, October 30, 1977, p. 16.

16. See, for example, Everett G. Martin, "Brazil Raises Exports of High Technology to Pace Third World," *Wall Street Journal*, October 6, 1981, and Stephen Haggard, "Taiwan's Experiments with High Technology," *Asian Wall Street Journal*, November 4, 1981.

17. "Arab Banks Grow: A Tool to Control World Capital," *Business Week*, p. 184. See also: "Arab Banking: Is an Encore Possible?" *World Business Weekly*, November 3, 1980, pp. 29-39; "Bypassing Euromarkets," *South*, November 1980, pp. 73-74; and "Saudi Arabia: Where the Very Rich Invest Their Money," *World Business Weekly*, May 25, 1981, p. 29.

18. For information on non-OPEC banks' going abroad, see: "Mexican Banks Look Abroad for Funds," *World Business Weekly*, May 4, 1981, p. 50; Norman Thorpe, "South Korean Banks Are Turning to CDs to Raise Money in Overseas Markets," *Asian Wall Street Journal*, July 6, 1981, p. 4; and "Bank Bumi Grows Tall, Literally," *Asian Finance*, July 15, 1981, pp. 32-33.

19. Robert A. Scalapino, "Emerging Trends in the Pacific-Asian Region," in

ASEAN and a Positive Strategy for Foreign Investment, edited by Lloyd R. Vasey (Honolulu: University Press of Hawaii, 1978), p. 32.

20. Lawrence R. Klein, "America's Competitive Position," an address delivered at the Conference on U.S. Competitiveness, Harvard University, Cambridge, Mass., April 25, 1980.

21. *Ibid.*

22. See Douglas F. Lamont, *Foreign State Enterprises: A Threat to American Business* (New York: Basic Books, 1979). Other selected books on this subject include: Stuart Holland (ed.), *The State as Entrepreneur* (London: Weidenfeld and Nicolson, 1972); Renato Mazzolini, *Government Controlled Enterprises: International Strategic and Policy Decisions* (New York: Wiley, 1979); Bridger M. Mitchell and Paul R. Kleindorfer (eds.), *Regulated Industries and Public Enterprises: European and United States Perspectives* (Lexington, Mass.: Lexington Books, 1980); Raymond Vernon and Yair Aharoni (eds.), *State-Owned Enterprise in the Western Economies* (New York: St. Martin's Press, 1981); William Keyser and Ralph Windle (eds.), *Public Enterprise in the EEC* (Groningen, The Netherlands: Sijthoff & Noordhoff, 1978); and Chalmers Johnson, *Japan's Public Policy Companies* (Washington, D.C.: American Enterprise Institute for Public Policy Research, 1978). There are also several excellent articles: "Public Sector Enterprise," *Economist,* December 30, 1978, p. 37; Kenneth D. Walters and R. Joseph Monsen, "State-Owned Business Abroad: New Competitive Threat," *Harvard Business Review,* March-April 1979, p. 160; Hugh D. Menzies, "U.S. Companies in Unequal Combat," *Fortune,* April 9, 1979, p. 102; John B. Rhodes, "Economic Growth and Government-Owned Multinationals," *Management Review,* February 1979, p. 31; Raymond Vernon, "The International Aspects of State-Owned Enterprises," *Journal of International Business Studies,* Winter 1979, p. 7; Yair Aharoni, "The State Owned Enterprise as a Competitor in International Markets," *Columbia Journal of World Business,* Spring 1980, p. 14; Yves Doz, "Multinational Strategy and Structure in Government Controlled Business," *Columbia Journal of World Business,* Fall 1980, p. 14; Renato Mazzolini, "Government Controlled Enterprises: What's the Difference?" *Columbia Journal of World Business,* Summer 1980 p. 28; Renato Mazzolini, "Government Policies and Government Controlled Enterprises," *Columbia Journal of World Business,* Fall 1980, p. 47; and Malcolm Gillis and Ignatius Peprah, "State-Owned Enterprises in Developing Countries," *Wharton Magazine,* Winter 1981-82, p. 32.

23. Walters and Monsen, p. 162.

24. See Eduardo White, "The International Projection of Firms from Latin American Countries," in *Multinationals from Developing Countries,* edited by Krishna Kumar and Maxwell G. McLeod (Lexington, Mass.: Lexington Books, 1981).

25. Louis Kraar and Stephen Blank, "Malaysia: The High Cost of Affirmative Action," *ASIA*, March-April 1980, p. 9.
26. Guido Goldman, "German Competitiveness," *The Proceedings of the Conference on U.S. Competitiveness*, Harvard University, April 25, 1980 (Washington, D.C.: U.S. Government Printing Office, August 1980), p. 23.
27. Johnson, *Japan's Public Policy Companies*.
28. "The Foreign 500," *Fortune*, p. 208.
29. See "Banco do Brazil's Extraordinary Growth," *World Business Weekly*, July 20, 1981, p. 51.
30. Charles C. Tillinghast, Jr., "Competing against State-Owned Companies," an address presented at the Academy of International Business Annual Meeting, Las Vegas, Nevada, June 17, 1979.
31. Paul Lewis, "National Oil Companies Crowd the 'Seven Sisters,'" *New York Times*, December 30, 1979, p. E2. See also Abderrahamane Megateli, *Investment Policies of National Oil Companies* (New York: Praeger, 1980).
32. See Mazzolini, *Government Controlled Enterprises*.
33. Menzies, "U.S. Companies," p. 106.
34. *Ibid.*, p. 102.
35. *Ibid.*, p. 105. See also "Bernard Lathiere: Airbus' High-Flying Frenchman," *World Business Weekly*, January 12, 1981, p. 21, and Patricia Painton, "For Frere Jacques, Profits Come First," *New York Times*, January 17, 1982, p. V3.
36. Menzies, "U.S. Companies," p. 102. See also "The Tycoons of Socialism," *Newsweek*, March 1, 1982, p. 62.
37. Renato Mazzolini, "European Government-Controlled Enterprises: Explaining International Strategic and Policy Decisions," *Journal of International Business Studies*, Winter 1979, p. 54.
38. Walters and Monsen, p. 169.
39. See my "Moscow Goes International," p. 48.
40. Martha Mautner, "Soviet Influence and Economic Interest in the Pacific," an address delivered at the University of Hawaii, Honolulu, November 6, 1978.
41. See Ann Hughey, "We Are a Soft Target," *Forbes*, September 15, 1980; "How Russian Snares High-Technology Secrets," *Business Week*, April 27, 1980; Harry Rositzke, "Industry and the K.G.B.," *New York Times*, July 22, 1981, p. A23; and "The KGB's Spies in America," *Newsweek*, November 23, 1981, p. 50.
42. See "The Red Tycoons," *Newsweek*, April 17, 1978, p. 84.
43. Hedrick Smith, *The Russians* (New York: Ballantine Books, 1976), p. 11.
44. John A. Miller (ed.), *Toward New World Trade and Investment Policies*, proceedings of a symposium conducted by Sperry Rand Corporation, 1978, p. 100. See also Mark R. Beissinger, "Soviet Factory Directors Go to Business School," *Wall Street Journal*, November 2, 1981, p. 25.

45. Andres Garrigo, "Growth of the Red Multinationals," *Profile,* vol. 14, 1978, p. 9.
46. See Edwin McDowell, "This Tractor Is Russian. It's Stalled," *New York Times,* March 9, 1980, p. F1, and Dan Balz, "Selling Soviet Tractors Is a Tough Row to Hoe," *Sunday Star-Bulletin and Advertiser,* September 6, 1981, p. A18.
47. Raymond Vernon, "Storm over the Multinationals: Problems and Prospects," *Foreign Affairs,* January 1977, p. 254.
48. See Howard V. Perlmutter for the first discussions of the "Emerging East-West Ventures: The Transideological Enterprise," *Columbia Journal of World Business,* September-October 1969.
49. George Feifer, "Russian Disorders," *Harper's,* February 1981, p. 41; "Soviet Imperialism Is in the Red," *Fortune,* July 13, 1981, p. 107; "Soviet Economy Faces Slower Growth in '80s, U.S. Agency Predicts," *Wall Street Journal,* September 4, 1981, p. 19; and "The Stalled Soviet Planning," *Business Week,* October 19, 1981, p. 72.
50. Herbert E. Meyer, "This Communist Internationale Has a Capitalist Accent," *Fortune,* February 1977, p. 148.
51. Cook, "A Game Any Number Can Play," p. 55.

CHAPTER FIVE

1. Senator Lloyd M. Bentsen, "Letter to the Editor," *Harvard Business Review,* November-December 1980, p. 212.
2. Robert Keatley, "Turning Malaysians into Fledgling Capitalists," *Wall Street Journal,* February 2, 1981, p. 17.
3. Chalmers Johnson, *Japan's Public Policy Companies* (Washington, D.C.: American Enterprise Institute for Public Policy Research, 1978).
4. David A. Heenan and Warren J. Keegan, "The Rise of Third World Multinationals," *Harvard Business Review,* January-February 1979, p. 101.
5. Raphall Pura, "Malaysian Times Set Up International Trading Concern," *Asian Wall Street Journal,* January 4, 1982, p. 3.
6. Andy McCue, "Singapore Looks to Japan Model to Push Exports," *Asian Wall Street Journal,* February 12, 1980, p. 1.
7. *Ibid.*
8. This point is made in Yoshi Tsurumi (with Rebecca R. Tsurumi), *Sogoshosa: Engines of Export-Based Growth* (Montreal: Institute for Research on Public Policy, 1980).
9. Howard V. Perlmutter, "The Multinational Firm and the Future," *Annals of the American Academy of Political and Social Science,* September 1972, p. 141. See also Renato Mazzolini, *European Transnational Concentration* (New York: McGraw-Hill, 1974), and Francis Fishwick and Michael Allen, *Multinational Companies and Economic*

Concentration in Europe (New York: Praeger, Holt, Rinehart and Winston/CBS, 1981).

10. David B. Tinnin, "Volvo Grabs for Growth—Again," *Fortune,* December 29, 1980, p. 54.

11. For a discussion of some managerial implications, see David A. Heenan and Howard V. Perlmutter, *Multinational Organization Development: A Social Architectural Approach* (Reading, Mass.: Addison-Wesley, 1979), chapter 5. Renato Mazzolini discusses the negative aspects of building corporate coalitions. See his "Obstacle Course for European Transnational Consolidations," *Columbia Journal of World Business,* Spring 1973, p. 53. Some disappointments are described in "The Romance Is Over for Dunlop and Pirelli," *Business Week,* May 11, 1981, p. 46; "Why Transnational Marriages Tend to End in Tears," *World Business Weekly,* June 1, 1981, p. 6; and Peter Norman, "Death Throes of the Transnational Experiment," *The Times,* May 11, 1981, p. 21. Also, see an interview with Peter F. Drucker on this subject in "Why Some Mergers Work and Many More Don't," *Forbes,* January 18, 1982, p. 34.

12. Peter F. Drucker, *Managing in Turbulent Times* (New York: Harper & Row, 1980), p. 97.

13. Mats Halvarsson, "The Business Marriage Bureau," *Profile,* vol. 23, 1981, p. 9. See also "The Common Market's Rush into Cartels," *Business Week,* March 27, 1978, p. 107.

14. Halvarsson, p. 10.

15. *Ibid.*

16. "European Strategies to Fight IBM," *Business Week,* December 17, 1979, p. 73. See also "The EC Goes after IBM," *World Business Weekly,* January 26, 1981, p. 7.

17. "European Strategies to Fight IBM," p. 73.

18. *Ibid.*

19. Marina v. N. Whitman, "Auto Industry's New Challenges," *New York Times,* September 3, 1980, p. D2. In a speech delivered at Washington University, Dr. Whitman adds: "[W]e are going to see—indeed, we are already seeing—a significant restructuring and rationalization in the global automobile industry. Over the next decade, there will be mergers of companies and joint production agreements of various kinds, such as those already being discussed or underway between American Motors and Renault, Chrysler and Peugeot, Nissan and Alfa Romeo, British Leyland and Honda, and Volkswagen and Nissan." See "The Global Economy in the 1980s," The Fourth Annual David R. Calhoun, Jr., Memorial Lecture, an address delivered at Washington University, St. Louis, April 7, 1981, p. 17.

20. Mike Knepper, "Le Boss," *Car and Driver,* September 18, 1980, p. 22.

21. Reginald A. Stuart, "Car Makers Forging New Alliances," *New York Times International Economic Survey,* February 3, 1980, p. 17.

22. See: Tracy Dahlby, "A Headlong Drive for Exports in a Race against the Clock," *Far Eastern Economic Review,* February 15, 1980, p. 40; Louis Kraar, "Japan's Automakers Shift Strategies," *Fortune,* August 11, 1980, p. 106; "Auto Industry Outlook as Cooperation Builds with Japanese Firms," *Business Asia,* October 10, 1980, p. 321; and Henry Scott Stokes, "Japan's Amazing Auto Machine," *New York Times,* January 18, 1981, p. F1. Also of considerable importance at the national level is the merger between Toyota Motor Co., Japan's largest carmaker, and Toyota Motor Sales Co., an independent company that serves as its marketing arm. See Akihiro Sato, "Toyota and Its Sales Arm Plan Merger to be More Responsible to Market Needs," *Wall Street Journal,* January 26, 1982, p. 26, and "Toyota Merger May Pose New Threat to Foreign Car Makers," *Asian Wall Street Journal Weekly,* February 8, 1982, p. 6.

23. See Edwin O. Reischauer, "The Japanese Way," *Across the Board,* December 1977, especially pp. 35-37.

24. Dahlby, p. 44.

25. See "How Japan Competes," *Dun's Review,* July 1979, pp. 65-87. See also "Japan's Strategy for the '80s," *Business Week,* December 14, 1981, pp. 39-120.

26. See "Renault Joins Forces with Volvo to Become a 'World Car' Producer," *World Business Weekly,* December 31, 1979, p. 5; Robert Ball, "Renault Takes Its Hit Show on the Road," *Fortune,* May 4, 1981, p. 275; and Allan Sloan, "Here Comes the Franglaismobile," *Forbes,* September 28, 1981, p. 42.

27. "Renault Joins Forces with Volvo to Become a 'World Car' Producer," p. 5.

28. "Hitachi Sets Own Color TV Plan in U.S. after Joint Venture with GE Is Blocked," *Wall Street Journal,* April 25, 1979, p. 6. Subsequently, both companies formed a laser manufacturing and marketing tie-up in worldwide robotics. See "Hitachi Robots Will Give GE a Helping Hand," *Business Week,* August 24, 1981, p. 45.

29. Steve Lohr, "Overhauling America's Business Management," *New York Times Magazine,* January 4, 1981, p. 15.

30. "Study: U.S. Productivity to Slip More," *Honolulu Advertiser,* May 30, 1981, p. A12.

31. Arnold R. Deutsh, "How to Discourage Job Hopping," *New York Times,* March 15, 1981, p. F3.

32. *Ibid.*

33. See Sharon Frederick, "Why John and Mary Won't Work," *Inc.,* April 1981, p. 73.

34. "Americans Failing to Reach Potential in Work, Poll Says," *Miami Herald,* April 21, 1981, p. B5.

35. Cited in Frederick, p. 73.

36. "Americans Failing to Reach Potential in Work, Poll Says," p. B5.

37. James Flanigan, "The Wrong Bottom Line," *Forbes*, May 25, 1981, p. 46.
38. See William G. Ouchi, *Theory Z: How American Business Can Meet the Japanese Challenge* (Reading, Mass.: Addison-Wesley, 1981).
39. Robert Mamis, "Theory Z: Making American Business More Productive," *Inc.*, April 1981, p. 130.
40. Regina Ordoñez, "The ASEAN Manager and Implications for Western Management Behavior," an address presented at the East-West Center Culture Learning Institute, Honolulu, Hawaii, Fall 1981.
41. Sam Jameson and John F. Lawrence, "Morita: U.S. Lacking Good Management," *Honolulu Advertiser*, November 1, 1980.
42. *Ibid.*
43. Robert H. Hayes and William J. Abernathy, "Managing Our Way to Economic Decline," *Harvard Business Review*, July-August 1980, p. 68.
44. John Kenneth Galbraith, "Corporate Senility," *Washington Post*, February 11, 1981, p. A19.
45. Steve Lohr, p. 43.
46. *Ibid.* See also Arch Patton, "Industry's Misguided Shift to Staff Jobs," *Business Week*, April 5, 1982, p. 12.
47. "Putting Production First," an interview with Dean Richard West, January 26, 1982.
48. Frederick W. Taylor, *Principles and Methods of Scientific Management* (New York: Harper & Brothers, 1911).
49. Robert Frosch, "Engineers' Role in Industry," *New York Times*, February 20, 1981, p. D2.
50. Donald S. MacNaughton, "The Act of Management," an address at the Graduate School of Business, Rutgers University, New Brunswick, N.J., March 1980, p. 7.
51. *Ibid.*
52. Mary Rowland, "All Business Schools Are Slipping," *Philadelphia Bulletin*, May 26, 1981, p. B3. See also Liz Roman Gallese, "Business Schools Try Harder to Find Jobs for More Demanding, Diverse Graduates, *Wall Street Journal*, April 1, 1982, p. 48.
53. Steve Lohr, p. 58.
54. Rowland, p. B3. For a discussion of the Japanese perspective of U.S. business schools, see "Japan Gives the B Schools an A—for Contacts," *Business Week*, October 19, 1981, p. 132.
55. Steve Lohr, p. 58. See also Walter Kiechel III, "Harvard Business School Restudies Itself," *Fortune*, June 18, 1979, p. 48.
56. Lloyd M. Bentsen, "America's Challenge," an address delivered to the Conference on U.S. Competitiveness, Harvard University, Cambridge, Mass., April 25, 1980 (Washington, D.C.: U.S. Government Printing Office, 1980), p. 88.
57. Frank A. Weil, "Management's Drag on Productivity," *Business Week*, December 3, 1979, p. 14.

58. Flanigan, p. 42. See also Peter F. Drucker, "Behind Japan's Success," *Harvard Business Review,* January-February 1981, p. 83.

59. Harold M. Williams, "The Economy and the Future—The Tyranny of the Short-Run," an address delivered to the Commonwealth Club, San Francisco, Calif., November 21, 1980, pp. 13-14. Contrast this with Japan's propensity for the long run. See Steven C. Wheelwright, "Japan —Where Operations Really Are Strategic," *Harvard Business Review,* July-August 1981, p. 67.

60. See "Letter from the Editor," *Harvard Business Review,* November-December 1980, p. 1.

61. Thomas H. Naylor, "Management Is Drowning in Numbers," *Business Week,* April 6, 1981, p. 16.

62. Alfred Rappaport, "A Fatal Fascination with the Short Run," *Business Week,* May 4, 1981, p. 22.

CHAPTER SIX

1. Edward Mason, "Interests, Ideologies and the Problem of Stability and Growth," *American Economic Review,* vol. 53, 1963, pp. 1-18.

2. *Ibid.*

3. George P. Schultz, "The Abrasive Interface," in J. Dunlop *et al.,* "Business and Public Policy," *Harvard Business Review,* November-December 1979, p. 85.

4. Robert Green McCloskey, *American Conservatism in the Age of Enterprise 1865-1910* (New York: Harper & Row, 1951), pp. 23-24. See also Samuel P. Huntington, *American Politics: The Promise of Disharmony* (Cambridge, Mass.: The Belnap Press of Harvard University Press, 1981).

5. For a lucid discussion of the historical underpinnings of U.S. government-business distrust, see David Vogel, "Why Businessmen Distrust Their State," *British Journal of Political Science,* January 1978, pp. 45-78.

6. *Ibid.,* p. 57.

7. Ezra F. Vogel, *Japan as Number One: Lessons for America* (Cambridge, Mass.: Harvard University Press, 1979), p. 252.

8. D. Vogel, p. 57.

9. George Cabot Lodge, *The New American Ideology* (New York: Knopf, 1975), p. 74.

10. D. Vogel, p. 64.

11. *Ibid.,* p. 59.

12. Alexis de Tocqueville, *Democracy in America,* vol. 2 (New York: Schocken Books, 1961), p. 298.

13. Henry Steele Commager, *The American Mind* (New Haven, Conn.: Yale University Press, ˙1950). Cited also in James Reston, "Where Are We Going?" *New York Times,* August 3, 1980, p. E19.

14. Interview.
15. E. Vogel, p. 55.
16. Detlav F. Vagts, "The United States and Its Multinationals: Protection and Control," *Harvard International Law Journal,* Spring 1979, p. 237.
17. D. Vogel, p. 67.
18. Arthur Okun, "Capitalism and Democracy: Some Unifying Principles," *Columbia Journal of World Business,* Winter 1978, p. 23.
19. Vagts, pp. 236-237.
20. E. Vogel, p. 54.
21. Lodge, p. 148.
22. Peter F. Drucker, *Managing in Turbulent Times* (New York: Harper & Row, 1980), p. 169.
23. George M. Taber, "Capitalism: Is It Working . . . ?" *Time,* April 21, 1980, p. 40.
24. George Gilder, *Wealth and Poverty* (New York: Basic Books, 1981), p. 24.
25. David Vogel, "The Political and Economic Impact of Current Criticisms of Business," *California Management Review,* Winter 1975, p. 90.
26. Cited in Taber, p. 46.
27. *Ibid.,* p. 55.
28. Norman Podohertz, "The New Defenders of Capitalism," *Harvard Business Review,* March-April 1981, p. 99.
29. *Ibid.,* p. 45.
30. Cited in Podohertz, p. 109. See also Irving Kristol, *Two Cheers for Capitalism* (New York: Basic Books, 1978).
31. *Ibid.*
32. Cited in Arthur Schlesinger, Jr., "Is Liberalism Dead?" *New York Times Magazine,* March 30, 1980, pp. 70-71.
33. *Ibid.*
34. *Ibid.*

CHAPTER SEVEN

1. Quoted by Leonard Curry, "U.S. Must Promote American Businesses Abroad, Javits Says," *Washington Star,* June 26, 1979, pp. 6-7.
2. Detlav F. Vagts, "The United States and Its Multinationals: Protection and Control," *Harvard International Law Journal,* Spring 1979, p. 239.
3. David Vogel, "Why Businessmen Distrust Their State: The Political Consciousness of American Corporate Executives," *British Journal of Political Science,* January 1978, p. 78.
4. Richard D. Robinson, *International Business Policy* (New York: Holt, Rinehart and Winston, 1964), p. 24. For an update, see Robinson, "Background Concepts and Philosophy of International Business from

World War II to the Present," *Journal of International Business Studies,* Spring-Summer 1981, pp. 13-21.

5. 49 Congressional Record 9 (1912).
6. W. A. Williams, *The Tragedy of American Diplomacy* (Cleveland: World Publishing Co., 1959), pp. 34-35. See also William G. Roy, "The Process of Bureaucratization in the U.S. State Department and the Vesting of Economic Interests, 1886-1905," *Administrative Science Quarterly,* vol. 26, 1981, pp. 419-433.
7. Robinson, *International Business Policy,* p. 34.
8. *Ibid,* p. 35.
9. J. Gilles Wetter, "Diplomatic Assistance to Private Investment: A Study of the Theory and Practice of the United States during the Twentieth Century," *University of Chicago Law Review,* vol. 29, 1962, p. 284.
10. Wetter, p. 283.
11. "The Decline of U.S Power," *Business Week,* March 12, 1979, p. 76.
12. *Ibid.*
13. Wetter, p. 286.
14. William E. Simon, *The Deteriorating Role of U.S. Business in the World* (Dallas: Center for International Business, 1980).
15. Peter Gabriel, "Management of Public Interests by the Multinational Corporation," *Journal of World Trade Law,* January-February 1977, p. 19.
16. *Ibid.*
17. David A. Heenan and Howard V. Perlmutter, *Multinational Organization Development: A Social Architectural Approach* (Reading, Mass.: Addison-Wesley, 1979), p. 6. See, too, many other sources on this subject. For example: Raymond Vernon, *Sovereignty at Bay* (New York: Basic Books, 1971), and his later *Storm over the Multinationals: The Real Issues* (Cambridge, Mass.: Harvard University Press, 1977); Richard J. Barnet and Ronald E. Müller, *Global Reach: The Power of the Multinational Corporations* (New York: Simon and Schuster, 1974); C. Fred Bergsten, Thomas Horst, and Theodore H. Moran, *American Multinationals and American Interests* (Washington, D.C.: Brookings Institution, 1978).
18. Thomas N. Gladwin and Ingo Walter, *Multinationals under Fire* (New York: Wiley, 1980).
19. Nancy Needham Wardell, "The Corporation," *Daedalus,* Winter 1978, pp. 97-110.
20. Peter L. Berger, "New Attack on the Legitimacy of Business," *Harvard Business Review,* September-October 1981, p. 89.
21. Heenan and Perlmutter, pp. 12-13.
22. Jethro K. Lieberman, *The Litigious Society* (New York: Basic Books, 1981).

23. Quoted in Robert B. Reich, "Regulation by Confrontation on Negotiation," *Harvard Business Review*, May-June 1981, pp. 82-92.
24. *Ibid.*
25. William E. Simon, "Free Enterprise and the Pols," *Wall Street Journal*, January 10, 1980, p. 22.
26. George A. Steiner, "Can Business Service Its New Environment?" *Business*, January-February 1980, p. 15.
27. Murray Weidenbaum, *The Future of Business Regulation* (New York: Amacom, 1979).
28. A confidential report prepared for the Asian Pacific Chamber of Commerce by A. J. Kearney, Inc., Tokyo, Japan, 1980.
29. "Senate Panel Rejects Plan to Soften Ban on Foreign Payoffs, Ducks Other Issues," *Wall Street Journal*, September 17, 1981, p. 5.
30. Karen W. Arenson, "Gains for Americans Who Work Abroad," *New York Times*, August 28, 1981, p. 1.
31. "The Decline of U.S. Power," p. 96.
32. Wardell, p. 107.
33. George P. Schultz, "Light Switch Diplomacy," *Business Week*, May 25, 1979, p. 24.
34. Cited in Judith Miller, "Dresser Jousts with U.S.," *New York Times*, July 21, 1978, p. D1.
35. "A Retreat on Soviet Trade," *Business Week*, August 10, 1981, p. 97.
36. "A Test Case on East-West Trade," *Business Week*, September 7, 1981, p. 111. See also "Trading with the Kremlin: What Rules Should Apply?" *New York Times*, July 19, 1981, pp. 4-5.
37. "The Decline of U.S Power," p. 76.

CHAPTER EIGHT

1. Ronald Reagan, "Government and Business in the '80s," *Wall Street Journal*, January 9, 1981, p. 18.
2. Ezra F. Vogel, "Guided Free Enterprise in Japan," *Harvard Business Review*, May-June 1978.
3. For more on this subject, see George Cabot Lodge, *The New American Ideology* (New York: Knopf, 1976).
4. William H. Batten, "The United States in a Competitive World: Americans Are Concerned," an address to the Conference on U.S. Competitiveness, Harvard University, Cambridge, Mass., April 25, 1980.
5. James O'Toole, "What's Ahead for the Business-Government Relationship," *Harvard Business Review*, March-April 1979, p. 103.
6. *Ibid.*, p. 99.
7. Peter F. Drucker, *Managing in Turbulent Times* (New York: Harper & Row, 1980), chapter 4.
8. Max Ways, "The Corporation and Society," The Institute for Constructive Capitalism, University of Texas at Austin, 1979, p. 3.

9. Cecil Heftel, "Decline in U.S. Productivity," *Honolulu Star Bulletin,* May 9, 1980, p. A20.

CHAPTER NINE

1. "Reindustrialization, What?" *New York Times,* June 2, 1980, p. A16.
2. Robert A. Leone and Stephen P. Bradley, "Toward an Effective Industrial Policy," *Harvard Business Review,* November-December 1981, p. 92. See also Paul W. McCracken, "A United States 'Industrial Policy,'" *Wall Street Journal,* January 12, 1981, p. 20; George Eads, "The Government and Industrial Policy: Picking Winners and Killing Dogs," *Wharton Magazine,* Fall 1981, pp. 33-41; and Robert B. Reich, "Why the U.S. Needs an Industrial Policy," *Harvard Business Review,* January-February 1982, p. 74.
3. See Philip J. Friedman (ed.), *America's Competitive Challenge: The Public's Response* (New York: The Garth Group, Inc., 1980).
4. Thornton Bradshaw, "My Case for National Planning," *Fortune,* February 1977, p. 104.
5. *Ibid.*
6. John F. Cunningham, "Readers Report," *Business Week,* August 11, 1980, p. 7.
7. *Ibid.*
8. "How Close Is a Planned Economy," *Wharton Magazine,* Fall 1977, p. 32.
9. *Ibid.*
10. Peter F. Drucker, *Managing in Turbulent Times* (New York: Harper & Row, 1980), especially pp. 143-150.
11. Amitai Etzioni, "Why U.S. Industry Needs Help," *Forbes,* August 18, 1980, p. 121. See also his "Reindustrialization: View from the Source," *New York Times,* June 29, 1980, p. F6; "Rebuilding Our Economic Foundations," *Business Week,* August 25, 1980, p. 16; and "Choose America Must —," *Across the Board,* October 1980, pp. 42-49.
12. Among the many criticisms of this approach are: "Why Reward Failure in Detroit," *New York Times,* March 1981, p. A22; "R.I.P.," *Wall Street Journal,* August 22, 1980, p. 20; James A. Rousmaniere, Jr., "Carter's New Auto Policy Produces Some Cheers and Some Skepticism," *Los Angeles Times,* July 15, 1980, p. 4, part 4; Hobart Rowen, "Carter's Stuck on His Own Band-Aids," *Sunday Star-Bulletin and Advertiser* (Honolulu), July 13, 1980, p. B13; "Motown and MITI," *Wall Street Journal,* July 10, 1980, p. 18; and Jerry Flint, "You Read It Here First," *Forbes,* June 23, 1980, p. 35.
13. Rowen, "Carter's Stuck on His Own Band-Aids." See also "A Leaf out of Europe's Industrial Book," *Economist,* August 9, 1980, pp. 21-22.
14. "Curing Ailing Industries," *Time,* July 14, 1980, p. 42.
15. Bruce R. Scott, an address delivered at the Conference on U.S. Compe-

titiveness, Harvard University, Cambridge, Mass., April 25-26, 1980. See also his "How Practical Is National Economic Planning?" *Harvard Business Review*, March-April 1978, pp. 137-145.

16. Interview, Cambridge, Mass., April 25, 1980.

17. Iqbal Mathur and Subhash Jain, "The Financial Manager and National Economic Planning," *University of Michigan Business Review*, November 1979, pp. 7-12.

18. *Ibid.*, p. 12.

19. Paul W. McCracken, "The Fading American Importance," *Wall Street Journal*, June 17, 1980, p. 22.

20. Quoted in Christoper Conte, "The U.S. Message for Ailing Industries," *Wall Street Journal*, April 6, 1981, p. 22.

21. Mark Shepherd, Jr., an address delivered at the Conference on U.S. Competitiveness, Harvard University, Cambridge, Mass., April 25-26, 1980.

22. *Ibid.*

23. "Reindustrialization, What?" *New York Times*, June 2, 1980, p. A16.

24. John E. Fleming, "A Possible Future of Government-Corporate Relations," *Business Horizons*, December 1979, pp. 43-47.

25. *Ibid.*, p. 46.

26. Leone and Bradley argue that, in the interim, public policy need not stand still. Their recommendations are contained in "Toward an Effective Industrial Policy," pp. 96-97.

27. Sidney Harman, "For an 'America, Inc.,'" *Newsweek*, March 12, 1979, p. 21.

28. See Karlyn Barker, "SES Executives Find Many Thorns, Few Roses," *Washington Post*, October 15, 1981, pp. 1-2. See also Richard Cavanagh, "Why the Government Isn't Businesslike," *Wall Street Journal*, July 27, 1981, p. 18. For an in-depth analysis, see Laurence E. Lynn, Jr., *Managing the Public's Business: The Job of the Government Executive* (New York: Basic Books, 1980).

29. Ezra F. Vogel, *Japan as Number One: Lessons for America* (Cambridge, Mass.: Harvard University Press, 1979), pp. 233-234.

30. "The Corporate Chiefs' New Class," *Time*, April 14, 1980, p. 87. See also Art Pine, "At the Top of Industry, a Look Back," *Philadelphia Inquirer*, February 11, 1981, p. D13, and J. Dunlop *et al.*, "Business and Public Policy," *Harvard Business Review*, November-December 1979, pp. 98-102.

31. For a commentary on the likelihood of *closer* cooperation between these two outstanding schools, see Clyde H. Farnsworth, "Harvard Unit Widens Study," *New York Times*, December 7, 1981, p. 24.

32. Cited in Harlan Cleveland, "The Public Executive: A Sense of Responsibility for the Whole," *Public Management*, December 1980, p. 3.

33. William F. Martin and George Cabot Lodge, "Our Society in 1985—

Business May Not Like It," *Harvard Business Review*, November-December 1975.

34. The Hodge study is cited in "'Me' on Campus," *Forbes*, May 25, 1981, p. 11. Robert S. McElvaine also concludes: "An insidious selfishnes gnaws at the cooperative aspects of our national life. . . . The evidence that the major—although certainly not the exclusive—thrust of the current generation is toward extreme egotistical individualism is abundant." See his "The Truly Greedy Set Today's Moral Tone" and *Down and Out: Letters from the 'Forgotten Man' in the Great Depression* (Chapel Hill: University of North Carolina Press, 1982).

35. H. Justin Davidson, "The Top of the World Is Flat," *Harvard Business Review*, March-April 1977, p. 95.

36. Christopher Lasch, *The Culture of Narcissism* (New York: Norton, 1978).

37. Marvin Harris, *Culture Materialism: The Struggle for a Science of Culture* (New York: Random House, 1979).

38. Daniel Bell, *The Cultural Contradictions of Capitalism* (New York: Basic Books, 1976).

39. See Michael Novak, *The American Vision: An Essay on the Future of Democratic Capitalism* (Washington, D.C.: American Enterprise Institute for Public Policy Research, 1979). See also Jane S. Shaw (ed.), "Private Enterprise Marches Forward, Then Falls Back," *Business Week*, April 13, 1981, p. 13.

40. Roger B. Smith, "Toward a New Partnership," an address delivered at the Conference on Business and Government, the Lyndon Baines Johnson Library, Austin, Texas, March 2, 1979, p. 2.

41. *Ibid.*

42. Daniel Seligman, "The Trouble with Partnership," *Fortune*, August 11, 1980, p. 97.

CHAPTER TEN

1. Quoted in George M. Taber, "Capitalism: Is It Working . . . ?" *Time*, April 21, 1980, p. 44.

2. James D. Hodgson, interview, Honolulu, Hawaii, May 8, 1980.

3. "Electronics Research Projects," *New York Times*, December 26, 1981, p. 19.

4. Douglas R. Sease and Robert L. Simison, "GM to Cut Prices of Cars if UAW Grants Savings," *Wall Street Journal*, January 13, 1982, p. 3.

5. "A Dose of Self-Help in Detroit," *New York Times*, January 14, 1982, p. A22.

6. Ambassador Hodgson suggests these contradictions may lessen over time as we integrate more fully the cultural lessons from Japan to American society. "Useful elements of Asian/Pacific culture will grad-

ually be woven into the fabric of our society," he argues. "America will experience still another massive cultural transfusion. The values and virtues of traditional Asian thought will become better known, appreciated and understood." James Day Hodgson, "The Pacific Basin: Its Role in America's Future," The Sixth Annual Boyd MacNaughton Memorial Lecture, College of Business Administration, University of Hawaii, Honolulu, November 2, 1981, p. 12.

7. "Report on the POQ Readership Survey," *Public Opinion Quarterly,* Spring 1980, p. 12.

8. Lester C. Thurow, *The Zero-Sum Society* (New York: Basic Books, 1980).

9. Lewis Foy, former chairman of Bethlehem Steel Corp., quoted in "Embattled America," *Saturday Review,* June 7, 1979, p. 32.

10. H. Justin Davidson, "The Top of the World Is Flat," *Harvard Business Review,* March-April 1977, p. 95. See also Sidney Blumenthal, "Whose Side Is Business On, Anyway?" *New York Times Magazine,* October 25, 1981.

11. Art Pine, "At the Top of Industry, a Look Back," *Philadelphia Inquirer,* February 11, 1981, p. D13.

12. Steven N. Brenner, "Business and Politics—An Update," *Harvard Business Review,* November-December 1979, p. 162. For an excellent discussion, see J. Ronald Fox, "Breaking the Regulatory Deadlock," *Harvard Business Review,* September-October 1981, pp. 97-105.

13. Richard G. Darman, "Government-Business Relations—And the Prospects for U.S. Competitiveness," a paper presented to the Conference on U.S. Competitiveness, Harvard University, Cambridge, Mass., April 25, 1980, p. 20.

14. Cited in Lillian W. Kay (ed.), *The Future Role of Business in Society,* a Special Report of Conference Proceedings (New York: The Conference Board, 1977), p. 46.

15. Leslie E. Grayson, interview. See also his "Executive Profile of the Top Officers of the Largest Oil Companies in the United States: 1950-1980" (with Allison Spencer) (Charlottesville, Va.: Energy Policies Center, University of Virginia, 1981).

16. "A Conversation with Roy L. Ash," *Organizational Dynamics,* Autumn 1979, p. 65.

17. Peter F. Drucker, *Managing in Turbulent Times* (New York: Harper & Row, 1980), p. 221. See also William H. Newman (ed.), *Managers for the Year 2000* (Englewood Cliffs, N.J.: Prentice-Hall, 1980).

18. "A Conversation with Roy L. Ash," p. 65.

19. See Howard V. Perlmutter and David A. Heenan, "How Multinational Should Your Top Managers Be?" *Harvard Business Review,* November-December 1974, p. 132. See also David A. Heenan and Howard V.

Perlmutter, *Multinational Organization Development: A Social Architectural Approach* (Reading, Mass.: Addison-Wesley, 1979), chapter 6.

20. Robert B. Reich, "Regulation by Confrontation or Negotiation?" *Harvard Business Review*, May-June 1981, p. 93.

21. See Kim McQuaid, "The Roundtable: Getting Results in Washington," *Harvard Business Review*, May-June 1981, pp. 114-123.

22. Steven V. Roberts, "Democrats: An Aye for Business," *New York Times*, March 1, 1981, pp. 4-5.

23. Paul Uselding, "Letters to the Editor," *Harvard Business Review*, July-August 1981, p. 197. For another negative perspective, see Paul W. MacAvoy, "The Business Lobby's Wrong Business," *New York Times*, December 20, 1981, p. F3.

24. See Judson Bemis and John A. Cairns, "In Minnesota, Business Is Part of the Solution," *Harvard Business Review*, July-August 1981, pp. 85-93. See also Kathleen Teltsch, "Minnesota a Model of Corporate Aid to Cities," *New York Times*, July 27, 1981.

25. Cited in Roger B. Smith, "Toward a New Partnership," an address at the Conference on Business and Government, the Lyndon Baines Johnson Library, Austin, Texas, March 2, 1979, p. 6.

26. This proposal is consistent with Harlan Cleveland's earlier notion of the "public executive." See his *Future Executive: Guide for Tomorrow's Managers* (New York: Harper & Row, 1972), and "The Public Executive: A Sense of Responsibility for the Whole," *Public Management*, December 1980, pp. 2-7. See also Barbara Gamarekian, "A Capital Sabbatical," *New York Times*, October 25, 1981, p. F7, and Susan Ferraro, "Time Off for Good Behavior," *American Way*, October 1981. For a contrary opinion of the merits of executive-on-loan programs, see Donald M. Kendall, "Letters to the Editor," *Harvard Business Review*, March-April 1981, p. 201. The board chairman of PEPSICO states: "With rare exception, I cannot envision a company 'lending' an up-and-coming executive to government for 2 or 4 years or this executive accepting the office. If his or her position is at all important to company operations, it would have to be filled during his or her absence by an equally qualified executive. I suspect also that a government employee who has spent 2 to 4 years in private industry would be reluctant to return to government if for no other than financial reasons."

27. Elmer B. Staats, "SMR Forum: Improving Industry-Government Cooperation in Policy Making," *Sloan Management Review*, Spring 1980, p. 65.

28. David Vogel, "Business, in Victory," *New York Times*, February 2, 1981, p. 23.

29. Irving S. Shapiro, "Business and Public Policy," *Harvard Business Review*, November-December 1979, p. 99.

30. Ezra F. Vogel, "Meeting the Japanese Challenge," *Wall Street Journal*, May 19, 1980.
31. Roberts, p. F4.
32. Winston Williams, "Taking the Shackles off Business," *New York Times*, March 1, 1981, sec. 3, p. F1.
33. "The End of Industrial Society," *Business Week*, September 3, 1979, p. 177.
34. "FTC Should Press Conventional Antitrust, Crop 'Misguided' Efforts, Stockman Says," *Wall Street Journal*, March 7, 1981, p. 2.
35. Stan Crock, "James Miller, FTC Nominee, Seeks Study on Necessity of Two Antitrust Agencies," *Wall Street Journal*, July 27, 1981, p. 9.
36. Robert Pear, "Clarifying Some Mixed Signals on Antitrust Law," *New York Times*, July 19, 1981, p. D2.
37. Robert E. Taylor and Stan Crock, "Reagan Team Believes Antitrust Legislation Hurt Big Business," *Wall Street Journal*, July 8, 1981, p. 1. See also Steve Lohr, "Antitrust: Big Business Breathes Easier," *New York Times*, February 5, 1981, p. F1; Edward Meadows, "Bold Departures in Antitrust," *Fortune*, October 5, 1981; Eleanor F. Fox, "From Antitrust to a Trust-in Business," *Across the Board*, November 1981, pp. 59-67; Laurence J. White, "The Merger Wave: Is It a Problem?" *Wall Street Journal*, December 11, 1981, p. 26; and Ralph Nader, "Ended: Big Antitrust," *New York Times*, March 4, 1982, p. 29.
38. Ruben F. Mettler, "Needed: A National Policy for Private Investment," *Dun's Review*, March 1980, p. 157.
39. Mark Shepherd, Jr., "The U.S. Corporation within the Competitive Environment," a paper presented to the Conference on U.S. Competitiveness, Harvard University, Cambridge, Mass., April 20, 1980 (Washington, D.C.: U.S. Government Printing Office, 1980), p. 70.
40. *Ibid.*
41. John A. Prestbo, "New Industrial Revolution Is Near, Economist Says, But U.S. May Lag," *Wall Street Journal*, June 4, 1981, p. 29.
42. See William Stockton, "The Technology Race," *New York Times Magazine*, June 28, 1981.
43. For specific thoughts, see William J. Abernathy and Balaji S. Chakravarthy, "Government Intervention and Innovation in Industry: A Policy Framework," *Sloan Management Review*, Spring 1979, pp. 3-18.
44. Simon Ramo, "SMR Forum: America's Technology Slip—A New Political Issue," *Sloan Management Review*, Summer 1980, p. 81.
45. "The Reindustrialization of America," *Business Week*, June 30, 1980, p. 102.
46. Staats, p. 61.
47. Lawrence R. Klein, "America's Competitive Position," a paper presented to the Conference on U.S Competitiveness, Harvard University, Cambridge, Mass., April 20, 1980 (Washington, D.C.: U.S. Government

Printing Office, 1980), p. 46. For an excellent overview of the productivity problem, see "The Productivity Crisis," *World,* Winter 1981, pp. 2-31. See also: John W. Kendrick and Elliott S. Grossman, *Productivity in the United States: Trends and Cycles* (Baltimore: Johns Hopkins University Press, 1980); National Research Council, Panel to Review Productivity Statistics, *Measurement and Interpretation of Productivity* (Washington, D.C.: National Academy of Sciences, 1970); Beta Gold, *Productivity, Technology, and Capital* (Lexington, Mass.: Lexington Books, 1979); William J. Abernathy, *The Productivity Dilemma: Roadblock to Innovation in the Automobile Industry* (Baltimore: Johns Hopkins University Press, 1978); Thibaut de Saint-Phalle, *U.S. Productivity and Competitiveness in International Trade* (Washington, D.C.: Center for Strategic and International Studies, Georgetown University, 1980); *The Decline in Productivity Growth: Proceedings of a Conference Held at Edgartown, Massachusetts, June 1980* (Boston: Federal Reserve Bank of Boston, 1980); Ali Dogramaci (ed.), *Productivity Analysis: A Range of Perspectives* (Boston: Martinus Nijhoff, 1981); John E. Ullmann (ed.), *The Improvement of Productivity: Myths and Realities* (New York: Praeger, 1980); and Ben S. Graham, Jr., and Parvin S. Titus (eds.), *The Amazing Oversight: Total Participation for Productivity* (New York: Amacom, 1979).

48. Staats, p. 61.
49. *Ibid.*
50. *Ibid.*
51. William F. Miller, "Internalizing the Challenge of Global Competition," *Stanford GSB,* Fall 1980-81, p. 19.
52. See Bernard Rostker, "Draft May Be Answer, But It Is No Panacea," *Honolulu Advertiser,* August 8, 1981, p. A7. See also "Considering National Service," *Philadelphia Inquirer,* September 24, 1980, p. A10, and Charles C. Moskos, "Making the All-Volunteer Force Work: A National Service Approach," *Foreign Affairs,* Fall 1981, pp. 17-34.
53. Steven Rattner, "Group Call for Greater Competition," *New York Times,* April 28, 1980, p. D1.
54. See Philip J. Friedman (ed.), *America's Competitive Challenge: The Public's Response* (New York: The Garth Group, Inc., 1980).
55. See William Serrin, "Where Are the Pickets of Yesteryear?" *New York Times,* May 31, 1981; "Hard Times for Big Labor," *Newsweek,* September 7, 1981, pp. 61-62; Anne Field, "Labor's Lost Love," *Forbes,* September 14, 1981, p. 70; Robert S. Greenberger, "Frustration in the House of Labor . . . ," *Wall Street Journal,* July 22, 1981, p. 22; Gerald P. Glyde, " 'Big Labor'—It's a Big Myth," *New York Times,* October 18, 1979, p. A23; and John T. Dunlop, "Past and Future Tendencies in American Labor Organizations," *Daedalus,* vol. 107, no. 1, 1978, pp. 79-96.
56. Robert L. Simison, "UAW Struggles with a New Idea: Cooperation,"

Wall Street Journal, April 14, 1981, p. 30. See also A. H. Raskin, "Needed: Alliance: Not Militance," *New York Times,* September 7, 1981, p. A15.
57. Quoted in Serrin, p. F1.
58. *Ibid.*
59. "The Reindustrialization of America," *Business Week,* p. 82.
60. Simison, p. 30.
61. *Ibid.*
62. *Ibid.*
63. "Experiment in Steel," *Business Week,* August 18, 1980, p. 130. See also Joseph C. Harsch, "U.S. Steel's Turnaround Sets an Example for the Auto Industry," *Philadelphia Inquirer,* February 28, 1981, p. A5, and "Steel's Comeback," *Business Week,* October 12, 1981, p. 180.
64. See Robert E. Cole, *Work, Mobility, and Participation: A Comparative Study of American and Japanese Industry* (Berkeley and Los Angeles: University of California Press, 1979).
65. "The New Industrial Relations," *Business Week,* May 11, 1981, p. 86. See also: Jay Hall, "Inspiring Workers," *New York Times,* September 18, 1981, p. 27; Gene Bylinsky, "A New Industrial Revolution Is on the Way," *Fortune,* October 5, 1981; and Kenichi Ohmae, "Quality Control Circles: They Work and Don't Work," *Wall Street Journal,* March 29, 1982, p. 18.
66. "The New Industrial Relations," p. 86.
67. Alice L. Ahmuty, "Organized Labor's View on Government Involvement in the Private Corporation" (Washington, D.C.: Congressional Research Service, Library of Congress, February 28, 1980), p. 11.
68. "Steel's Tripartite Idea May Spread," *Business Week,* July 7, 1980, p. 22.
69. "The Reindustrialization of America," p. 96.
70. Cole, p. 260.
71. Note, for example, the automobile workers' rekindled interest in job security in Douglas R. Sease and Robert L. Simison, "UAW Switch on Revising Contracts Reflects Growing Concern for Jobs," *Wall Street Journal,* December 21, 1981, p. 21; William Serrin, "Unions Yielding 'Givebacks' to Employees at Rising Rate," *New York Times,* October 12, 1981, p. 1; John Holusha, "U.A.W. to Stress Job Security in '82 Bargaining, Fraser Says," *New York Times,* September 15, 1981; and Hobart Rowen, "Some Hope on Economic Front," *Honolulu Advertiser,* December 24, 1981, p. A10.
72. Leonard Silk, "A Social Role for Business," *New York Times,* March 27, 1981, p. D2.
73. *Ibid.*

Selected Bibliography

Abegglen, James C. *Management and Worker: The Japanese Solution.* Tokyo: Sophia University, in cooperation with Kodansha International, 1973.

———, Thomas Hout, and C. Tait Ratcliffe, *Japan in 1980.* London: The Financial Times, 1974.

Agmon, Tamir, and Charles P. Kindleberger (eds.). *Multinationals from Small Countries.* Cambridge, Mass.: M.I.T. Press, 1977.

Ahmuty, Alice L. "Worker Participation in Management Decision-Making in Western Europe: Implications for the United States." Washington, D.C: Congressional Research Service Report No. 79-136, April 23, 1979.

"American Renewal." *Fortune,* March 9, 1981, pp. 71-115.

Apter, David E. "Charters, Cartels, and Multinationals—Some Colonial and Imperial Questions." In *The Multinational Corporation and Social Change,* edited by David E. Apter and Louis Wolf Goodman. New York: Praeger, 1976.

Balassa, Bela. *The Newly Industrializing Countries in the World Economy.* Elmsford, N.Y.: Pergamon Press, 1981.

Baranson, Jack. *The Japanese Challenge to U.S. Industry.* Lexington, Mass.: Lexington Books, 1981.

Barnet, Richard J. *The Lean Years.* New York: Simon and Schuster, 1981.

———, and Ronald E. Müller. *Global Reach: The Power of the Multinational Corporations.* New York: Simon and Schuster, 1974.

Barraclough, Geoffrey, and Takeo Kuwabara. "The Limits of Westernization." *World Press Review,* March 1981, pp. 24-26.

269

SELECTED BIBLIOGRAPHY

Beissinger, Mark R. "Soviet Factory Directors Go to Business School." *Wall Street Journal,* November 2, 1981.

Bell, Daniel. *The Coming of Post-Industrial Society.* New York: Basic Books, 1973.

———. *The Cultural Contradictions of Capitalism.* New York: Basic Books, 1975.

———. "The New Class: A Muddled Concept." *Transaction/Society,* January-February 1979.

Berger, Peter L. "New Attack on the Legitimacy of Business." *Harvard Business Review,* September-October 1981, pp. 82-89.

Bergsten, C. Fred, Thomas Horst, and Theodore H. Moran. *American Multinationals and American Interests.* Washington, D.C.: Brookings Institution, 1978.

Blumberg, Paul. *Inequality in an Age of Decline.* New York: Oxford University Press, 1980.

Blumenthal, Sidney. "Whose Side Is Business On, Anyway?" *New York Times Magazine,* October 25, 1981, pp. 29-31.

Bolling, Richard, and John Bowles. *America's Competitive Edge: How to Get Our Country Moving Again.* New York: McGraw-Hill, 1982.

Bradshaw, Thornton. "My Case for National Planning." *Fortune,* February 1977, pp. 100-104.

Brenner, Steven N. "Business and Politics—An Update." *Harvard Business Review,* November-December 1979, pp. 149-163.

Business International (in collaboration with J. J. Boddewyn). *International Divestment: A Survey of Corporate Experience.* Geneva: Business International, 1976.

Childs, David, and Jeffrey Johnson. *West Germany: Politics and Society.* New York: St. Martin's Press, 1981.

Cleveland, Harlan. *The Future Executive: A Guide for Tomorrow's Managers.* New York: Harper & Row, 1972.

———. "The Public Executive: A Sense of Responsibility for the Whole." *Public Management,* December 1980.

Cline, Ray S. *World Power Assessment 1977: A Calculus of Strategic Drift.* Boulder, Colo.: Westview Press, 1977.

Cole, Robert E. *Japanese Blue Collar: The Changing Tradition.* Berkeley and Los Angeles: University of California Press, 1971.

———. *Work, Mobility, and Participation: A Comparative Study of American and Japanese Industry.* Berkeley and Los Angeles: University of California Press, 1979.

Commager, Henry Steele. *The American Mind.* New Haven, Conn.: Yale University Press, 1950.

Cook, James. "A Game Any Number Can Play." *Forbes,* June 25, 1979, pp. 49-55.

Davidson, H. Justin. "The Top of the World Is Flat." *Harvard Business Review,* March-April 1977, pp. 89-99.

"The Decline of U.S. Power: The New Debate over Guns and Butter." *Business Week*, March 12, 1979, pp. 36-96.

Denison, Edward F., and William K. Chung. *How Japan's Economy Grew So Fast: The Sources of Postwar Expansion.* Washington, D.C: Brookings Institution, 1977.

Diebold, William, Jr. *Industrial Policy as an International Issue.* New York: McGraw-Hill, for the Council on Foreign Relations/1980s Project, 1980.

Dore, Ronald P. *British Factory, Japanese Factory: The Origins of National Diversity in Industrial Relations.* Berkeley and Los Angeles: University of California Press, 1973.

Drucker, Peter F. "Behind Japan's Success." *Harvard Business Review,* January-February 1981, pp. 83-90.

———. "Japan Gets Ready for Tougher Times." *Fortune,* November 3, 1980, pp. 108-112.

———. *Managing in Turbulent Times.* New York: Harper & Row, 1980.

———. "What We Can Learn from Japanese Management." *Harvard Business Review,* March-April 1971, pp. 110-122.

Dunlop, John T. "Past and Future Tendencies in American Labor Organizations." *Daedalus,* Winter 1978, pp. 79-96.

——— (ed.). *Business and Public Policy.* Cambridge, Mass.: Harvard University Press, 1981.

———, Alfred D. Chandler, Jr., George P. Schultz, and Irving S. Shapiro. "Business and Public Policy." *Harvard Business Review,* November-December 1979, pp. 85-102.

Eads, George. "The Government and Industrial Policy: Picking Winners and Killing Dogs." *Wharton Magazine,* Fall 1981, pp. 33-41.

"An Economic Dream in Peril." *Newsweek,* September 8, 1980, pp. 50-69.

Eells, Richard S. F. *The Political Crisis of the Enterprise System.* New York: Macmillan, 1980.

"Embattled America: The Struggle for Global Markets." *Saturday Review,* July 7, 1979, pp. 18-22.

"The End of the Industrial Society." *Business Week,* September 3, 1979, pp. 2-4.

Etzioni, Amitai. "Choose America Must—." *Across the Board,* October 1980, pp. 42-49.

———. "Rebuilding Our Economic Foundations." *Business Week,* August 25, 1980, p. 16.

———. "Reindustrialization: View from the Source." *New York Times,* June 29, 1980, p. F6.

———. "Why U.S. Industry Needs Help." *Forbes,* August 18, 1980, pp. 120-121.

Feldstein, Martin (ed.). *The American Economy in Transition.* Chicago: University of Chicago Press, 1980.

Fleming, John E. "A Possible Future of Government-Corporate Relations."

Business Horizons, December 1979, pp. 43-47.

Fox, J. Ronald. "Breaking the Regulatory Deadlock." *Harvard Business Review,* September-October 1981, pp. 97-105.

Franko, Lawrence G. "Multinationals: The End of U.S. Dominance." *Harvard Business Review,* November-December 1978, pp. 93-101.

Friedman, Milton, and Rose Friedman. *Free to Choose: A Personal Statement.* New York: Harcourt Brace Jovanovich, 1980.

Friedman, Philip J. (ed.). *America's Competitive Challenge: The Public's Response.* New York: The Garth Group, Inc., 1980.

Galbraith, John Kenneth. *The Affluent Society.* Boston: Houghton Mifflin, 1958.

―――. "Corporate Senility." *Washington Post,* February 11, 1981, p. A19.

Garrigo, Andres. "Growth of the Red Multinationals." *Profile,* 1978, p. 9.

Gibney, Frank. *Japan, the Fragile Superpower.* New York: Norton, 1975.

Gilder, George F. *Wealth and Poverty.* New York: Basic Books, 1981.

Gilpin, Robert. *U.S. Power and the Multinational Corporation: The Political Economy of Foreign Direct Investment.* New York: Basic Books, 1975.

Gladwin, Thomas N., and Ingo Walter. *Multinationals under Fire: Lessons in the Management of Conflict.* New York: Wiley, 1980.

Grayson, Leslie E., and Allison Spencer. "Executive Profile of the Top Officers of the Largest Oil Companies in the United States: 1950-1980." Charlottesville, Va.: Energy Policies Center, University of Virginia, 1981.

Harman, Sidney. "For an 'America, Inc.'" *Newsweek,* March 12, 1979, pp. 20-21.

Hartrich, Edwin. *The Fourth and Richest Reich.* New York: Macmillan, 1980.

Hatvany, Nina, and Vladimir Puick. "Japanese Management Practices and Productivity." *Organizational Dynamics,* Spring 1981, pp. 4-21.

Hayes, Robert H. "Why Japanese Factories Work." *Harvard Business Review,* July-August 1981, pp. 56-66.

―――, and William J. Abernathy. "Managing Our Way to Economic Decline." *Harvard Business Review,* July-August 1980, pp. 66-77.

Heenan, David A. "Ideology Revisited: America Looks Ahead." *Sloan Management Review,* Winter 1982, pp. 35-46.

―――. "Moscow Goes International." *Harvard Business Review,* May-June 1981, pp. 48-50.

―――, and Warren J. Keegan. "The Rise of Third World Multinationals." *Harvard Business Review,* January-February 1979, pp. 101-109.

―――, and Howard V. Perlmutter. *Multinational Organization Development: A Social Architectural Approach.* Reading, Mass.: Addison-Wesley, 1979.

Heilbroner, Robert L. *Beyond Boom and Crash.* New York: Norton, 1978.

―――, and Lester C. Thurow. *The Economic Problem.* 5th ed. Englewood Cliffs, N.J.: Prentice-Hall, 1979.

SELECTED BIBLIOGRAPHY

Ho Kwon Ping. "Thailand, Inc., an Open Door for the World's Multinationals." *Far Eastern Economic Review*, May 23, 1980, pp. 40-41.

Hodgson, James D. *The Wondrous Working World of Japan*. Washington, D.C.: American Enterprise Institute, 1978.

Huntington, Samuel P. *American Politics: The Promise of Disharmony*. Cambridge, Mass.: The Belnap Press of Harvard University Press, 1981.

International Business Information, Inc. *Japanese Corporate Finance, 1977-1980*. Prepared by C. Tait Ratcliffe. London: Financial Times, 1977.

Johnson, Chalmers A. *Japan's Public Policy Companies*. Washington, D.C.: American Enterprise Institute, 1978.

Johnson, M. Bruce (ed.). *The Attack on Corporate America: The Corporate Issues Sourcebook*. New York: McGraw-Hill, 1978.

Johnson, Richard Tanner, and William G. Ouchi. "Made in America (Under Japanese Management)." *Harvard Business Review*, September-October 1974, pp. 61-69.

Kahn, Herman, and Thomas Pepper. *The Japanese Challenge: The Success and Failure of Economic Success*. New York: Thomas Crowell, 1979.

Kaufman, Michael T. "Sri Lanka Lures Business, Singapore-Style." *New York Times*, November 12, 1980, p. D18.

Kindleberger, Charles P. *Economic Response: Comparative Studies in Trade, Finance, and Growth*. Cambridge, Mass.: Harvard University Press, 1978.

Kobayashi, Noritake. "The Japanese Approach to 'Multinationalism.'" *Journal of World Trade Law*, March-April 1976, pp. 177-184.

Kojima, Kiyoshi. *Japan and a New World Economic Order*. Tokyo: Tuttle Press, 1977.

Komiya, Ryutaro. "Planning in Japan." In *Economic Planning, East and West*, edited by Morris Bornstein. Cambridge, Mass.: Ballinger, 1975.

Kraar, Louis. "Make Way for the New Japans." *Fortune*, August 10, 1981, pp. 176-184.

Kristol, Irving. *Two Cheers for Capitalism*. New York: Basic Books, 1978.

Kumar, Krishna, and Maxwell G. McLeod (eds.). *Multinationals from Developing Countries*. Lexington, Mass.: Lexington Books, 1981.

Lamont, Douglas F. *Foreign State Enterprises, a Threat to American Business*. New York: Basic Books, 1979.

Lecraw, Donald. "Direct Investment by Firms from Less Developed Countries." *Oxford Economic Papers*, November 1977, pp. 442-457.

Leone, Robert A., and Stephen P. Bradley. "Toward an Effective Industrial Policy." *Harvard Business Review*, November-December 1981, pp. 91-97.

Lewis, Paul. "National Oil Companies Crowd the 'Seven Sisters.'" *New York Times*, December 30, 1979, p. E2.

Lieberman, Jethro K. *The Litigious Society*. New York: Basic Books, 1981.

273

Lindblom, Charles E. *Politics and Markets.* New York: Basic Books, 1977.

Lodge, George Cabot. *The New American Ideology.* New York: Knopf, 1975.

Lohr, Steve. "Japan's Challenge to U.S. Is Policies, Not Products." *New York Times,* January 3, 1982, p. E3.

———. "Overhauling America's Business Management." *New York Times Magazine,* January 4, 1981, pp. 14-17.

Lynn, Laurence E., Jr. *Managing the Public's Business: The Job of the Government Executive.* New York: Basic Books, 1981.

McCloskey, Robert Green. *American Conservatism in the Age of Enterprise, 1865-1910.* New York: Harper & Row, 1951.

McCracken, Paul W. "The Fading American Importance." *Wall Street Journal,* June 17, 1980, p. 22.

———. "A United States 'Industrial Policy.'" *Wall Street Journal,* January 12, 1981, p. 20.

McCue, Andy. "Souring of the 'Sweetness' of the Singapore Model." *Asian Wall Street Journal,* January 4, 1980, p. 4.

MacLeod, Celeste. *Horatio Alger, Farewell: The End of the American Dream.* New York: Seaview Books, 1980.

McQuaid, Kim. "The Roundtable: Getting Results in Washington." *Harvard Business Review,* May-June 1981, pp. 114-123.

Magaziner, Ira C., and Robert B. Reich. *Minding America's Business: The Decline and Rise of the American Economy.* New York: Harcourt Brace Jovanovich, 1982.

Marsh, Robert M., and Hiroshi Mannari. *Modernization and the Japanese Factory.* Princeton, N.J.: Princeton University Press, 1976.

Martin, William F., and George Cabot Lodge. "Our Society in 1985— Business May Not Like It." *Harvard Business Review,* November-December 1975, pp. 143-152.

Mason, Edward. "Interests, Ideologies and the Problem of Stability and Growth." *American Economic Review,* March 1963, pp. 1-18.

Mathur, Igbal, and Subhash Jain. "The Financial Manager and National Economic Planning." *University of Michigan Business Review,* pp. 7-12.

Mazzolini, Renato. "European Government-Controlled Enterprises: Explaining International Strategic and Policy Decisions." *Journal of International Business Studies,* Spring-Summer 1980, pp. 48-58.

———. *European Transnational Concentrations.* New York: McGraw-Hill, 1974.

———. *Government Controlled Enterprises: International Strategic and Policy Decisions.* New York: Wiley, 1979.

———. "Government Controlled Enterprises: What's the Difference?" *Columbia Journal of World Business,* Summer 1980, pp. 28-37.

———. "Government Policies and Government Controlled Enterprises." *Columbia Journal of World Business,* Fall 1980, pp. 47-54.

Mettler, Ruben F. "Needed: A National Policy for Private Investment." *Dun's Review,* March 1980, pp. 157-158.

Meyer, Herbert E. "This Communist Internationale Has a Capitalist Accent." *Fortune,* February 1977, pp. 134-148.

Miller, William F. "Internalizing the Challenge of Global Competition." *Stanford GSB,* Fall 1980-81, pp. 17-19.

Ministry of International Trade and Industry (MITI). *Japan's Industrial Structure—A Long Range Vision: Report BI-23.* Tokyo: MITI, 1976.

———. *Japan's Industrial Structure—A Long Range Vision: Report NR-140 (77-26).* Tokyo: MITI, 1977.

Mintz, Morton, and Jerry S. Cohen. *America, Inc.: Who Owns and Operates the United States.* New York: Dial, 1971.

Müller, Ronald E. *Revitalizing America: Politics for Prosperity.* New York: Simon and Schuster, 1980.

Nakane, Chie. *Japanese Society.* Berkeley and Los Angeles: University of California Press, 1970.

Naya, Seiji, and Richard Schatz. "Trade, Investment, and Aid: The Role of the U.S. and Japan in Asian Economic Development." In *Pacific Basin Development,* edited by Harald B. Malmgren. Lexington, Mass.: Lexington Books, 1972.

Naylor, Thomas H. "Management Is Drowning in Numbers." *Business Week,* April 6, 1981, pp. 14-16.

Neal, Alfred C. *Business Power and Public Policy.* New York: Praeger, 1981.

Newman, Barry. "Can Singapore Become Japanese?" *Wall Street Journal,* January 1, 1981, p. 23.

Newman, William H. (ed.). *Managers for the Year 2000.* Englewood Cliffs, N.J.: Prentice-Hall, 1978.

Norman, Peter. "Death Throes of the Transnational Experiment." *The Times,* May 11, 1981, p. 21.

Novak, Michael. *The American Vision: An Essay on the Future of Democratic Capitalism.* Washington, D.C.: American Enterprise Institute, 1978.

Ohkawa, Kazushi, and Henry Rosovsky. *Japanese Economic Growth.* Palo Alto, Calif.: Stanford University Press, 1973.

Okochi, Kazuo, Bernard Karsh, and Solomon B. Levine. *Workers and Employers in Japan: The Japanese Employment Relations System.* Princeton, N.J.: Princeton University Press, 1974.

Okun, Arthur M. "Capitalism and Democracy: Some Unifying Principles." *Columbia Journal of World Business,* Winter 1978, pp. 22-30.

O'Toole, James. *Making America Work: Productivity and Responsibility.* New York: Continuum, 1981.

———. "What's Ahead for the Business-Government Relationship." *Harvard Business Review,* March-April 1979, pp. 94-105.

Ouchi, William G. *Theory Z: How American Business Can Meet the Japa-*

nese Challenge. Reading, Mass.: Addison-Wesley, 1981.

Ozawa, Terutomo. "Japanese World of Work: An Interpretive Survey." *MSU Business Topics,* Spring 1980, pp. 45-55.

———. "Japan's New Resource Diplomacy: Government-Backed Group Investment." *Journal of World Trade Law,* January-February 1980, pp. 3-13.

———. "Japan's Resource Dependency and Overseas Investment." *Journal of World Trade Law,* January-February 1977, pp. 52-74.

———. "Multinationalism—Japanese Style." *Columbia Journal of World Business,* November-December 1972, pp. 33-42.

———. *Multinationalism, Japanese Style: The Political Economy of Outward Dependency.* Princeton, N.J.: Princeton University Press, 1979.

Pascale, Richard Tanner, and Anthony G. Athos. *The Art of Japanese Management.* New York: Simon and Schuster, 1981.

Patrick, Hugh, and Henry Rosovsky (eds.). *Asia's New Giant: How the Japanese Economy Works.* Washington, D.C.: Brookings Institution, 1976.

Perlmutter, Howard V. "Emerging East-West Ventures: The Transideological Enterprise." *Columbia Journal of World Business,* September-October 1969, pp. 39-50.

———. "The Multinational Firm and the Future." *Annals of the American Academy of Political and Social Science,* September 1972, pp. 139-152.

———. "The Tortuous Evolution of the Multinational Corporation." *Columbia Journal of World Business,* January-February 1969, pp. 9-18.

———, and David A. Heenan. "How Multinational Should Your Top Managers Be?" *Harvard Business Review,* November-December 1974, pp. 121-132.

Podohertz, Norman. "The New Defenders of Capitalism." *Harvard Business Review,* March-April 1981, pp. 96-106.

Prestbo, John A. "New Industrial Revolution Is Near, Economist Says, But U.S. May Lag." *Wall Street Journal,* June 4, 1981, p. 29.

Rabushka, Alvin. *The Changing Face of Hong Kong: New Departures in Public Policy.* Washington, D.C.: American Enterprise Institute, 1973.

———. "Sri Lanka's Experiment in Economic Liberalism." *Wall Street Journal,* May 18, 1981, p. 27.

Rapp, William V. "Japan's Industrial Policy." In *The Japanese Economy in International Perspective,* edited by Isaiah Frank. Baltimore: Johns Hopkins University Press, 1975.

Rappaport, Alfred. "A Fatal Fascination with the Short Run." *Business Week,* May 4, 1981, pp. 20-22.

Reagan, Ronald. "Government and Business in the '80s." *Wall Street Journal,* January 9, 1981, p. 18.

Reich, Robert B. "Regulation by Confrontation or Negotiation." *Harvard Business Review,* May-June 1981, pp. 82-93.

———. "Why the U.S. Needs an Industrial Policy." *Harvard Business Review*, January-February 1982.

The Reindustrialization of America. New York: McGraw-Hill, 1982.

"The Reindustrialization of America." *Business Week*, June 30, 1980, pp. 56-142.

Reischauer, Edwin O. *The Japanese.* Cambridge, Mass.: Harvard University Press, 1977.

———. "The Japanese Way." *Across the Board*, December 1977, pp. 34-42.

Reston, James. "Where Are We Going?" *New York Times*, August 3, 1980, p. E19.

Robertson, James Oliver. *American Myth, American Reality.* New York: Hill & Wang, 1980.

Robinson, Richard D. "Background Concepts and Philosophy of International Business from World War II to the Present." *Journal of International Business Studies*, Spring-Summer 1981, pp. 13-21.

———. *International Business Policy.* New York: Holt, Rinehart and Winston, 1964.

The Role of Trading Companies in International Commerce. Tokyo: Japan External Trade Organization, 1977.

Roy, William G. "The Process of Bureaucratization in the U.S. State Department and the Vesting of Economic Interests, 1886-1905." *Administrative Science Quarterly*, September 1981, pp. 419-433.

Saxonhouse, Gary R. "Industrial Restructuring in Japan." *Journal of Japanese Studies*, Summer 1979, pp. 273-320.

Scalapino, Robert A. "Emerging Trends in the Pacific-Asian Region." In *ASEAN and a Positive Strategy for Foreign Investment*, edited by Lloyd R. Vasey. Honolulu: University Press of Hawaii, 1978.

———(ed.). *The Foreign Policy of Modern Japan.* Berkeley and Los Angeles: University of California Press, 1977.

Schlesinger, Arthur, Jr. "Is Liberalism Dead?" *New York Times Magazine*, March 30, 1980, p. 42.

Schwartz, Gail Garfield, and Pat Choate. *Being Number One: Rebuilding the U.S. Economy.* Lexington, Mass.: Lexington Books, 1980.

Scott, Bruce R. "How Practical Is National Economic Planning?" *Harvard Business Review*, March-April 1978, pp. 131-145.

Seligman, Daniel. "The Trouble with Partnership." *Fortune*, August 11, 1980, p. 97.

Servan-Schreiber, Jean-Jacques. *The American Challenge.* New York: Avon Books, 1969.

———. *The World Challenge: OPEC and the New World Order.* New York: Simon and Schuster, 1980.

Silk, Leonard. "A Social Role for Business." *New York Times*, March 27, 1981, p. D2.

Smith, Hedrick. *The Russians.* New York: Ballantine Books, 1976.

277

Staats, Elmer B. "SMR Forum: Improving Industry-Government Cooperation in Policy Making." *Sloan Management Review,* Spring 1980, pp. 61-65.

Stockton, William. "The Technology Race." *New York Times Magazine,* June 28, 1981, pp. 14-20.

Taber, George M. "Capitalism: Is It Working . . . ?" *Time,* April 21, 1980, pp. 40-55.

Thurow, Lester C. *Generating Inequality: Mechanisms of Distribution in the U.S. Economy.* New York: Basic Books, 1975.

————. *The Zero-Sum Society: Distribution and the Possibilities for Economic Change.* New York: Basic Books, 1980.

Tocqueville, Alexis de. *Democracy in America.* Vol 2. New York: Schocken Books, 1961.

Tsurumi, Yoshihiro. *The Japanese Are Coming: A Multinational Interaction of Firms and Politics.* Cambridge, Mass.: Ballinger, 1976.

————, and Rebecca R. Tsurumi. *Sogoshosa: Engines of Export-Based Growth.* Montreal: Institute for Research on Public Policy, 1980.

Vagts, Detlev F. "The United States and Its Multinationals: Protection and Control." *Harvard International Law Journal,* Spring 1979, pp. 235-251.

Vernon, Raymond. "Gone Are the Cash Cows of Yesteryear." *Harvard Business Review,* November-December 1980, pp. 150-155.

————. "International Investment and International Trade in the Product Life Cycle." *Quarterly Journal of Economics,* May 1966, pp. 190-207.

————. *Sovereignty at Bay: The Multinational Spread of U.S. Enterprise.* New York: Basic Books, 1971.

————. "Storm over the Multinationals: Problems and Prospects." *Foreign Affairs,* January 1977, pp. 243-262.

————. *Storm over the Multinationals: The Real Issues.* Cambridge, Mass.: Harvard University Press, 1977.

————, and Yair Aharoni (eds.). *State-Owned Enterprise in the Western Economies.* New York: St. Martin's Press, 1981.

Vogel, David. "Business, in Victory." *New York Times,* February 2, 1981, p. 23.

————. "The Political and Economic Impact of Current Criticisms of Business." *California Management Review,* Winter 1975, pp. 86-92.

————. "Why Businessmen Distrust Their State." *British Journal of Political Science,* January 1978, pp. 45-78.

Vogel, Ezra F. "Guided Free Enterprise in Japan." *Harvard Business Review,* May-June 1978, pp. 161-170.

————. *Japan as Number One: Lessons for America.* Cambridge, Mass.: Harvard University Press, 1979.

Walters, Kenneth D., and R. Joseph Monsen. "State-Owned Business Abroad: New Competitive Threat." *Harvard Business Review,* March-April 1979, pp. 160-170.

Ways, Max. "The Corporation and Society." Austin: The Institute for Constructive Capitalism, University of Texas at Austin, 1979.

Wells, Louis T., Jr. "Foreign Investment from the Third World: The Experience of Chinese Firms from Hong Kong." *Columbia Journal of World Business*, Spring 1978, pp. 39-49.

Wheelwright, Steven C. "Japan—Where Operations Really Are Strategic." *Harvard Business Review*, July-August 1981, pp. 67-74.

Whitman, Marina v. N. "Auto Industry's New Challenges." *New York Times*, September 3, 1980, p. D2.

Williams, William A. *The Tragedy of American Diplomacy*. Cleveland: World Publishing Co., 1959.

Wilson, Arlene. "Foreign Investment in U.S. Industry." Issue Brief No. IB78091. Washington, D.C.: Library of Congress, Congressional Research Service, November 18, 1980.

———. "Major Structural Differences between the Economies of the United States, Germany and Japan: An Overview." Washington, D.C.: Library of Congress, Congressional Research Service, October 31, 1979.

Wood, Robert C. "Economic Brief: Japan's Industrial Vision." *Asia*, January-February 1982, pp. 8-9.

Yoshino, Michael Y. *Japan's Managerial System: Tradition and Innovation*. Cambridge, Mass.: M.I.T. Press, 1968.

———. *Japan's Multinational Enterprises*. Cambridge, Mass.: Harvard University Press, 1976.

———. "Multinational Spread of Japanese Manufacturing Investment since World War II." *Business History Review*, Autumn 1974, pp. 357-381.

Index

DATE DUE

JUN 1 5 1984	
DEC 1 5 1984	
NOV 01 '89	
BRODART, INC.	Cat. No. 23-221